WITHDRAWN

# HELLENISTIC CIVILISATION

BY

## W. W. TARN

Author of "Antigonos Gonatas," etc.

LONDON

## EDWARD ARNOLD & CO.

1927

Made and Printed in Great Britain by
Butler & Tanner Ltd., Frome and London

To
MY WIFE

# PREFACE

This book is neither a history nor a textbook, but an attempt to get a general picture of the civilisation of the Hellenistic period, covering all the main subjects and as detailed as space permits. The neglect in Britain of this period, in spite of its varied interest, has been notorious, and there is no work in English to which anyone who desires a connected view of the Greek world during these three centuries can turn. I hope that parts of this book will in consequence possess a certain freshness for some readers in this country ; and if much of it is only a summary of existing knowledge, a few sections, I hope, are rather more than that, notably in chapter III. Possibly to some the more favourable view here presented of certain things in the Greek world after Alexander may seem a little unfamiliar ; but it is desirable in any period to take both men and movements seriously.

As to the plan of the book, the historical outline in chapter I is merely meant as a guide to the subsequent chapters ; and to save space I have practically omitted certain outlying branches of Hellenism—Italy and Sicily, South Russia, and the kingdoms in Bactria and India— and kept to the centre of things, the world between the Adriatic and the Tigris. In conclusion, I should like to thank the publishers for giving me the opportunity of writing this book, and as it is written practically without notes or acknowledgements I would here express my gratitude generally to all the scholars, living and dead, whose work has rendered it possible.

W. W. TARN.

Muirtown, Inverness.
*August* 1927.

# CONTENTS

# HELLENISTIC CIVILISATION

## CHAPTER I

## HISTORICAL OUTLINE

This book aims at giving, in brief outline, a sketch of the civilisation of the three Hellenistic centuries, from the death of Alexander in 323 to the establishment of the Roman empire by Augustus in 31 B.C.[1] These limits are of course conventional, for the germs of certain phenomena of Hellenism begin to appear before Alexander, and in some respects Augustus represents no real break. But they do serve to emphasise two facts : the creative impulses evoked by Alexander's career forbade anything ever to be quite the same again as before, and, after the Hellenistic world had finally gone down in the ruin of the Roman civil wars, with the Empire it began to be built up afresh on different lines ; civilisation became Graeco-Roman. Throughout this book Rome and Roman history are taken for granted, and we are concerned simply to see what Hellenism was and what kind of world the Roman Republic found when it came eastward. Unlike the Empire, that Republic, in its contact with Hellenistic civilisation, was purely receptive ; the Greece that taught Rome was not the older Greece but contemporary Hellenism, and so far as modern civilisation is based on Greek it is primarily on Hellenism that it is based.

What now does Hellenism mean ?[2] To one, it means a

[1] All dates and centuries throughout the book are B.C. unless otherwise stated.

[2] 'Hellenism,' though incorrect in form, has long done duty as the substantive of Hellenistic, Hellenisticism being an impossible word in any language.

new culture compounded of Greek and Oriental elements ;
to another, the extension of Greek culture to Orientals ;
to another, the continuation of the pure line of the older
Greek civilisation ; to yet another, that same civilisation
modified by new conditions.  All these theories contain a
truth, but none represents the whole truth ; and all are
unworkable the moment one comes down to details, such
(for example) as that Hellenistic mathematics were purely
Greek, while the sister-science, astronomy, was Graeco-
Babylonian.  To get a true picture we must look at all
the phenomena, and Hellenism is merely a convenient label
for the civilisation of the three centuries during which Greek
culture radiated far from the homeland ; [1]  no general
definition will cover it all.  Moreover, in some respects,
these three centuries represent, not one phase of civilisation,
but two :  the earlier phase creative in science, philosophy,
literature, political state-forms, and much else, with an
independent Graeco-Macedonian world extending its civilisation to Asia ; the later phase distinguished by the exhaus-
tion of the creative impulse and the reaction, both spiritual
and material, of the East against the West, while the
Graeco-Macedonian world is caught between that reaction
and Rome, until Rome, having destroyed the Hellenistic
state-system, is ultimately compelled to take its place
as the standard-bearer of Greek culture.  The two phases
cannot always be definitely separated ; but the lines of
the evolution of any particular matter are easier to understand if the above broad distinction be kept in mind.
There are, however, many respects in which the Hellenistic
period does form a connected whole, and as such we may
for a moment glance at it.

The world of Hellenism was a changed and enlarged
world.  Though the particularism of the Greek city-state
was to remain vigorous enough in fact, it had broken down

[1] One school would now include under Hellenism the contemporary civilisation of the Roman Republic.  It is not so included
in this book ; but I am not expressing an opinion here on that
view.

in theory ;  it was being replaced by universalism and its
corollary, individualism.   The idea emerges of an *oecumene*
or ' inhabited world ' as a whole, the common possession
of civilised men ;  and for its use there grows up the form
of Greek known as the *koine*, the ' common speech,' which
was also used by many Asiatics ;  Greek might take a man
from Marseilles to India, from the Caspian to the Cataracts.
Nationality falls into the background ;  common speech
and education promote a common culture in every city
of the ' inhabited world' ;  literature, learning, above all
philosophy, do to some extent envisage a larger world
than Greece, and the upper classes in Rome and parts of
Asia come to feel that Greek culture is a thing a man must
have, at least in externals.   Commerce is internationalised.
Most of the barriers are down :  thought is free as it was
not to be again till modern times ;  race hatred is a thing
of the past, except perhaps among the native Egyptians
and some Jews ;  religious persecution on religious ground
is unknown (for Antiochus' attack upon the Jews was a
political measure) ;  morality is a matter for science, not
for authority.   The personality of the individual has free
scope.   It is an age of specialists, from the scientific
worker to the carpenter who makes a door but requires
another man to hang it ;  when Poseidonius tries for the
last time to take all learning for his province, as Aristotle
had done, his superficiality in certain fields is apparent.
And even the creative third century differs from its fore-
runners in this, that, though the Greek spirit was still of
supreme importance, it can no longer be said that every
fruitful idea was Greek ;  for, quite apart from religion and
astronomy, the single greatest creation of the age, the
Stoic philosophy, originated with one who, whether he had
some Greek blood or not, was certainly to his contemporaries
a Phoenician.

The resemblance of this world to our own is at first
sight almost startling.   There was the same complex of
states, big and little, with different state-forms, some more
advanced than others, working within the bounds of a

common civilisation ; and, beside some of the phenomena noticed above, there were many others which look very modern. Such are the eternal trouble of prices and wages ; Socialism and Communism, the strike and the revolution ; the growth of ideas of humanity and brotherhood combined with savage quarrelling ; the emancipation of woman and the restriction of population ; questions of franchise and (possibly) representation, of emigration and the proletariat ; exact learning and crass superstition side by side ; a vast literature dealing with every sphere of human activity, often competent, but no longer producing writers equal to the great names of the past ; the spread of education, resulting in the manufacture of masses of the half-educated ; the more conscious emergence of propaganda ; the growth of all the half-worlds that cling to the skirts of science, of history, and of religion. I am not much concerned to draw parallels with the modern world, and have usually left this to the reader. But such parallels must not be drawn too far. Though many things had a certain likeness to the things of to-day, they were seldom the *same* ; for example, there is little resemblance between an Egyptian and a modern strike, or between modern and Stoic Communism. And underlying everything were two radical and crucial differences : it was a world empty of machines and full of slaves. This last fact cannot be over-emphasised. To see Hellenistic society as it existed, the slave background must never be lost sight of ; and such aspirations as freedom and brotherhood—even the very revolutions—too often convey a sense of unreality when it is remembered that a large part of the population was, by most people, excepted from their scope.

The Hellenistic period has often been treated as one of decline, even of decay ; but probably few would now care to argue that this was true of the third century. Such terms can only apply, if at all, to what I have called the later phase ; and even there it must, I think, largely depend on the point of view. For example, if physical science, or art, be all-important, then the later phase was one of decline ;

but if the emergence of certain religious instincts and feelings, such as might pave the way for something greater, be at least equally material, then it was one of growth. What we *do* seem to see in the later phase is a mass of contradictions ; for example, which really represents the late second century, the slave-market at Delos or the manumissions at Delphi ? Are we to argue from the peripatetic magician, or from the Stoic who believed that virtue was its own reward ? I myself venture to entertain considerable doubts whether the true Greek, the racial aristocracy of the Aegean, really degenerated. This is not the more usual view ; but I have given the facts as they appear to me, and they should enable the reader to form his own conclusions. Much too which at first sight looks like decline can be accounted for by two general considerations. One is the steady diminution in the numbers of the true Greek after *c.* 200, combined with the intrusion, or admixture, of alien stocks, which, whatever their latent capabilities, often had not at the time the intellectual, political, or social energy of the Greek. The other is the behaviour of the Roman Republic, which tended to break the Greek spirit and probably ended by convincing many people beside the kings of Syria and Egypt that efforts doomed beforehand to be fruitless were not worth while. Mere subjection by greatly superior force, by whomsoever wielded, naturally has no bearing on the question ; it is not the business of history to cheer for the big battalions.

One remark needs making here about the literary sources. More important than their fragmentary nature is the fact that they are so often hostile to what they are describing (Plutarch is an exception) ; even Polybius has small claims to impartiality. To copy out party propaganda, such as is represented by (say) Pausanias on the end of the Achaean League or Justin on Ptolemy Euergetes II, and call it history, is merely misleading ; we are still some way from a proper answer to the question, what is much of the tradition *worth* ? There are plenty of figures and events

in this period which, I imagine, we do not see at all; we
see only a literary smoke-screen. But we have one steadily
increasing source which can be trusted, the contemporary
inscriptions and papyri; and the smoke does gradually
tend to clear.

     \*     \*     \*     \*     \*

Alexander's empire at his death embraced Macedonia,
Egypt, and most of Asia from the Aegean to the Punjab,
south of the Caucasus-Caspian line, except Arabia, Armenia,
and northern Asia Minor; while most of the Greek cities
of Greece and Asia were his allies, whose relations to himself were regulated by the League of Corinth, the chief
exceptions being Sparta and the Black Sea cities. He
left no heir, and had made no arrangements for carrying
on the government. Once the uprisings of Greece in the
Lamian war and of the Greeks in the far east were defeated,
a struggle for power started among his generals, in the
shape of war between the satraps (territorial dynasts) and
whatever central power aimed at general control; the battle
of Ipsus in 301 definitely decided that the Graeco-Macedonian world could not be held together, and that world
presently returned very much to the political shape it had
before Alexander, though under different rulers and a
different civilisation. By 275 three dynasties, descended
from three of his generals, were well established; the
Seleucids ruled much of what had been the Persian empire
in Asia, the Ptolemies Egypt, and the Antigonids Macedonia.
A fourth European dynasty, not connected with Alexander,
the Attalids of Pergamum, subsequently grew up in Asia
Minor at Seleucid expense, and became great by favour of
Rome. In 212 Rome began to take part, at first tentatively,
in Hellenistic affairs, and ultimately absorbed the whole
Mediterranean world, the last independent state, Egypt,
coming to an end in 30 B.C.

The complicated story of the struggle among the generals
down to 301, largely waged with mercenaries of every
nationality, can only be briefly indicated. The arrangements made by the army after Alexander's death vested

the kingship jointly in his idiot half-brother Philip III
and his posthumous son by Roxane, Alexander IV : his
general Perdiccas had the effective control in Asia, and
Antipater in Europe, where he had been governing Macedonia and supervising Greece for Alexander. Various
satrapies were allotted afresh among the generals ; in
the division Ptolemy, a wise and far-seeing man, secured
Egypt, Antigonus the One-eyed, satrap of Phrygia, obtained
further territory, and Lysimachus received Thrace. War
broke out in 321 with a combination of Antipater, Antigonus, and Ptolemy against Perdiccas, who professedly
stood for the kings but was accused of aiming at the throne ;
he was ultimately murdered, and the united Macedonian
armies made Antipater regent. He was the last of the
generals of Philip II, and the universal respect felt for him
enabled him to hold the empire together till his death in
319 ; during this time Antigonus, who, as his general,
commanded a large force, crushed Perdiccas' party till
only one leader survived, the Greek Eumenes of Cardia,
Alexander's secretary. On Antipater's death Polyperchon
was locally elected regent in Macedonia ; Antigonus began
to work for his own hand, and Eumenes joined Polyperchon
to uphold the kings. War blazed up again ; in Asia the
protagonists were Eumenes and Antigonus, who was
supported by Ptolemy and others ; in Europe, Polyperchon
and Antipater's son Cassander, who was Antigonus' ally.
The war in Europe ended in 316 with the complete success
of Cassander, a man of remarkable ability, who became
master of Macedonia and much of Greece, including Athens ;
Philip III and Alexander's mother Olympias perished in
the struggle, and Cassander obtained possession of the
young Alexander IV. The fight made under great difficulties by Eumenes, resourceful and absolutely loyal, is
one of the romances of history ; he captured Babylon,
secured the help of the far eastern satraps, and defeated
Antigonus more than once, but early in 316 he was betrayed
to Antigonus by his own troops and put to death. With
his death the cause of Alexander IV was definitely lost.

Antigonus, a man of enormous capacity and unlimited ambition, now held the strongest position of any of the generals, and claimed to stand in Alexander's place; he began striking down the eastern satraps, and Seleucus, satrap of Babylon, only saved his life by escaping to Ptolemy. The smaller men were by now largely eliminated, and the principal rulers—Cassander, Ptolemy and Lysimachus—formed a coalition against Antigonus, on the ground, which was true, that he was aiming at the empire; but the war (315–311) was indeterminate, though in 312 Ptolemy restored Seleucus to Babylon. Antigonus however in 314 secured the moral support of the Greek democracies by a proclamation, which for years he carried out honestly, that all Greek cities should be free, ungarrisoned, and self-governing; it was a revival of Alexander's policy, directed against Cassander's system of governing the cities through oligarchies and garrisons (Chap. II). One result was that Delos revolted from Athens, and remained free till 166. After the peace of 311 between Antigonus and the coalition, which left Antigonus master of Syria, Asia Minor, and Mesopotamia, he attempted to crush Seleucus, but failed, though he half-ruined Babylon, and Seleucus subsequently secured everything east of Babylon, though he had to cede the Indian provinces to the Mauryan Chandragupta; in return he obtained 500 war elephants. In 310 Cassander murdered Alexander IV, a step which the other dynasts had invited by the terms of the treaty of 311; and all now became independent rulers.

In 307 Antigonus and his brilliant son Demetrius, a man of great and varied talents but unstable character, began a second struggle to secure the whole empire, a struggle which ultimately involved the entire military strength of every part of the Hellenistic world. Since 317 Cassander had governed Athens through Demetrius of Phalerum, a Peripatetic; the city had had peace and prosperity, and Demetrius had made laws in Aristotle's spirit, but his government had favoured the well-to-do. In 307 Antigonus' son Demetrius freed Athens and restored democratic government, and in 306 utterly defeated Ptolemy in a naval battle off Salamis in Cyprus and secured the command of the sea ; his father and he, who trusted each other absolutely, thereon each took the title of king, as joint monarchs of Alexander's empire. But Antigonus' attempt to invade Egypt and destroy Ptolemy failed, and in 305 Ptolemy and the other dynasts also took the royal title, as kings in their separate territories ; and a year wasted by Demetrius over his famous and unsuccessful siege of Rhodes enabled Cassander to begin reconquering Greece. Demetrius drove Cassander off, freed most of Greece, and in 303 re-formed Alexander's League of Corinth with his father and himself as Presidents in Alexander's seat. Cassander, Lysimachus, and Ptolemy then secured Seleucus' help, and in 302, while Demetrius moved on Macedonia with a great force, Lysimachus, with reinforcements sent by Cassander, crossed to Asia. Antigonus, who failed to crush him, had to recall Demetrius, and in 301, at Ipsus in Phrygia, the two gave battle to the combined forces of Lysimachus and Seleucus, who had 480 elephants in action ; Antigonus was defeated and killed, but Demetrius escaped.

The victors divided the spoils, Lysimachus taking Asia Minor north of Taurus and Seleucus Mesopotamia and Syria ; Ptolemy however had occupied Syria south of Aradus and Damascus during the Ipsus campaign, and Seleucus, who never forgot that he owed to Ptolemy both life and kingdom, did not demand its retrocession, though he preserved his claim. Cassander, the soul of the coalition, was content with Macedonia ; Demetrius still ruled the sea, and held Tyre and Sidon, some cities in Asia Minor, and parts of Greece. The mutual distrust of the victors was of advantage to Athens, still the greatest of Greek cities except Syracuse, and Cassander's forbearance left her her liberty till Demetrius conquered and garrisoned her in 295. Cassander died in 297, and quarrels between his sons enabled Demetrius in 294 to seize the throne of Macedonia, a throne he held for six years, during which he reduced most of Greece except Sparta, Aetolia, and

Pyrrhus king of Epirus, and built his name-city Demetrias (p. 60). The position of the parties in the Greek cities meanwhile clarified, and henceforth, while the democracies usually stood for national independence, the wealthy looked to Macedonia for support, as later they were to look to Rome. Demetrius however, though he could conquer, could not govern ; he compared badly with the statesmanlike Cassander, and never secured his people's affection, for he treated Macedonia merely as a base for the reconquest of Asia. In 289 his naval preparations alarmed the other kings, and they combined against him ; in 288 Lysimachus and Pyrrhus overran and partitioned Macedonia, Athens revolted with Ptolemy's aid, and Demetrius was again reduced to some Greek cities and his fleet. Nevertheless he invaded Asia, flung himself without much success against Lysimachus, his bitter personal enemy, and finally, driven over the Taurus, became engaged in a heroic struggle with Seleucus. At one moment it looked as if he would yet rule Asia ; but he fell ill, his army deserted, and in 285 he was forced to surrender. Two years later the most brilliant of Alexander's Successors had drunk himself to death in his captivity.

On Demetrius' fall part of his fleet went over to Ptolemy, who with it secured Tyre and Sidon, the Island League (p. 63), and the command of the sea. But Lysimachus, who in 285 expelled Pyrrhus from his half of Macedonia, gained most ; master of Macedonia, Thessaly, Thrace, and much of Asia Minor, he was now really stronger than Seleucus. He was a cautious statesman and an excellent general and financier ; though he ruled his Greek cities after Cassander's fashion he was not always unpopular, and he fostered trade, particularly in the Black Sea, which possibly he hoped to make his lake. His capital was at first his new city Lysimacheia, near Gallipoli ; later he probably transferred his seat to Macedonia. Demetrius' last campaign had revealed a growing distrust between Lysimachus and Seleucus which foreshadowed a contest for the lordship of Asia, and in 283 Seleucus made over-tures to Antigonus Gonatas, Demetrius' son by Antipater's daughter Phila. Antigonus was ruling his father's Greek cities, and in 281 reduced Athens, independent since 288.

Ptolemy's house played its part in Lysimachus' ultimate fall. Ptolemy had married Antipater's daughter Eurydice, and her long struggle with her maid-of-honour Berenice, who was Ptolemy's mistress, had ended before 287 in Ptolemy repudiating Eurydice and marrying Berenice. Eurydice's son Ptolemy, afterwards called Keraunos, the Thunderbolt, was exiled, and when in 283 Ptolemy died— the only Successor who died in his bed—his son by Berenice succeeded peacefully as Ptolemy II. Keraunos went to Lysimachus, who had married as his third wife Ptolemy II's sister Arsinoe, Berenice's daughter ; and round these two centred (in the tradition) the obscure intrigues which ended in Lysimachus murdering his eldest son Agathocles, and driving all discontented elements in his kingdom into Seleucus' arms. Seleucus ultimately crossed the Taurus, defeated and killed Lysimachus in 281 at Corupedion in Lydia, and for a moment, last and most fortunate of Alexander's companions, saw all Alexander's empire except Egypt at his feet. But early in 280 he was assassinated by Keraunos, whom Lysimachus' army accepted as Lysimachus' avenger and made king of Macedonia. Keraunos managed to hold his kingdom against his numerous rivals, defeating Antigonus Gonatas at sea, winning over Pyrrhus by help for his Italian expedition, and getting rid of Arsinoe, who held Cassandreia, by first marrying and then expelling her. Antiochus I, Seleucus' son by his Sogdian wife Apama, was fully involved at home : Ptolemy II, who had a footing in Caria, was threatening him, Northern Syria was in revolt, and he was cut off from Europe and the Black Sea by the Northern League, a combination of Heraclea, Byzantium, Chalcedon, Cius, Tios, the Persian prince Mithridates of Pontus, and Nicomedes of Bithynia, who were fighting for their independence. He was also attacked by Antigonus from Greece.

This was the situation when the migrating Galati, Gallic

tribes who had followed the Danube valley, reached the Macedonian frontier, bringing their families with them. Early in 279 a body under Bolgius burst into Macedonia and defeated and killed Keraunos, but subsequently retired with their plunder; but a second body under Brennus had entered the country and, failing to establish themselves, passed southward late in the year to invade Greece. Brennus, who cannot have had over 30,000 fighting men, successfully turned the defenders of Thermopylae, but failed in an attempt to raid Delphi with a flying column, while his main force was checked and then driven north with heavy loss by the Aetolians, who acquired a well-deserved reputation as the saviours of Greece. The danger to Greece induced Antigonus and Antiochus to make a real peace, and their treaty (autumn 279) remained for long a cardinal point of Hellenistic politics; it bound Antiochus not to interfere in Macedonia and Greece, or Antigonus in Thrace and Asia; and for long the two dynasties remained friends. In 278 three tribes of Gauls, the Tolistoagii, Trocmi, and Tectosages, 20,000 strong, reached the Dardanelles, and were taken into service by Nicomedes and Mithridates to attack Antiochus; they ravaged Asia Minor for two years and created a panic, but in 275 Antiochus, having settled Syria, gave the country some rest by defeating the Gauls with the aid of 16 elephants sent by his general in Bactria. Nicomedes and Mithridates then settled the Gauls in northern Phrygia (Galatia) as a buffer against him. Meanwhile another body had invaded Thrace; in 277 part of these reached the sea and were destroyed in battle near Lysimacheia by Antigonus. With the prestige of this victory Antigonus entered Macedonia, which was in anarchy, was accepted as king, and by the end of 276 was master of the kingdom and married Antiochus' half-sister Phila. Apart from Galatia, the Gauls managed to found two kingdoms which affected Greek history, that of the Scordisci in Serbia and that called Tylis in Thrace.

From 275 we can follow the history of the three Mace-

donian dynasties as separate units ; Lysimachus' kingdom
never revived, and in the Black Sea he had no successor.
Of the new kings, Antiochus I was a great city-builder
and administrator whose history is lost. Tradition makes
Ptolemy II a valetudinarian and dilettante ; he was
really, though no general, a strong ruler of aggressive
ambition, highly educated, an able diplomat and skilled
organiser. Antigonus, the second founder of Macedonia,
was a blunt straightforward character, of dogged tenacity
and with the full family loyalty of his house ; friend and
pupil of the philosophers Menedemus and Zeno, his Stoic
sympathies made him the first king whom philosophy
could claim as her own. Egypt's foreign policy, which
aimed at the empire of the Aegean and its coasts, and her
great strength, were bound to bring her into conflict with
the other two kingdoms, while the Seleucids could not forget
their claim to southern Syria, which Egypt held. The
result was the long series of the so-called Syrian Wars
between Egypt and the Seleucids, conjoined with wars
between Egypt and Macedonia. These wars helped to
prevent Greek civilisation establishing itself as firmly in
Asia as it might otherwise have done.

It was Ptolemy II who began the first Syrian War.
Possibly he became aggressive as soon as Seleucus was
dead, for Miletus, Seleucid in 280, was Egyptian in 279 ;
certainly in 276 his army invaded Seleucid Syria, but was
defeated and driven out by Antiochus I, who was then able to
defeat the Gauls and besiege Miletus (275) ; he allied himself with Magas, Ptolemy II's half-brother who governed
Cyrene. In winter 276–5, however, Ptolemy repudiated
his wife (Lysimachus' daughter Arsinoe I) and married his
full sister Arsinoe II, widow of Lysimachus and Keraunos,
probably because he needed her brains. Arsinoe took the
lost war into her strong hands, turned it into a sweeping
success, and ended (273 or 272) in possession of all Phoenicia
and most of the coast of Asia Minor from Miletus to the
Calycadnus in Cilicia ; she was to receive unexampled
honours both as woman and goddess. The years till her

death in 270 were Egypt's golden age, and Callimachus prophesied that Ptolemy would rule the world from the rising to the setting sun. Arsinoe wished to make Ptolemaeus, her son by Lysimachus, king of Macedonia, but she died too soon; she had, however, prevented Antigonus interfering in the war by subsidising Pyrrhus, who had returned from Italy and desired to attack him. In 273 Pyrrhus momentarily conquered Macedonia, but quitted it for adventures in Greece; he tried and failed to take Sparta, and was finally killed (272) in street fighting at Argos, leaving Antigonus arbiter of Greece.

Antigonus showed moderation. His position in Greece depended on holding Corinth, which prevented Greece uniting against him, (for a united Greece would have been stronger than Macedonia), and Piraeus, which ensured that Athens should informally be his spiritual capital; he conquered enough to ensure their communications with Demetrias, but sought no further possessions in Greece (p. 58). In 267, however, Athens, Sparta, and other cities, encouraged by Ptolemy, allied themselves with Egypt to attack him; this severe struggle (266–262), called the Chremonidean War from the Athenian statesman Chremonides, ended in Antigonus' victory and the capture of Athens, which henceforth ceased to play any prominent part in politics. The leading men of Antigonus' party also seized power as tyrants in Argos, Megapolis, and other Peloponnesian cities, and acted in his interest and with his support as a check on Sparta. Antigonus, a good ruler, subsequently restored Macedonia to its fullest boundaries and gave his dynasty a position in the country which nothing could shake. In 262 Antiochus I died, after losing Ephesus to Egypt.

His son Antiochus II and Antigonus, probably in alliance, took their revenge on Ptolemy II in the Second Syrian War (259–255); Antiochus recovered Ephesus, Miletus, much of the coast of Asia Minor, and Phoenicia down to Berytus, while Antigonus defeated Ptolemy's fleet off Cos and secured the Island League and command of the sea; for a time his half-brother Demetrius the Fair ruled Cyrene. But the revolt c. 252 of Alexander, his general in Corinth and Euboea, with Egypt's support, crippled him at sea, and he only recovered Corinth in 246 after Alexander's death ; while Ptolemy in 252 won over Antiochus, who sent away his wife Laodice and married Ptolemy's daughter Berenice. On Antiochus' death (late 247) a struggle began between the rival queens ; Berenice and her son were killed, but their deaths were concealed, and in 246 Ptolemy III (son of Arsinoe I), who in January had succeeded his father Ptolemy II, occupied Northern Syria and Cilicia, made a military parade through the distracted kingdom professedly as champion of the rightful king, Berenice's son, and reached Seleuceia on the Tigris. He met little resistance, but he described his exploit as the subjection of Seleucid Asia. In the ensuing war, the Third Syrian or Laodicean (to 241), Laodice's son Seleucus II recovered Cilicia, Northern Syria (inland), and the east, but failed to recover Seleuceia in Pieria and Phoenicia, and again lost the coast of Asia Minor, along which Ptolemy later extended his power and even occupied the coast of Thrace. Ptolemy's fleet however was defeated by Antigonus off Andros (246 or 245) ; Antigonus recovered Delos and some islands, and Egypt was never again supreme at sea, but apparently the Island League broke up. Subsequently the Seleucid empire was paralysed by civil war between Seleucus II and his brother Antiochus Hierax, who allied himself with the Galatians. Cappadocia had already become an independent native kingdom ; and during this period Bactria, Parthia, and the provinces beyond Parthia were finally lost, and the victorious Galatians again became a threat.

That threat brought Pergamum into prominence. A eunuch from Tios, Philetaerus, half a Paphlagonian, governor of the fortress of Pergamum, after betraying Antigonus I and Lysimachus in turn, had made himself semi-independent under Antiochus I, and on his death in 263 left a little principality on the Caïcus to his nephew Eumenes, who in 241 again bequeathed it, considerably enlarged, to his nephew Attalus I. The eclipse of Seleucid power in Asia Minor gave Attalus his chance ; he challenged the Galatians by refusing the tribute which they exacted even from the Seleucids as a condition of refraining from raids, broke them in two battles (before 230), took the royal title, and then drove Hierax out of Asia Minor and from 228 to 223 ruled the whole Seleucid territory north of Taurus. Seleucus II, who was trying to reconquer Parthia, died in 226 and his son Seleucus III in 223 without having been able to deal with him.

Meanwhile Greece had been witnessing the growth of the two great Leagues (Chap. II). Aetolia, already mistress of Delphi, began to expand after 279 ; she promised Antigonus her neutrality and kept her promise, and as compensation began to include in her League the little Amphiktyonic states ; she apparently met with intermittent opposition from Phocis and Boeotia, but in 245 she broke Boeotia's power at Chaeronea, and that country never regained its former importance. The expansion of the League of the eleven Achaean cities began in 251, when a young Sicyonian exile named Aratus surprised Sicyon by night, expelled its tyrant, and for security joined Sicyon to the Achaean League. Aratus was a strange character, a compound of heroism and nervous weakness, unscrupulous, but with an amazing power over his fellow citizens ; for a generation he almost *was* the League, whose general he became every alternate year from 245 onwards. In 243 he embarked on the crusade which was his life's purpose, to free the Peloponnese from Antigonus and the tyrants he supported ; he surprised Macedonia's key position, Corinth, by night in time of peace and captured Acrocorinthus. Antigonus died in 240-39 without recovering Corinth, and the two Leagues at once went to war with his son Demetrius II. Demetrius curtailed Aetolia's influence, but did not damage her badly ; but the Aecheans won over city after city, including Megalopolis and Argos, whose tyrants laid down their power and became League officials.

In 229 Demetrius II died, after being severely defeated

by Macedonia's northern neighbours the Dardanians, who
invaded the country.  Philip, his son by his second wife,
the Epirote princess Phthia, was a child, and the army
ultimately crowned Philip's guardian Antigonus Doson,
son of Demetrius the Fair, an able ruler ;  he drove out the
Dardanians and restored Macedonia.  But the Leagues
had seized their opportunity ;  in the confusion of 229
Aetolia was able to stretch from sea to sea (p. 65), and now
regarded herself as Macedonia's equal, while Aratus expelled
every trace of Macedonian influence from the Peloponnese.
By 228 the Achaean League had reached its zenith ;  it
comprised Achaea, Sicyon, Corinth, Megara, Aegina, Argos
and the coastal cities, Megalopolis and most of Arcadia,
*i.e.* practically all of the Peloponnese which Cassander
and Demetrius I had ruled ;  it had none but willing citizens,
and was completely independent, for its nominal alliance
with the now inactive Ptolemy III did not shape its policy.
These years mark the culmination of the federal movement ;
Doson did not meddle with the Peloponnese, and contented
himself with obtaining Aetolia's neutrality.   Athens also
recovered her freedom on Demetrius' death ;  none interfered with her, and except for the one episode of Philip's
attack she fought no more wars till 88 ;  she was almost
as it were neutralised by universal consent, for she was a
brilliant University town and the cultural centre of Greece,
whose honours were sought by many kings as the highest
expression of civilised approbation.

But the Achaean League could neither conquer nor win
over Sparta ;  on this rock it was ultimately to founder.
The young king of Sparta, Cleomenes III, quarrelled with
the League, enrolled mercenaries, and in 227, having thus
secured the necessary force, carried through his revolution
(p. 105), restored (as he thought) Lycurgus' Sparta, and
enormously increased his country's strength.  He then
invaded Achaea, and his victory at Hecatombaion laid the
League at his feet ;  city after city, including Corinth and
Argos, seceded to him, for the common people everywhere
thought he would carry out social revolution and give them

the land. In reality he was intensely ambitious, and was aiming at the headship of Peloponnese ; as a beginning he demanded the generalship of the League, which he would have made the kernel of a new confederacy. To save what remained of the League, Aratus, who was desperate, made the great betrayal ; having expelled the Macedonians from Peloponnese, he decided to bring them back. He asked Doson's help, which Doson gave in return for the cession of Corinth, henceforth again a Macedonian fortress. Doson re-formed the League of Corinth as a Hellenic League of Leagues (p. 62) ; but as it did not include the Aetolian League, Sparta, Athens, Elis, and Messenia, Greece was really split in half, though Doson's conception was statesmanlike. Cleomenes made a good fight, but was defeated by Doson at Sellasia (222) and fled to Egypt, where he died. Doson occupied Sparta, never before taken, undid the revolution, restored the old régime, and made Sparta Macedonia's ally. In 221 he died, a heavy loss to Macedonia ; he had taken care to secure Philip's succession.

Polybius' history formally begins with the accession of new kings in all the kingdoms ; in Syria Antiochus III, the younger son of Seleucus II (223) ; in Egypt Ptolemy IV Philopator (221) ; and Philip V in Macedonia. Ptolemy III had allowed his army to decay, and his son Ptolemy IV was an art-loving voluptuary, who left the government to his strong and unscrupulous minister Sosibius. Antiochus III, later called " the Great," young, energetic, and sensible, found a shattered kingdom, which he set to work to restore ; by 220 his cousin Achaeus had reconquered Seleucid Asia Minor from Attalus, and he himself had suppressed a revolt of his generals in Media and Persis ; once master in his own house, he set out to wrest southern Syria from the inactive Philopator. But the Syrian fortresses delayed him, and Sosibius held him off by negotiations while he brought generals from Greece and created an army ; he, or Philopator, also took the dangerous step of enrolling 20,000 native Egyptians in the phalanx, no native having borne arms since Ptolemy I's experiment in 312. This

war, the Fourth Syrian, ended with the battle of Raphia
(22 June 217) ; Philopator left his pleasures to take command, and a hard-fought day was decided by his leadership
and the bravery of the Egyptian phalanx. Philopator
retained southern Syria and Phoenicia ; but for his dynasty
the victory was not all gain, since from it dates the resur-
gence of the native element in Egypt against the Greek.

In Macedonia the accession of Philip V, gifted and
attractive, roused high hopes ; the unbridled temper which
was to mar his life only revealed itself later. The Aetolians
under Scopas had broken loose on Doson's death, and in 220
their raids on other states brought on the so-called Social
War (War of the Allies), in which they and their allies
Sparta and Elis opposed Philip and his Hellenic League.
Philip, who was watching the actions of Rome in Illyria,
did not want war, but loyally defended his allies ; he made
one daring raid on Thermum, Aetolia's federal centre, which
he sacked. The war, which produced no result, ended in
217 with the peace of Naupactus, the peace conference
being notable for the appeal made by the Aetolian Agelaus
for Hellenic unity in face of the ' cloud rising in the west,'
the ultimate victor in the war between Carthage and Rome.
The popularity of Philip, the ' darling of Hellas,' in 217 was
so marked that for a moment he seemed to have a better
chance of unifying Greece than any of his predecessors ;
but he threw the chance away, if chance it were, and
Aratus' death in 214-3 removed his best counsellor, for
Aratus seemingly had learnt through misfortune. In 215
Philip allied himself with Carthage and attempted to expel
the Romans from Illyria ; the result was that alliance of
Rome and Aetolia (212) which ushered in the First Macedonian War. This was the Social War over again, with
one great difference : Aetolia was aided by Roman and
Pergamene squadrons, Attalus having joined Rome's
alliance, while Philip's new allies, Carthage and Prusias I
of Bithynia, gave him little help. The once powerful
Macedonian fleet had decayed, and Philip was helpless at
sea ; all his activity could hardly counter enemies who

struck where they would. His one gain was that Philopoemen of Megalopolis reformed the incompetent Achaean
army. Philopoemen, a soldier and little more, had fought
with distinction at Sellasia, but had then, with a curious
lack of patriotism, gone to Crete as an adventurer ; he
returned in 210, and in 207 the new Achaean army under
his lead defeated Machanidas, who had seized power at
Sparta, and thus gained confidence. One other consequence
the war had : the Greek world, accustomed to Macedonian
warfare, which had grown relatively humane, saw with fear
or anger how Romans treated a captured city. In 205 the
inconclusive war ended with the general peace of Phoenice.

Debtor and creditor troubles at once broke out in Aetolia ;
Scopas tried to cancel debts, failed, and went to Ptolemy
to command his army. Sparta, left masterless by Machanidas' death, was seized by Nabis, a distant collateral of the
royal house ; the revolution he carried through (p. 106)
again strengthened Sparta enormously, and he secured
some sea-power by Cretan alliances. Whatever his mis-
deeds, he was very popular with large classes, and it is our
loss that we only possess hostile notices. The decay of the
Macedonian fleet had left the Aegean masterless, and by
200 Rhodes had seized the vacant position and created a
new Island League under her own presidency.

Ptolemy IV died in 203, leaving as heir a child, Ptolemy
V Epiphanes ; Polybius has left a wonderful picture of the
rising in Alexandria which overthrew the hated minister
Agathocles and gave the child new guardians. Philip and
Antiochus, whose dynasties had both suffered much at
Egypt's hands, at once formed an alliance to divide up
Egypt's foreign possessions. Antiochus had a fixed purpose,
the restoration of Seleucus' empire ; after Raphia he had
recovered Asia Minor from his revolted cousin Achaeus,
and had then made his famous eastern expedition. He
had conquered part of Armenia, made Arsaces of Parthia
tributary, defeated Euthydemus of Bactria, and penetrated
the Cabul valley ; and he had shown statesmanship by
leaving Euthydemus his throne as a necessary bulwark of

civilisation against the nomads. His compact with Philip seemingly gave Philip Cyrene, Ionia, and the Cyclades, while he himself was to have Cyprus, southern Syria, and the other Egyptian possessions in Asia Minor. Antiochus in 202 invaded southern Syria (the Fifth Syrian War), defeated Scopas in 200 at Panion near the source of the Jordan, and by 198 was master of the whole country (including Phoenicia), which his dynasty was to retain. Philip, having built a fleet, attacked the Straits in 202, took Lysimacheia, Chalcedon, and Cius, and destroyed Cius with a brutality displayed later at Abydos and Maroneia ; he was trying Roman methods, and evoked general distrust, even hatred. In 201 he turned south and seized Samos ; but he had foolishly antagonised Rhodes by stirring up Crete against her, and the Rhodians, to whom he had promised to spare Cius, now combined with Egypt's friend Attalus against him ; their united fleets defeated him off Chios, and though he subsequently managed to defeat the Rhodians alone at Lade, and conquered part of Caria, he never recovered at sea from his heavy losses at Chios.

The conquest of Carthage in 202 had freed Rome's hands, and in 200 Egypt, Rhodes, and Attalus appealed to her for help ; it was not unnatural, but it gave Rome that position of arbiter in the Eastern Mediterranean which she was never again to quit. Rome had as yet no deliberate purpose of reducing the east, and so far her interventions had been provoked ; but she had henceforth a consistent block of supporters,—Egypt, Pergamum, Rhodes, and Athens. Athens desired peace only, Egypt self-preservation, Rhodes the freedom of the Greeks and of the sea ; but Pergamum, to whom Seleucid power was a standing threat, was usually ready to egg Rome on. Macedonia, the Seleucids, and subsequently Aetolia, came to represent the more nationally-minded opposition to Rome's advance. Rome in 200 had no grievance against Philip, but seemingly she was afraid, —afraid that Philip and Antiochus would conquer and control Egypt and its resources, and launch against Italy all Alexander's empire. It was a chimaera ; the two

kings, though allies, profoundly distrusted each other, and
Philip would never have allowed Antiochus to cross to
Greece. Rome's plan, to meet the imagined danger, was
to free Greece and make it her outpost against the kings ;
she declared war (the Second Macedonian) and sent a large
army to Illyria. The Aetolians, Philip's consistent foes,
joined her in 198, and Philip even made an enemy of peaceful
Athens, who welcomed Attalus, and whose suburbs Philip
cruelly ravaged. The Achaeans deserted him, and his
other allies were of little account. He held out for two
years ; but Macedonia was becoming so exhausted that in
197 he could only raise 26,000 men by enrolling boys and
grey-beards, and was decisively defeated at Cynoscephalae
in Thessaly by the proconsul T. Quinctius Flamininus and
the Aetolians.

The Aetolians clamoured for Philip's destruction ; but
Flamininus refused. Philip had to surrender the ' fetters
of Greece '—Corinth, Chalcis, and Demetrias—withdraw
altogether from Greece and Thessaly, give up his cities in
Asia, which became free, and pay an indemnity ; and he
became Rome's ally. Rome paid for this alliance with
Aetolia's scarcely-veiled hostility, for Aetolia did not obtain
for her League all the cities she claimed. But Flamininus
kept his theatrical masterstroke for the Isthmian games of
196, when to a great concourse his herald proclaimed that
all Greeks formerly subject to Philip or members of the
Hellenic League should be free. It resembled the proclamation of Antigonus I in 314 ; like Antigonus, Rome acted
from political motives, not sentiment, and meant what she
said—at the start. The enthusiasm in Greece was enormous, the subsequent disillusionment correspondingly bitter.
Doson's Hellenic League was thus dissolved, and its constituent members, including the Achaean League, became
Rome's allies, as did Acarnania ; the synoecism of Demetrias (p. 60) was broken up, and the Magnesian cities
again made autonomous and united in a League with
Demetrias as federal centre ; other new Leagues now formed
were the Thessalian, Perrhaebian, and Euboean.

There remained Nabis. Philip had tried to win him during the war by giving him Argos; Nabis took Argos and concluded an alliance with Rome. The loss of Argos, however, made the inextinguishable hostility between Achaea and Sparta blaze up afresh; both were Rome's allies, but Flamininus declared for Achaea. He paid Nabis, who had raised 15,000 men, the compliment of calling up all Rome's Greek allies; he ultimately had 50,000 troops in Laconia. Nabis made a good fight, and when the Romans finally tried to storm Sparta (195) his general Pythagoras fired the threatened quarter and drove them out; but Nabis lost his nerve and made terms. He surrendered Argos and the coast, but kept Sparta; Flamininus neither 'freed' the city nor restored the Spartans exiled in the revolution. The reason of his forbearance was partly his desire to settle Greece before a successor could interfere, and partly Antiochus.

Antiochus, far from helping Philip, had used 197 to conquer the coast of Asia Minor from Cilicia to the Hellespont; he also annexed the acquisitions made by Attalus, who died that year, and left to Attalus' son, Eumenes II, only the original Pergamene territory; naturally Eumenes became and remained his bitter enemy. In 196 Antiochus crossed the Dardanelles and began to subdue the Thracian coast. Both Greeks and Romans exaggerated his strength; he had had a career of singular success, ruled an enormous territory, and represented to Rome the danger of the unknown. Roman envoys met him at Lysimacheia with a demand that he should evacuate Europe. Antiochus replied that he was only reoccupying Seleucus' possessions: he did not interfere with Italy, and Rome must not interfere with Asia. For three years negotiations continued, with the same deadlock; Antiochus only wanted to be let alone, and Rome, her hands full in Spain, did not desire war. But two powers did desire war: Eumenes, who feared Antiochus, and Aetolia, who wanted vengeance upon Rome. The Roman armies had quitted Greece in 194; the country had suffered greatly, if merely from feeding such large forces, and the democracies were disillusioned, for it was the well-to-do who favoured Rome, as they had once favoured Macedonia, and everywhere Rome had brought them to power.

In 193–2 Antiochus married his daughter Cleopatra I to Ptolemy V, and secured Bithynia, Cappadocia, and Galatia as allies ; but, though Rome in 193 sent him an ultimatum, he had made no real preparation for war when an Aetolian embassy arrived, described the feeling in Greece, begged him to cross, and promised him Philip and Nabis as allies. Hannibal, who had taken refuge with him when exiled from Carthage in 195, naturally urged him to attack Rome in Italy ; but Antiochus, as was also natural from his own standpoint, was not inclined to convert the defence of Thrace into a life and death struggle, and favoured the Aetolian plan ; his minister Menippus in turn made Aetolia absurd promises. Aetolia struck at once ; she surprised and secured Demetrias, a sensational event, but failed to surprise Sparta. However, she killed Nabis, and Philopoemen seized the opportunity to force Sparta into the Achaean League ; in 191 he also incorporated Elis and Messenia, and the League embraced all Peloponnese, but Sparta and Messenia were unwilling members and merely sources of weakness. Antiochus, once a sensible man, but deceived by Aetolia and Menippus, exercised no foresight ; his army was not ready, but in 192 he crossed to Demetrias with 10,000 men, enough to provoke war but too few to wage it. The battle-cry was the liberation of Greece from the Romans ; but the promised upheaval did not take place, and though Antiochus secured Euboea and part of Thessaly, both Philip and Achaea held to Rome, and in 191 a Roman army, co-operating with Philip, recovered Thessaly and destroyed Antiochus' force at the usual death-trap, Thermopylae, the king escaping to Asia almost alone.

In 190 the consul L. Cornelius Scipio, accompanied by his brother Africanus, the conqueror of Hannibal, as the real commander, prepared to invade Asia ; they were greatly aided by Aetolia requesting a truce, and with Philip's help advanced through Thrace, while the Roman fleet appeared in the Aegean and was joined by those of Eumenes and Rhodes. Antiochus' admiral, the Rhodian exile Polyxenidas, fought well ; he was defeated at Corycus by the Romans and Eumenes, but subsequently destroyed a Rhodian squadron, and in the final battle of Myonnesus, probably the only sea-fight ever fought by Rome against odds, he might have defeated the Romans alone, but the skill of the Rhodian contingent with them turned the day. This battle ended the predominance of the Macedonian kingdoms at sea, which had endured since the downfall of Athens' navy at Amorgus in the Lamian war (322). Meanwhile Antiochus had collected his army, but after Myonnesus he lost his head and abandoned the defence of the strong Lysimacheia and the Dardanelles ; he seems to have believed that Fortune had deserted him. With Eumenes' help the Scipios crossed the Dardanelles and late in 190 Antiochus was completely defeated at Magnesia, much of the credit belonging to Eumenes. In 189 a Roman force entered Phrygia and overthrew Antiochus' allies the Galatians, while in Greece Philip and the Romans were conquering Aetolia. The heroic resistance of Ambracia secured for Aetolia moderate terms ; she again became Rome's ally, but her League was considerably curtailed, and she lost Delphi. In 188 peace was made at Apamea between Antiochus and Rome ; Antiochus had to surrender all Seleucid Asia Minor except eastern Cilicia, give up his elephants and fleet, and pay a large indemnity. Rome also demanded Hannibal, who escaped to Bithynia.

The peace of Apamea altered the face of the Hellenistic east ; Rome was now the predominant power, and in Greece itself no state was really independent of her. The time that followed was one of constant Roman interference ; every weaker disputant, every person aggrieved, appealed to Rome, and Roman commissioners were perpetually travelling eastward ; and in the cities the democracies, which stood for national independence, at least internally, now tended to look to Macedonia, while the well-to-do favoured submission to the wishes of Rome. Eumenes reaped his reward at the peace ; he received Seleucid Asia Minor north of Taurus and the Maeander, with parts of the Pamphylian and Thracian coasts ; he must too have received western Cilicia, but he could never master the wild country of Pisidia and the Taurus. He reached the Black Sea at Tios, and held his enemy Bithynia in his arms. He had a war with her, which in 183 Rome settled in his favour ; Rome then again demanded Hannibal, who took poison to avoid being surrendered by Prusias. Eumenes also fought with Pharnaces of Pontus, who however took Sinope and made it his capital ; but Eumenes made himself suzerain of Galatia—a success perhaps commemorated by the great altar at Pergamum (p. 262)—and extended his influence even to Cappadocia and Armenia. His relations with his Greek cities are noticed elsewhere (p. 132). He grew great, but was everywhere disliked as being Rome's jackal, the traitor to Hellenism. Rhodes received Lycia and Caria south of the Maeander ; she had now reached her zenith, was head of a powerful city confederacy, and ruled the sea ; but the Lycians revolted again and again, and were an open sore in her side. Antiochus, for all his losses, still retained a great empire, though his suzerainty over Parthia naturally lapsed ; but he had trouble over raising the indemnity, and in 187 was ingloriously killed while trying to plunder a temple in Elymais (Elam). His son Seleucus IV waged no wars, the best thing he could do, and was murdered in 175 by his minister Heliodorus, who apparently also removed the son who succeeded him. His younger son, Demetrius, was a hostage in Rome, and the crown was seized the same year by his gifted brother Antiochus IV Epiphanes.[1]

The Achaean League, like Rhodes, now enjoyed a high reputation ; Philopoemen stood for friendship with Rome

[1] To alter Epiphanes' number to Antiochus V (W. Otto, *Helio-dorus* in Pauly-Wissowa) is incorrect, the name of Seleucus IV's son being unknown. Demetrius' name suggests *two* elder brothers.

but complete independence outside the League's obligations as Rome's ally. But, as Lycia to Rhodes, so Sparta was an open sore to Achaea, and in 188 Philopoemen attempted to settle the matter by brute force ; he took Sparta, razed the wall, restored the men exiled by Nabis and his predecessors, abolished the Lycurgan institutions, removed many of Nabis' new citizens to Achaea, and sold as slaves 3,000 who refused to go ; he thus manufactured more exiles, who began appealing to Rome. In 183 Messene revolted and was not subdued till she had captured and poisoned Philopoemen ; Lycortas continued his policy, and it was Lycortas' young son, the historian Polybius, who bore Philopoemen's urn when his ashes were brought home. In 181 Rome intervened on Sparta's behalf, and Lycortas' opponent Callicrates, head of the Roman party in Achaea, at Rome's behest restored all the Spartan exiles, the wall, and the Lycurgan institutions. Polybius naturally has little good to say of Callicrates ; but some settlement of the Spartan troubles was forced on Rome, and was one of her most justifiable acts.

Philip during the war with Antiochus had by Rome's leave retaken Demetrias and parts of Thessaly and Thrace ; Demetrias he kept, but Rome ordered him to retire from Thrace and Thessaly. He obeyed, with bitter hate in his soul. He had helped Rome greatly, and had received what was to become the usual reward of her friends. All that had happened to Macedonia itself had been defeat in one battle ; and Philip sat down to prepare for a second war. He still had his outbursts of madness—the massacre at Maroneia when he quitted it, and the murder of his younger son Demetrius for favouring Rome, the first murder in the Antigonid house ; and he became more arbitrary than ever. But his talents showed brighter in misfortune than in fortune ; he restored Macedonia to strength and prosperity, stopped infanticide, introduced settlers, opened new mines, acquired large control in Thrace, and when he died in 179 he left to his son Perseus a Macedonia better populated and wealthier than she had been since Cassander's reign.

One plan was cut short by his death ; he meant to use the friendly Bastarnae, a powerful Gallic confederacy on the lower Danube, to destroy the Dardanians, and then employ them and their relatives the Scordisci to invade Italy while he reconquered Greece. Owing to his death only part of the Bastarnae started, but Greeks were alarmed and Perseus was accused of designs upon Greece ; thereon he withheld the expected support, and the Dardanians defeated the Bastarnae and for a time broke their power.

Unhappily Perseus was the least gifted of the Antigonids, with a lack of decision and will-power. But he soon attracted universal goodwill ; he married a daughter of Seleucus IV and the Rhodian fleet escorted the bride ; all the national or democratic parties in Greece looked to him, and he had much support even in Rhodes and Aetolia. Eumenes alone was irreconcilable, and in 172 went to Rome in person to urge her to destroy Macedonia. Doubtless it looked to Rome as if Perseus might form a great confederacy ; she had no grievance against him, but she listened to Eumenes, and when on his way home Eumenes was nearly murdered in some private quarrel, Rome accused Perseus and welcomed the pretext for war. Eumenes was believed to be dead, and his brother Attalus took his kingdom and his wife Stratonice ; he surrendered both on Eumenes' return, Eumenes merely remarking that he had married in some haste (p. 37).

Rome declared war in 171, and called out all her allies ; by 168 she had 100,000 men in Macedonia and Greece, against Perseus' 43,000. Perseus' only allies were Cotys of Thrace, Epirus, and later Genthius of Illyria. Their governments kept the Greek states quiet ; their real interest lay, not in Perseus' victory, but in his survival to balance Rome. Perseus has been accused of irresolution and miserliness. Possibly however he believed that defeating Roman armies would only harden Rome's resolve, and that his one chance was to conserve his resources and protract the war till Rome wearied of the useless effort. For three years, aided by minor victories and Roman incompetence, he was successful, and only at the end of 169 did the consul Q. Marcius Metellus cross his frontier from Thessaly. But in 168 Rome sent to the army of Macedonia a better man, the consul L. Aemilius Paullus, while Perseus lost the invaluable help of 20,000 Bastarnae by haggling over their pay. Paullus manœuvred Perseus out of his impregnable position, and at Pydna succeeded in inducing him to attack. The Macedonian phalanx swept the Roman advance-guard before them, and Paullus confessed that he trembled as they came down on him, tossing his men aside on their spear-points ; but the attacking formations were not properly synchronised, some Roman troops thrust in between the phalanx and the hypaspists, and taken in flank the phalanx was helpless ; the end was massacre. Perseus fled while the Macedonians were dying, and lost all standing with his people ; he did not even destroy his papers, which incriminated many Greeks ; finally, forsaken by all, he surrendered, was led in triumph, and died miserably in a Roman prison.

Both the growing deterioration of the Roman character and the temporary eclipse of Roman Philhellenism were reflected in the settlement. Macedonia was forcibly broken up into four republics, and further weakened by economic restrictions. The national parties in Greece, who had only aided Perseus with good wishes, suffered heavily, and many men everywhere were exiled ; even from Achaea, which had offered Rome her army, 1,000 leading men, including Polybius, were transported to Italy. The Aetolian League was dismembered, Aetolia reduced to her original boundaries, and the whole Council exiled. Epirus, in revenge for Pyrrhus' invasion of Italy, was ruined for ever ; the multitude sold as slaves was so great that an Epirote could be bought for a few shillings ; three Greek cities which had joined Perseus were also sold up. Perseus' fleet had used Delos, which Delos was powerless to prevent ; she was punished by being given back to Athens, who exiled the Delians and colonised the island with Athenian cleruchs. Rhodes, a consistent friend of Rome, was tricked

by the consul Metellus ; he suggested she should offer
mediation, which she did, and for this Rome deprived her
of most of her possessions on the mainland, and ended her
commercial predominance by making Athenian Delos a
free port.  Even Eumenes, Rome's more than ally, suffered
for having grown strong ; on the suspicion that he had
intended to offer mediation—the facts are obscure—Rome
incited the Galatians against him ; when he went to Italy
to plead his cause he was turned back unheard, and when
in 166, after a severe struggle, he broke the invading Galatians, Rome promptly declared them autonomous ; in 163
P. Sulpicius Galba sat in Pergamum for ten days listening
to complaints against him.  No service or subservience to
the Roman Republic could secure the genuine friendship
of that immoral State ; and few of the excesses or in-
justices of any ruler of Macedonian blood can compare
with the practice of that Republic in its later days.  The
effect of Rome's anger was to render Eumenes less unpopular
with the Asiatic Greeks.  In 160–59 he died ; his brother
succeeded as Attalus II, and again married Stratonice.

Ptolemy V, after mastering for the time the native
revolts which culminated in his reign, was poisoned in
181–0, leaving three small children.  The elder son, Ptolemy
VI Philometor, subsequently married his sister Cleopatra
II ; the younger was afterwards Ptolemy VIII Euergetes
II.[1]  In 173 the boy-king's ministers made preparations
for recovering southern Syria ; but Antiochus Epiphanes
anticipated their design.  Antiochus, the ' Saviour of Asia',
was one of the most remarkable men of his house.  He
had lived 14 years in Rome, and was her convinced friend
and imitator ; he was an Athenian citizen and a passionate
admirer of things Greek ; he adorned Athens and many
other cities with gifts of temples and buildings, added to
Antioch, refounded many towns as Greek cities (Chap. IV),
and brought in new settlers.  Magnificent and munificent,
ready to play the democrat or the jester or seek nocturnal

----

[1] The numbering of the Ptolemies after Philometor is uncertain,
as some ephemeral reigns defy exact location.

adventures in the streets of the capital, but popular and a
king, some called him mad ; but he raised his kingdom to
a high pitch of efficiency, and the reorganisation he attempted later was no unworthy one. In 169 he invaded
Egypt, took Pelusium and Memphis, and extended his
protectorate over Ptolemy VI. He then returned to
Syria (for his relations with Judaea see Chap. VI) ; but the
Alexandrians made Euergetes king, Philometor recognised
him, and Egypt had two kings together. In 168 Antiochus
returned and besieged Alexandria. But Pydna had been
fought, and Rome, following her consistent policy of weakening the Seleucids, intervened ; the envoy G. Popilius
handed Antiochus the Senate's order to quit Egypt, drew
a circle round him in the sand with his stick, and told him
to decide before quitting the circle. It was an unheard-of
insolence, though perhaps matched later when Scipio
Aemilianus made Ptolemy Euergetes II accompany him on
foot through Alexandria and deliberately walked too fast in
order to shame his unwieldy host before his subjects. Antiochus stood dumbfounded ; then he slowly replied that
he would do as Rome wished. He quitted Egypt, and devoted the rest of his life to trying to strengthen his kingdom
to resist Rome ; but in 163 he died on a very successful
campaign in the east, and with him ended all chance of
his empire playing any further part as a world-power.

Rome took advantage of his son Antiochus V being a
child to demand the destruction of the Syrian war-fleet
and elephants ; the sight of the hamstrung elephants so
moved the populace that one Leptines murdered the Roman
envoy Octavius, an incident Rome merely saved up for
future use. But the boy did not reign long. In 162
Demetrius, son of Seleucus IV, escaped from Rome with
Polybius' help, easily overthrew the unpopular regent
Lysias, and took the crown as Demetrius I Soter. He
displayed energy, recovering Media and Babylonia from
the general Timarchus, who had revolted and been recognised by Rome, and setting up a new king in Cappadocia
in place of his enemy Ariarathes V. But he was unpopular

with his people ; Attalus II restored Ariarathes, and the
two combined with Philometor of Egypt against him ;
and a pretender appeared, one Alexander Balas, who claimed
to be a son of Epiphanes. Rome and Philometor both
recognised him ; with Egyptian support he invaded Syria,
and Demetrius was defeated and killed (150).

In Egypt the joint reign of the brothers Philometor and
Euergetes was brief ; in 163 the Alexandrians drove out
Philometor. But Rome gave him some help, a change of
opinion brought him back, and under Roman mediation
the kingdom was divided, Philometor obtaining Egypt and
Cyprus, Euergetes Cyrene and Libya. The tradition makes
Philometor one of the best Ptolemies. Rome, with her
own difficulties, was ceasing to be interested in Egypt or
the Seleucids, provided neither grew too strong ; and
Philometor turned his thoughts to Syria. Having supported Balas, he gave him after his victory his daughter
Cleopatra Thea, and virtually exercised a protectorate over
the Seleucid kingdom. But Balas was incompetent, and
Demetrius' son Demetrius II came back with Cretan mercenaries and disputed the throne. Philometor occupied
the Syrian coast himself, but fell out with Balas and transferred his patronage and his daughter to Demetrius. Balas
attacked him in 145, and was defeated and soon afterwards
killed ; but Philometor died of his wounds, and Euergetes
thereon became king of the whole Egyptian empire, and
married his sister Cleopatra II, Philometor's widow. Greek
tradition makes him a blood-stained tyrant, who committed many crimes. Much of this is obvious propaganda,
poorly attested, and completely contradicted by his great
series of decrees, which cannot be gainsaid ; though possibly his character, like Augustus', changed in later life.
Much of his reign was occupied in civil war with his sister ;
the causes and responsibility are obscure, the changes of
fortune not worth narrating. He married Philometor's
daughter, another Cleopatra (III), and both Cleopatras
often appear with him in official acts ; whether the elder
nominally remained his wife also, and what were the real

changes in the relationships of the three, can hardly be unravelled. But the interest of his reign lies in other matters than personal questions (Chap. V). He died in 116, the last of the great succession of the Ptolemies.

In Syria the excesses of Demetrius' Cretan troops at once provoked opposition, and Balas' general Diodotus set up as king Balas' young son Antiochus VI ; in 142 he murdered the boy and himself took the diadem and the name Tryphon. Demetrius could not overthrow him ; he left his wife Cleopatra Thea as regent in Syria and turned eastward, where Mithridates I of Parthia had extended his rule from the Punjab to the Tigris, and was threatening Babylonia. The Greek cities had called on Demetrius for help, and doubtless he hoped to return with resources sufficient to overthrow Tryphon. He found much support, and rescued Babylonia, but was finally captured and held in honourable captivity by Mithridates, and married to his daughter ; Mithridates now annexed Babylonia (141). But Thea held out, and in 139 Demetrius' brother Antiochus VII Sidetes came to her from Rhodes, married her as her third husband, and disposed of Tryphon. Sidetes was the last strong man of his line ; the only fault attributed to him is drink. He unified and strengthened his kingdom, subdued the long-lost Judaea (p. 189), and finally crossed the Euphrates with a large army. The Greek cities received him with enthusiasm ; he re-conquered Mesopotamia and Babylonia, drove the Parthian king Phraates out of Media, and seemed about to restore the empire of Antiochus III. But the cities grew lukewarm under the burdens of war, and early in 129 the Parthian surprised him in his winter quarters, defeated and killed him, and recovered his conquests ; our last document from Seleucid Babylon is dated in June 130. Phraates sent Sidetes' body home, and Syria made a great mourning, as though she knew that the effective history of her dynasty was ended.

Macedonia after Pydna had a troubled existence for some years, till a man named Andriscus claimed the crown, asserting that he was Perseus' son Philip, who had really died in Italy. Rome, fully involved in Spain, paid little attention to the ' false Philip ', who secured support in Thrace and in 149 invaded Macedonia, whereon the whole country accepted him. He invaded Thessaly in 148 and defeated a Roman force ; but he had alienated the Macedonians by playing the despot, and was defeated by the praetor Q. Caecilius Metellus, taken to Rome, and executed ; and Macedonia, first of the Hellenistic states, became a Roman province, which dated from 148 as her era. Another ' false Philip ' did appear, but had little success ; and the history of the province was chiefly one of repeated incursions by the northern barbarians, which culminated, though they did not end, with the great invasion of the Scordisci and Thracians in the first Mithridatic war, when they destroyed Delphi and Dodona. The Roman failure to keep out the barbarians contrasted badly with the record of the Antigonid kings in this respect.

Greece found it hard to recover from the chastisement she had received and the loss of her best men by exile ; in some districts, too, the increase of the Greek population was becoming insufficient to balance losses. But there was one fight still to come. The last struggle of the Achaean League is obscure ; most of Polybius, here frankly pro-Roman, is lost, and Pausanias' account merely reflects the view-point of Rome's partisans, though fortunately inscriptions help ; when we hear that the League was deteriorating and the leading men corrupt it is well to reserve judgment. For years Callicrates was the leading statesman, and worked entirely in Rome's interest ; but by 150 the surviving exiles, 300 only, had (except Polybius) returned from Italy and the democrats captured the government and made general Diaeus of Megalopolis, who stood for independence ; Callicrates died that year, and Rome's difficulties in Spain, Macedonia, and Africa seemed to afford the hope of a revived policy. There was again trouble with Sparta, who formally seceded in 148 ; the League declared war, and Rome intervened and summoned both parties to a congress at Corinth in 147. There the

Roman envoys announced that the League must give up,
not only Sparta, which would have been fair enough, but
Corinth, Argos, and Orchomenos, for generations integral
parts of the League ; the League had consistently supported Rome, and Rome now meant to destroy it as she
had destroyed the Aetolian. The Achaeans threatened
the envoys, but the story that they assaulted them is
recognised as untrue. In spring 146 the League voted
war ; it could do nothing else, unless a small country has
no right to fight for its liberties against a big one. It
was a people's war ; a moratorium was proclaimed, men
enlisted freely, and clubs of ' patriots ' appeared in the
cities ; at Troezen, and doubtless elsewhere, the members
put all their property at the city's disposal ; even Polybius
admits that feeling ran like a torrent. Boeotia, Euboea,
Phocis, and Locris joined Achaea. The general Critolaus
advanced northward to join his allies, but was defeated
and killed by Metellus, who hurried from Macedonia ; the
defeated took refuge in Corinth, where the consul L. Mummius took over command from Metellus. Diaeus, who
succeeded as general, raised a general levy, ordered 12,000
slaves to be freed and armed, and hastened to Corinth
with 14,600 men, perhaps the largest army the League
ever raised. He defeated Mummius' advance-guard, and
this induced him, though heavily outnumbered, to give
battle ; the Achaean phalanx fought desperately, but were
defeated by the superior Roman cavalry laying bare their
flank ; Diaeus, who escaped, committed suicide with his
family. Achaea had no cause to be ashamed of her last
fight, and she was not ashamed ; the cities set up their
rolls of honour, and we happen to possess that of Epidaurus, 156 dead in the battle from one small town. Mummius occupied Corinth and, though it had not resisted,
treated it like Carthage ; the men were killed, the women
and children sold, and the city razed to the ground. It
was a deliberate warning to Greece (p. 211), like Alexander's
destruction of Thebes. Chalcis and Thebes also suffered
heavily ; but in many places Mummius did not behave badly.

Greece after 146 became a Roman protectorate, supervised from Macedonia ; some documents date from this year as an era, but Greece was not yet a province. Polybius now obtained leave to return, and did good service by mitigating the first severity of Achaea's fate and afterwards superintending the transition period ; for all the Leagues which had fought, including the Achaean, were now dissolved into their component parts. Greece had no more wars or foreign politics, except boundary disputes. Timocracies—governments of the wealthy—were set up in many cities, and attempts to alter the constitution prohibited. Antigonus I had once claimed, in certain cities, to ' reprehend and punish ' those who proposed laws which he considered inexpedient, but Rome now made ' new laws ' punishable by death, an illustration of the difference between Roman and Macedonian rule. Nevertheless in Greece, if anywhere, the Roman Republic for a time justified itself ; it gave peace and prosperity, even if enforced. Some territories—Corinth, Euboea, Boeotia—were taxed ; but Athens, Sparta, and some other cities were tax-free, and probably there was no general system of tribute till after 88. Athens enjoyed an Indian summer of material wealth, and the facts known about Messene (p. 95) suggest a widespread well-being by c. 100. There was too a religious revival ; to this period belong the great legislative decree for the mysteries of Andania (91), the restoration of the oracle and service of Apollo Koropaeus, the publication at Lindus in 99 of its religious records, the ' Lindian chronicle '. Athens and Boeotia led the way ; the Boeotian Ptoia became quadrennial, and Tanagra founded her Serapieia ; Athens revived at Delos the great quadrennial Delia, omitted since 314, and at intervals sent to Delphi magnificently equipped religious processions, the Pythaids, to bring back the sacred fire to purify the city. All these things helped to re-establish the national consciousness.

At Pergamum the reign of Attalus II Philadelphus, a good ruler, was uneventful, save for the usual war with Bithynia ; but his fleet supported Rome in 148 and 146.

Under him the kingdom reached its greatest prosperity.
He died in 139–8, and was succeeded by Attalus III, a
natural son of Eumenes II, legitimised by him and adopted
by the childless Stratonice ; Attalus II may have married
Stratonice, who was not young, in loyalty to Eumenes,
to safeguard his son's succession,[1] which would explain
the haste he shewed in 172 and Eumenes' lack of resent-
ment. Attalus III was a man of disordered nerves, both
vain and cruel, who put many prominent men to death
and confiscated their estates ; subsequently, perhaps
through remorse, he lived in retirement, practising sculpture
and studying poisons. He died childless early in 133,
leaving a famous will : he gave freedom to Pergamum
and probably to his Greek cities generally, and bequeathed
his kingdom to Rome, which means that he gave to Rome
the King's Land, the royal treasure, and the right to act
as king of Pergamum vis-à-vis the other elements in the
country. His reason is conjectural ; hatred of his heir,
his half-brother Aristonicus, has been suggested, but more
probably he merely anticipated the fact that Rome would
take the kingdom when she chose. Rome accepted the
bequest. The Pergamenes, fearing a slave rising, enfranchised large classes (p. 136) ; but in 132 Aristonicus raised
a national revolt against Rome and threw in his lot with
the slaves. He easily defeated Rome's allies, the rulers
of Pontus, Bithynia, Cappadocia, and Paphlagonia ; and
though Pergamum itself forsook him, he had success enough
to overrun Caria, besiege Cyzicus, invade the Chersonese,
and early in 130 destroy the consul Crassus and his army.
But the new consul, M. Perperna, defeated and shut him
up in Stratonicea ; he had to surrender, and was taken
to Rome and killed. Even so, the war was not over, and
in 129 the consul M'. Aquilius had hard fighting both in
Caria and Mysia. The interest of this war lies in the theories
which Aristonicus sought to translate into action (p. 107).

[1] Precisely as Doson, in loyalty to Demetrius II, married
Philip V's mother by adoption, Demetrius' widow Chryseis, to
safeguard Philip's succession.

The war freed Rome from Attalus' will; she had conquered the kingdom, and in 130 she made part of it the Roman province of Asia. The cities which had aided Aristonicus became subject and were taxed; but many, like Miletus, were free and Rome's allies. Following Hellenistic precedent, Rome eased taxation at first; subsequently it was re-imposed by the Sempronian law of G. Gracchus. The status of the individual cities, however, often altered, for better or worse; the ambition of all was to obtain immunity from Roman taxes. Those taxes themselves were not oppressive; what was oppressive was the manner of collection. Instead of being collected by responsible officials, they were farmed out, *i.e.* the collector (*publicanus*) bought the right to collect the taxes from a district, and what he actually collected was limited only by his own greed; it was the worst system ever devised, especially as the publican on the spot was often only the agent of a company in Rome. Down to 88, however, some restraint was exercised, and the cities as a rule, especially the free ones, continued to prosper.

In 88 there opened the struggle which presaged the ruin of Hellenism, the first war between Rome and that remarkable barbarian, Mithridates Eupator of Pontus. These wars belong to Roman history; all that can be noticed here is their effect. Round Mithridates crystallised all the hatred felt for Rome and the Roman publican; when in 88 he overran the province of Asia many Greek cities joined him, and when he ordered a general massacre of all ' Romans ' it was largely obeyed. There were cities, like Rhodes, which saved the Romans and their honour; but great numbers perished,—80,000 or 150,000 in the tradition,—largely inoffensive traders and their families; Mithridates' general Archelaus killed 20,000 more in Delos and the islands. Even in Greece Mithridates found allies— Achaea, Laconia, Boeotia, and, most notable of all, the Athenian democracy. Athens had had an oligarchic revolution *c.* 103, and the democracy desired to recover power; but the city, harmless and historic, had made no pretence of waging war for generations, and its open espousal of Mithridates' cause is as eloquent of the hatred felt by Greeks for their Roman masters as the massacre in Asia. Athens fought desperately when besieged by Mithridates' conqueror Sulla, and never fully recovered from the consequent ruin. In Asia, Mithridates' deportation of the Chians caused many cities to desert his cause, and he attempted to regain them by stirring up social revolution in his favour; he proclaimed abolition of debts, enfranchisement of metics (aliens without the franchise residing in a city), and liberation of the slaves; he imitated Aristonicus in trying to use revolution as a weapon with which to fight Rome.

With Mithridates the material reaction of Asia against western rule, begun by Cappadocia and Parthia and continued by Judaea and Armenia, came to a head; and Rome, who had done so much to weaken or destroy the Graeco-Macedonian states, was ultimately forced to take their place as champion and protector of Greek civilisation in the East. But Hellenism had first to pass through a stage of distress and destruction. Caught between Rome and Pontus, and suffering heavily from both, both Greece and Asia were badly damaged; beside actual war exactions and losses, Sulla plundered temples at Olympia and elsewhere, Archelaus sacked Delos, and Mithridates' barbarian allies Delphi; the Cilician pirates, who aided Mithridates, added to the general misery. Sulla's exactions in both countries were severe, as were later those of M. Antonius Creticus in the Cretan war; and in all these wars Greek cities had to provide the Roman fleets. Before any recovery was possible, the Greek east was inextricably caught in the Roman Civil Wars.

Greece itself had no chance; its suffering culminated in Antony's deliberate attempt so to ruin the Peloponnese as to render it useless to Sextus Pompeius. Whole districts were half depopulated; Thebes became a village, Megalopolis a desert, Megara, Aegina, Piraeus heaps of stones; in Laconia and Euboea individuals owned large tracts,

perhaps worked only by a few herdsmen ; Aetolia, like
Epirus, was ruined for ever. Relief ultimately came when
in 27 Augustus made the country the province of Achaea.
Two new trading cities, Caesar's Corinth and Augustus'
Patrae, were to flourish ; Athens was still to be a leading
university ; Elis and Boeotia ultimately regained some
material prosperity, and Boeotia still had enough vitality
to produce Plutarch ; various cities were partially to recover. But for Greece, taken as a whole, Augustus' peace
came too late.

Heavily as Asia Minor suffered, its fate was to differ
from that of Greece. The intermediate period was bad ;
many cities lost their freedom after 88 ; a new generation
of publicans, perhaps not unnaturally, showed themselves
more oppressive than the old. Whereas under some Greek
laws a debtor's person could not be seized, debtors were
now sometimes not only seized but tortured, and their
children sold. Provincial governors extorted great sums ;
Cicero expounds the difficulties incurred by one who
favoured common honesty. Some cities, having exhausted
their temple funds, were driven to borrow from Roman
bankers at usurious rates ; Lucullus checked usury for a
moment, but in the civil wars it returned in full force.
None of the contending generals except Caesar (who temporarily abolished tax-farming) cared for anything but
their own success, while all needed money ; a few instances
of the extortion practised are noted elsewhere (p. 97).
But the great cities were not actually destroyed, and short
of that were too strong and too wealthy to go under ; and
once settled government returned they more than recovered their prosperity.

The other countries of Asia Minor fell to Rome one
by one, the transition sometimes being smoothed over by
the rule of a client king. Phrygia was added to Asia in
116. In 74 Nicomedes IV, imitating Attalus III, bequeathed
Bithynia to Rome ; and after Mithridates' final defeat
Pompey made it a province, together with part of Pontus.
In Galatia, where Mithridates had massacred most of the

nobility, one Deiotaurus made himself king; in 36 his secretary Amyntas secured Antony's favour and the kingdom, which he greatly extended to the southward; in 25 he fell in battle with the Homadenses of the Taurus, and his kingdom passed to Rome. Another of Antony's kings, Polemon, ruled Pontus from the Iris to Colchis and founded a dynasty; his kingdom only became Roman in A.D. 63, and Cappadocia, the last quasi-independent state, under Vespasian. The complicated details and changing boundaries of the Roman provinces in Asia Minor need not be noticed here; what matters is that Augustus partly returned to the Seleucid system (Chap. IV). Much land had become *ager publicus* under the Republic, and some Romans had seized great estates; Augustus made it Crown Land again, abolished the publican, and collected the taxes through government officials as the Seleucids had done.

Seleucid rule survived Sidetes' death for 46 years; but Commagene and Edessa were lost, and the line became a local dynasty in North Syria, which tore itself and the country to pieces in domestic quarrels. Phraates had released Demetrius II before Sidetes' defeat; he recovered Syria and his former wife Cleopatra Thea, who had meanwhile borne Sidetes five children. But the over-married and disillusioned woman could not endure Demetrius' incompetence after his brother, and when a pretender, Alexander Zabinas, defeated him she apparently prevented him escaping to safety. She now meant to hold the power herself. When her eldest son by Demetrius seized the throne she poisoned him; subsequently she set up as coruler the second, Antiochus VIII Grypus, who anticipated his fate by killing her first. Endless civil war followed between Grypus and Sidetes' son Antiochus IX Cyzicenus and their respective descendants; the great cities had to look after themselves, petty tyrants and Arab chieftains established principalities throughout the country, the Ituraeans of the Lebanon raided where they would, and for a time the advancing Nabataeans even held Damascus. In 83 Tigranes, who had united all Armenia, conquered most of the country and ended Seleucid rule ; though unpopular, he at least supplied a government, but after his overthrow by Lucullus there was sheer anarchy, and it was well for the sorely tried Hellenism of Northern Syria when in 64 Pompey made the country a Roman province.

Though no king of Egypt after Euergetes' death was in any way distinguished, the country still produced wealth and possessed many elements of strength, as is shewn by the continued exploration and advance southward (Chap. VII). Euergetes' widow, Cleopatra III, and his sons, the colourless Ptolemy X Soter II (Lathyros) and Ptolemy XI (Alexandros), ruled Egypt and Cyprus with various changes and combinations till 81–0 ; Cyrene he left to his illegitimate son Ptolemy Apion, who in 96 bequeathed it to Rome. The death of Lathyros' daughter in 80 ended the legitimate line, but the Alexandrians made Lathyros' illegitimate son king as Ptolemy XIII Neos Dionysos, nicknamed Auletes, the Fluteplayer ; in the tradition he was a vicious dilettante of Nero's type, who by servility towards Rome ruled till 51, after losing Cyprus in 58. Two of his children, the young Ptolemy XIV and his eldest sister Cleopatra VII, jointly succeeded. The boy-king and Alexandria between them made a good fight against Caesar and came near to ending his career ; but a unique glamour has been thrown over the fall of the dynasty by the name of Cleopatra. Cleopatra's courage is as indisputable as is the complete absence of moral scruple in her use of her person and her lovers for her one end. But what she really was, and what that end was, it seems impossible to know : whether she was a mere courtesan, crazy to be empress of the Roman world, or whether she was a great patriot, who with a woman's weapons all but reversed Fortune's wheel at the eleventh hour and almost succeeded in avenging Rome's treatment of the Hellenistic states by making her Hellenistic kingdom Rome's co-partner in empire. Whatever her aim, Antony's defeat at Actium (31) cut it short ; with her suicide next year the last Macedonian line ended, and Augustus sat in the seat of the Ptolemies.

# CHAPTER II

## MONARCHY, CITY, AND LEAGUE

The old Macedonian monarchy had retained some of the characteristics of the heroic monarchy, known from Homer and the Teutonic sagas. The god-descended king, with his subject princes and his free peers, ruled a national kingdom, but claimed an allegiance as much personal as patriotic; Alexander's Companions were the last remnant of the heroic retinue; the old bond of union, the idea of the Kin, was not yet quite dead in his time. The original meeting of the free men in arms, the army, remained, and they clung tenaciously to their powers; in Macedonia these powers were possibly older than the monarchy, which was not absolute, but limited by the rights of the people under arms; it has even been called quasi-constitutional. The king could not appoint his successor; on his death the vacant crown passed to the army, who elected the new king; naturally this was generally the eldest son, but not necessarily so. Were the king a child, the army alone could appoint a regent or guardian. In a trial for treason, where the king was virtually a party, the army represented the State, heard the case, and gave judgment; but probably the king could execute even a free-born Macedonian for murder without calling on the army. As the army elected the king, it could also depose him, though with a strong king this might entail going over to the enemy. But over policy the army had no voice; if they wanted one, they could only get it by mutinying, as sometimes happened.

The army was fully representative of the people, as all free Macedonians served, but these did not officially constitute part of the Macedonian State; subject to their powers above indicated, the king was the State, and alone represented Macedonia in its foreign relations. Thus in the League of Corinth Alexander held a double position, not always understood : the League was composed of the Greek states and of Alexander, who was officially the Macedonian State, while the man Alexander, King of Macedonia, was President. This position endured until Antigonus Doson, who made the Macedonian people the ' Commonwealth of the Macedonians,' and therewith made them part of the State, which was now no longer, in official language, ' King Antigonus,' but ' King Antigonus and the Macedonians.' It was only a name, and gave the people no extended rights ; indeed Philip V sometimes acted more arbitrarily than any other Macedonian king.

The Macedonian conquest of Egypt and Asia brought new problems. During the wars of the Successors the Macedonians in the armies abroad maintained their rights for a time, but probably these were lost after 300, the Macedonians having become only small minorities in mixed armies of mercenaries ; and the absolute monarchies of the Seleucids and the Ptolemies exhibit no Macedonian constitutional traits of any kind. If under the later Ptolemies their army sometimes interfered, its interference was that of a Praetorian Guard, and had nothing to do with the old Macedonian constitution ; indeed it would hardly contain one free-born Macedonian. If Macedonia made the monarchies of the Seleucids and the Ptolemies, Asia and Egypt made them what they were ; these kings *were* the State, absolutely and for all purposes, as much as Darius I or Thutmose III ; they were not national rulers, and there was no imperial citizenship in their realms, as there was to be in the Roman. One justification of these two dynasties was that only an absolute monarchy, standing above and apart from Greeks and Orientals, had any chance of uniting east and west ; this Rome ultimately discovered, for the Republic failed in governing Hellenistic countries. Both Seleucids and Ptolemies often made the crown prince co-

ruler with his father in the latter's lifetime; among the
Ptolemies dynastic murder was not uncommon, and for
over a century prevented civil war.

Every king, however, was affected by Greek ideas, and
desired to have some basis for his rule beyond mere conquest, or, as regards the early kings, the fact that they were
the most competent men alive and the right people to
govern. In Asia and Egypt this basis was ultimately
found in the king's divinity; but in considering the history of this idea, the worship of the kings by Greek cities
must be distinguished from the official cults instituted by
the kings themselves. Alexander's deification during his
life was not an official cult; it was a *political* measure
only, limited to the Greek world which deified him; he
desired it in order to obtain a footing in, and some necessary authority over, Greek cities who were his free allies
and in whom, as a king, he could otherwise find no place.
Long before Alexander some Greeks had claimed divinity
and been worshipped during life, and when the cities began
worshipping his Successors, these welcomed the political
advantage it was to them, as it had been to him; Antigonus I, Demetrius I, Lysimachus, Seleucus I, Ptolemy I,
even Cassander, were all worshipped in various cities, but
none of them officially became gods during life in their
kingdoms. Three Greeks in Egypt, saved from some danger, did indeed honour Ptolemy I and his consort Berenice
as 'saviour gods,' but this need not imply official deification. Alexander, however, was worshipped in Alexandria
as the city's founder, as other city founders were often
worshipped; after his death Eumenes and his Macedonian
army worshipped him, and possibly there was, as the coins
suggest, an official worship of him in Lysimachus' kingdom; but the worship which gave the precedent to the
world was the official worship of the great Macedonian
instituted in Egypt by Ptolemy I, probably soon after he
took the crown in 305. Soon after 280 Ptolemy II instituted at Alexandria a great festival in worship of his father,
Ptolemy I, and Antiochus I followed by deifying Seleucus

as Zeus Nikator; and therewith was established the further principle that the kings, like Alexander, officially became gods after death.

Probably it was Ptolemy II who took the final step; his sister and consort Arsinoe II was officially deified as the goddess Philadelphus, probably even before her death, and with her Ptolemy II (who was never called Philadelphus) himself officially became a god during his life. After his death each succeeding Ptolemy officially became a god during life as a matter of course, and took his place in the official worship. At the head of that worship stood Alexander, whose priesthood was held by the greatest in the land; his name was followed by the list of the deified kings and their consorts under their cult-names—the gods Adelphoi (Ptolemy II and Arsinoe II), the gods Euergetae, the gods Philopatores, and so on; Ptolemy I and Berenice ultimately took their place in the list next after Alexander as the gods Soteres, probably under Ptolemy IV. Arsinoe II had also a separate priestess for her own worship, as had afterwards Berenice, wife of Ptolemy III, and Arsinoe, wife of Ptolemy IV. Among the Seleucids Antiochus II perhaps officially became a god during life, though this is uncertain; but from his reign there seems to have been an official worship of the dynasty, including the living king, located in the capitals of the satrapies but with local variations of form. Divine pedigrees were invented for both dynasties; the Seleucids descended from Apollo, the Ptolemies from Heracles and Dionysus. The rulers of Pergamum, though after Attalus I took the crown they were worshipped during life in various cities and were officially deified after death, never officially became gods during life, and therefore could never claim divinity as the basis of their rule.

Macedonia was on a different footing. She was a national monarchy, and the Antigonid kings were not conquerors, but national kings constitutionally chosen by the army; there was no question of an official worship of these kings, and no Antigonid was ever a god to Macedonians, though he might be deified in Greek cities or in cities in Macedonia which had retained their Greek character; thus Demetrius I was worshipped in Athens, Euboea, Sicyon, and elsewhere, Antigonus Doson in Sicyon, Histiaea, and Laconia, Philip V in Amphipolis, just as Cassander and Lysimachus had been in Cassandreia. One king, Antigonus Gonatas, was an exception even to this, and exhibits the strange phenomenon of a monarch who was apparently never worshipped by anybody anywhere. His Stoic training and sympathies seemingly caused him to regard the thing as a sham, and he may have inherited the feeling of his grandfather Antipater, a Macedonian of the old school who had refused to worship Alexander. Gonatas himself preferred to seek the theoretic basis of his power in satisfying the requirements of philosophy, and his famous definition of his kingship as a ' noble servitude ' shows that in his eyes that basis was the duty of service : the king must be the servant of his people.

What now was the meaning of king-worship ? Wendland has called it a ' political religion,' and this expresses a truth, provided the emphasis be placed on ' political ' ; for it had nothing to do with religious feeling. To the king, it was a political measure which gave him a footing in Greek cities and ensured the continuing validity of his acts after death ; and it was rendered possible by the general disbelief of the educated classes, for the Olympian religion was spiritually dead, and when king-worship was established nothing else had yet taken its place. To talk about the arrogance of these rulers simply misses the point ; no king ever thought he *was* a god, or apparently (unless Antiochus Epiphanes) set much store by his own worship. Antipater in an older world had thought king-worship impious ; in the third century men would have smiled at such an idea, though Gonatas probably thought it silly. For (as the common man might argue) what was a god ? Two prominent gods of the time, Apollo and Dionysus, had had mortal mothers, even as Alexander or Ptolemy ; others, like Asclepius, had been men ; and

Euhemerus' theory that *all* had once been men was widely known. True, they were immortal; but was not Alexander, whose spirit still inspired the world, by that fact immortal also? The Olympians conferred no personal salvation, no hope of immortality, little spirituality; and as guardians of the higher morality they were mostly sad misfits. And one had to take so much on trust; one might believe in the power and splendour of Zeus, but one could see the power and splendour of Ptolemy. The local god could not feed you in a famine; but the king did. Perhaps Dionysus saved Themisonium from the Gauls; Antiochus I, for the time, certainly saved all Asia Minor. Apollo could not help the managers of his temple at Delos to get in his debts from the islands; Ptolemy, when appealed to, sent his admiral, who got them in at once. Had not then a king powers denied to a god? So at least men thought. The popular song in which the Athenians invoked Demetrius' protection against Aetolia ran: "The other gods either are not, or are far away; either they hear not, or they give no heed; but thou art here, and we can see thee, not in wood or stone, but in very truth."

This was why the common man took to king-worship; and the cult-names of the earlier kings—Soter the Saviour, Euergetes the Benefactor—express the fact that they were worshipped for what they *did*; Athens worshipped Demetrius because he saved her from Cassander, Rhodes and the islands worshipped Ptolemy I because he saved them from Demetrius, Ionia worshipped Antiochus I because he saved her from the Gauls and Miletus Antiochus II because he put down a tyrant; the typical function of kingship was held to be *philanthropia*, helpfulness to subjects. It must be remembered that such worship was not confined to kings, but was extended to private benefactors, such as Diogenes, who aided Athens to freedom in 229 and was worshipped there beside Ptolemy III, and Diodorus, priest of Zeus at Pergamum, to whom in his lifetime a temple was erected and splendidly inaugurated at Philetaireia for the salvation which he had brought to Pergamum in the troubles after 133 ; he even became eponymous hero of a tribe, an honour otherwise confined to gods or kings. At the same time the Athenian ephebes began to sacrifice to ' the benefactors ' of the city generally. In the Achaean League both Aratus and Philopoemen received cults after death ; and the cult of men after death as heroes was common, and much older than Hellenism.

Besides Saviour and Benefactor, most of the royal cult-names were drawn from family relationships—Philadelphus, Philopator, Philometor ; but there was one which stood on a different footing, Epiphanes, the god manifest. It was first bestowed on Ptolemy V at his coronation in 203 ; as he was a little child, and was also perhaps the first of his line to be crowned in Egyptian fashion by the priests, the title must be of Egyptian origin ; to Egyptians the child really was the Sun-god manifest upon earth. To the Greek world this was unimportant ; but the name became significant in the hands of its second wearer. Antiochus IV Epiphanes was perhaps the one monarch who took his divinity seriously ; but whether this was in any sense personal, and whether his brilliance really at times overstepped the line which we call insanity, can hardly be said. But certainly his reasons were mainly political ; he saw that, to withstand Rome, his kingdom must become homogeneous in culture and cult, which could both only be Greek ; and just as he turned native towns into cities with Greek forms on an extensive scale, so he possibly looked to the worship of himself as Zeus manifest for a means of unification ; he was the first Seleucid to use his cult-name and divine title on his coinage. In the later period all cult-names lost any particular significance, and even Epiphanes meant no more than The Most Christian King once meant.

As Rome gradually became the dominant factor in Hellenistic politics, the Greek cities began to transfer to her the phenomena of king-worship ; the ' goddess Rome '—the sum total of Romans—was worshipped at Smyrna in 195 and Alabanda in 170, in each case as a display of

E

gratitude for ' salvation,'—protection against Antiochus III ; after the creation of the province of Asia, the same worship is found at Miletus, Elaea, and elsewhere. It gave Rome the same footing in free Greek cities as the deified kings had possessed. It was accompanied by the worship of Roman ' benefactors '—of Flamininus, conqueror of Philip V, at Chalcis, and M'. Aquilius, who settled Asia, at Pergamum. In the first century Roman governors were worshipped indiscriminately, and Cicero had much trouble in preventing it in his own case ; and here certainly the servility of fear showed itself, for these people often did little but harm. The culminating point was the worship of Caesar at Ephesus as a god manifest ; finally everything passed into the official provincial worships of Rome and Augustus.

As regards marriage, the Successors of the first generation were frankly a law to themselves. Antigonus I and Cassander were apparently convinced monogamists ; Seleucus, like Alexander, had two legitimate queens at once ; Demetrius and Pyrrhus were free polygamists ; Lysimachus and Ptolemy seemingly always sent the then queen away before marrying her successor. After the first generation, the custom of one wife only at a time became absolute, though she could be repudiated at will and another taken ; some kings kept mistresses, some apparently did not. Queens were generally of some royal house, though the lesser dynasties of Asia Minor counted ; Berenice, the ultimate wife of Ptolemy I, may be an exception, but possibly she was related to Antipater ; later exceptions were the marriages of Attalus I with the much-praised Apollonis, daughter of a citizen of Cyzicus, and of Antiochus III with a girl of Chalcis. In Egypt, after Arsinoe II Philadelphus set the example, the queen's head always appeared on the coinage with her husband's ; and both Arsinoe II and her mother Berenice wore the diadem. From Arsinoe's time onward the queens in Egypt were officially styled ' sister queen ', a style which the Seleucids for other reasons also adopted and which has led to some

misunderstanding ; of the first five Ptolemies only two
married their sisters. These Macedonian princesses are an
interesting study, not merely because of their capabilities,
their ambitions, and (often) their loyalties, but because, at
least in the third century, there is little even hinted against
their morality ; no lover is anywhere recorded. It would
seem as if, with a woman like Arsinoe II, ambition left no
room for anything else ; as if she knew her own powers
and meant somehow to get free scope for them. She got
it after her marriage with Ptolemy II, when she became
co-ruler in name and ruler in fact ; and the way in which
she pulled round the lost war against Antiochus I and
turned it into a sweeping Egyptian triumph might rank,
if we knew the details, as one of the biggest things a woman
ever did. Even when the dynasties were wearing out the
women kept their vigour longer than the men ; Cleopatra
Thea, the only Seleucid queen who coined in her own
name, almost made kings at her pleasure, and the last
Cleopatra of Egypt was feared by Romans as they had
feared no one since Hannibal.

Certain features were common to all the kingdoms.
The king was the State ; ministers and officials were only
his men, whom he made or removed at pleasure ; his
council of ' Friends ' was purely advisory. He was the
fount of law ; and if the officials acted on rules laid down
for them in his rescripts, he laid down what rules he chose.
He had a secretarial department to draft rescripts, and the
Secretary kept an official Journal, checked daily by the
king, which recorded military and political events of importance ; between Journals and rescripts a secretarial
language grew up, whose influence can be seen in Polybius.
The provinces, home or foreign, were normally governed
by *strategoi*, generals with military powers, though the
Antigonids never used the system in Macedonia proper and
Thessaly and very sparingly in Greece ; the Ptolemies
and Seleucids also had a Lord High Admiral (*nauarchos*),
the Egyptian nauarch under Ptolemy II being almost a
Viceroy of the Sea. But, speaking generally, the system

of delegation was inadequate; the work that fell on
a conscientious monarch—military, administrative, legal,
commercial, even to the mere writing—was overwhelming; the apparent slackness in later life of certain once
energetic kings doubtless means that they were worn out.

Since in Macedonia, when the king died, the crown was
in the hands of the army till it appointed the new king,
it followed that the State was in abeyance with each death,
and that all treaties made by or with, and grants made
by, the dead king came to an end unless and until his successor renewed them. The new king usually renewed
grants on payment of a fine, the ' crown tax '; but the
other party to a treaty got a free hand, a bad system
whose ill-effects can be seen in the actions of Aetolia when
her treaties of neutrality with Gonatas and Doson ended
with their respective deaths. On the other hand, the acts
of a Seleucid or a Ptolemy, once he was a god, must have
remained valid after his death; but these kings nevertheless retained the theory that grants ended with the demise
of the Crown, for the purpose of imposing the crown tax.

The kings had the ordinary apparatus of a Court, and
the military arrangements usual since Alexander,—an
*agema* or guard, a corps of Royal Pages, boys of good
birth training for commissions, and officers called Bodyguards. Alexander's Bodyguards had been his Staff; but
by the second century this term, together with Friends
and Kinsmen, had merely become Court titles conferred
by the king in a definite precedence, Kinsmen being the
highest. The outward expression of kingship was the
diadem, a band of white linen round the head; kings
sometimes granted to others, officials or play-actors, the
right to wear the royal purple of Macedonia, now known
to have been violet, not crimson. The recognition of the
secondary kingdoms of Asia as royal favoured the formation
of an international royal caste; a certain amount of royal
correspondence remains, and the time-honoured opening
" Hoping this finds you well as it leaves me," now extinct
or confined to the uneducated, was then the formula with

which the kings of the earth regularly began letters to one another.

The army and navy were the king's. At sea there was a race in building great warships, beginning in 314 with the invention in Phoenicia, possibly by Demetrius, of the *hepteres*, a galley whose power-ratio to that of a quinquereme would be expressed by 7 : 5, and which proved its value at Salamis in 306. When Demetrius lost the sea in 285 his flagship, which Ptolemy I possibly dedicated at Delos, had already a ratio of 15 : 5. Ptolemy II built in Cyprus two vessels whose ratios were 20 and 30, and honoured the designer, Pyrgoteles ; Ptolemy IV possessed one whose ratio was 40, with a double prow and stern like the old Calais-Douvres. Vessels of the ratio of 8, 9, and 10 are often recorded in action, and Demetrius' flagship was highly efficient ; another famous vessel was Antigonus Gonatas' flagship Isthmia, which he dedicated at Delos after his victory at Cos, a heavy ship, perhaps with three decks and equipped primarily for a boarding fight ; but we cannot say what was the largest vessel actually in action, as details of the battles between Gonatas and Egypt are lost. That up to 10 at any rate the ratios mean so many men to an oar, like the five of a quinquereme, is most probable ; what a ratio of 30 or 40 implied is unknown. There were two definite theories of sea-fighting throughout the third century ; speaking very roughly, the Athenian-Phoenician tradition of swift ships manœuvring for the ram was adopted by Carthage, Rhodes, and probably Egypt (which held Phoenicia), the Corinthian-Syracusan tradition of heavier ships seeking to grapple and board by Macedonia and Rome. In the second century the standard quadriremes and quinqueremes saw their greater sisters die out in the Aegean, possibly a matter of expense and man-power rather than efficiency ; while Philip V created a revolution in 201 by successfully putting in line light Illyrian galleys (*lembi*) with rams, precursors of the Roman Liburnian. The great Hellenistic ships lingered on in Egypt, and Antony for a moment

revived their use ; but Rome never adopted them, and
the Empire's return to triremes and Liburnians closed a
rather extraordinary chapter in naval history.

Land warfare had been transformed by Alexander's use
of heavy cavalry ; and from Issus in 333 to Sellasia in
222 cavalry was king. Alexander had been a master in
the combination of arms,—heavy and light infantry of
various types, heavy and light cavalry ; his Successors
retained all the types and added war-elephants, which he
never used. While his influence lasted, the typical formation of the line was the phalanx of heavy infantry in the
centre, light-armed and cavalry on the wings ; the cavalry
opened, and sometimes ended, the fighting, there being
battles where the heavy infantry never engaged at all.
For a century after his death war was largely waged by
means of mercenaries, drawn from every people of Europe
and Asia ; after 278 Gallic mercenaries were much in
favour, being brave and, at first, cheap. The kings welcomed the use of mercenaries, as they could thus spare
their national home-troops who formed the phalanx ; also
mercenaries rarely fought to the death, and war often
meant compelling the enemy's mercenaries to surrender
and then enlisting them. But by 222 the mode of warfare was changing, and the phalanx, the national Macedonian arm, coming back into first place ; Sellasia in 222
and Raphia in 217 were both decided by the clash of
national phalanxes, who fought as men fight when national
feeling is involved. It was unfortunate for Macedonia
that, when she encountered Rome, Alexander's methods
had been forgotten. Alexander's phalanx had been an
active and flexible body, organised in numerous battalions,
its spears resembling cavalry lances in length ; even so,
he took enormous care to guard its flanks, and it was more
than once in trouble through failure to keep line. But
at Cynoscephalae Philip V was using a phalanx which had
grown rigid and non-flexible with the weight of the length-
ened spears, everything being sacrificed to having as many
spearheads as possible projecting before the front rank,

while the vital need of very strong flank guards was being
neglected.   Certainly the phalanx scarcely had a fair chance
at either Cynoscephalae or Pydna, as both battles started
irregularly ;   and doubtless *under its own conditions*—level
ground  and  impregnable  flank  guards—it  would  have
beaten the legions or anything else.   But such conditions
were rare, and did not in fact happen against Rome ;   and
the ability of the legion to fight well under most conditions was conclusive.   The phalanx, like the deinosaurs,
perished of overspecialisation.

The age of giant warships at sea was the age of elephant-
warfare on land ;   all Alexander's generals, impressed by
the desperate battle with Porus, valued elephants highly,
and the arrival of the different batches from India between 324 and 275 can still be traced.   By about 275
Ptolemy II was beginning to hunt African elephants ;   his
unique embassy to the Mauryan Vindusara was doubtless
sent to obtain Indian trainers and mahouts, and the
Ptolemies trained Africans till the second century.   But
the Seleucids were the true ' elephant-lords ' ;   it was
largely the 480 elephants of Ipsus which gave Seleucus
Asia, and when Rome in 163 tried to disarm the dynasty
it was the destruction of the elephants which enraged the
people most.   Elephants were deadly the first time, against
troops who had never met them ;   against experienced
infantry they soon lost effectiveness, but were often useful
against cavalry.   Indians and Africans met once, at Raphia,
and the Africans were beaten ;   but no deductions can be
drawn, as they were heavily outnumbered.

Administration in the kingdoms in Asia and Egypt is
dealt with elsewhere ;   but Macedonia under the Antigonids may be noticed here.   This national state retained
its vigour to the end ;   it depended on its national army,
mercenaries being used merely to spare the Macedonians
where possible.   Court life was simpler than in the other
kingdoms, the amount of wealth small in comparison—the
land tax produced little over 200 talents a year—and the
throne, till the later years of Philip V, was occupied by

kings of a high type ; their family loyalty was proverbial, and the dynasty knew no murders till Philip V, while Gonatas' interest in philosophy and history, and the circle of literary men he collected, were one of the features of his age. Pella was again the capital; no attempt was made to build a rival to Alexandria or Antioch. Probably there was no King's land in Macedonia proper, and the Macedonian peasant owned his farm ; but in conquered districts, like Chalcidice and Paeonia, the land passed to the State, *i.e.* the king. The Antigonids treated their King's land much as did the Seleucids (Chap. IV) ; they gave estates to nobles, and ' lots ' of the usual type to military settlers and time-expired mercenaries ; but seemingly they never gave the absolute property in the land, as the Seleucids often did, but retained a right of escheat. King's land not in grant was cultivated by tenants, and the kings owned the mines and forests.

Macedonia, or at least its upper classes, became thoroughly hellenised in the third century ; the Macedonian dialect was replaced either by Attic Greek or the ' common speech ', and the native pantheon by the Olympians. In spite of their mixture of blood the Macedonians were now one people, able to assimilate foreign settlers ; and the country had become only one more unit of the Greek circle, more powerful than others, though it never again raised such armies as in the fourth century. Men in the Greek coastal cities were now calling themselves Macedonians ; Pella, and doubtless the other old Macedonian towns, had become autonomous cities with Greek city-forms. The Antigonids built a few cities of secondary importance, but the principal new cities in the country were both founded by Cassander : Thessalonica (Salonica), and Cassandreia on the site of Potidea. Both were Greek cities with Greek organisation, and the Cassandreians never called themselves Macedonians. Macedonia seemed strange in Greek eyes because the country had no religious centre and the people were convinced monarchists ; the Antigonid house, thanks to Gonatas, so secured the people's

affections that the dynasty only fell through the overwhelming power of a foreign enemy. But for all the great
men Macedonia produced, perhaps the greatest thing about
the little country was the plain Macedonian peasant, free,
loyal, and entirely competent in peace and war alike ;
Macedonia fell before Rome solely because there were so
few Macedonians.

For the existing Greek cities, the period bridges the
transition from free city-states to municipalities of the
Roman Empire. It opens with two conflicting theories of
the relations of the monarchy and the city. Alexander
had treated the Greek cities as free allies, Antipater had
desired to treat them as subjects, garrisoning those he chose
and maintaining in power oligarchies or tyrants favourable
to himself ; and the conflict of these rival policies lasted
long. Cassander, Lysimachus, the Ptolemies, and the
Attalids, all essentially followed Antipater in treating the
cities as subjects. Antigonus I, as a political weapon
against Cassander, revived Alexander's methods, and for
years really treated the cities as free ; but later he began
to interfere with them, and at the end was garrisoning
those he desired. Demetrius followed the same course,
beginning with freedom and ending with subjection ; he
and Lysimachus introduced a new feature, taxation, probably developed out of the nominally voluntary war ' con-
tributions ' received by Alexander and Antigonus I from
their allied cities. Gonatas employed every system as
expediency might dictate ; Doson returned frankly to
Alexander. Under Seleucus and Antiochus I the cities
were subject allies and probably taxed ; the restoration of
freedom to Ionia by Antiochus II was a landmark. Perhaps on the whole a tendency to treat the cities as subjects was dominant, varied by strenuous revivals of Alexander's policy of free alliance ; but the matter is enormously complicated with every kind of variation and
exception, and of course there were cities and (in Greece)
countries which never had any connection with any monarchy at all. Free alliance was not unconditioned free-

dom, for the city's foreign policy was shaped by its more powerful ally; but it was complete internal freedom. As time went on taxation became more and more the sign of subjection, and absence of taxation of freedom; and Antipater's methods were replaced by the royal *epistates* or city governor, a system not necessarily oppressive in good hands. Another method occasionally employed was for the king to appoint one or more of the chief magistrates himself, as the Attalids did at Pergamum and probably the later Ptolemies at Ptolemais in Egypt; Gonatas did this at Athens from 261 to 255, perhaps the only instance in an old Greek city.

As an example of the complication referred to, Gonatas' reign may be taken. Old Macedonia and Thessaly (p. 63) he governed directly; their cities were under city governors, but their Assemblies were not controlled. Chalcidice he governed through a general; Thessalonica had a city governor who controlled the Assembly, but Cassandreia was probably fully autonomous. In Greece the city Assemblies were never controlled, but Corinth, Chalcis, and Piraeus were garrisoned and, with Megara and Euboea, were under generals; but Histiaea in Euboea was fully autonomous. Athens, though governed by his friends, the pro-Macedonian Athenians, was at first so free that we cannot even say if Gonatas was suzerain; from 261 to 255 there was a garrison and *epistates*, and Gonatas appointed the magistrates; after 255 Athens was free and ungarrisoned again, but Gonatas was now definitely suzerain. Argos, Megalopolis, and perhaps other Peloponnesian cities were ruled in his interest by partisans of his own who had seized power as tyrants; the rest of Greece had no connection with him and did as it pleased. This kind of thing cannot be summed up under any sweeping phrases about the subjection of Greece. There was much interplay of forces going on, as there always had been; the real difference was that *certain* cities, like Corinth, now got little chance of freedom. But it must be remembered, in talking about freedom, that Greeks too often meant by it merely freedom to

destroy each other, and nothing ever restrained them but
a king or a League ; when in 217 Agelaus appealed for
Greek unity against Rome one of the inducements he offered
was retention of the right to fight each other without interference, and even late in the period Byzantium, being
independent, practically destroyed Callatis, the most flourishing Greek city of the western Euxine. Indeed even
Federalism, though it might restrain, could not abolish
that spirit of particularism which was the curse of Greece.

Considered from without, the constitution of the self-
governing Greek city, in the third century, looked much
the same as it had always done ; it had its Assembly,
Council, and magistrates, its jurisdiction over its citizens,
its immature finance, its intestine quarrels. In Northern
Greece there was even a steady increase in the number
of autonomous cities, especially in Aetolia. But in reality
modification was going on, due to the root fact that the
actual political life of the city, considered as a thing in
which all shared, was losing its former importance and
interest (Chap. III). By the second quarter of the third
century oligarchy and democracy, as political faction-
theories, were dead ; the real line of cleavage took other
directions. In Asia it might be pro-Seleucid and pro-
Ptolemy, in any city the King's party and the Nationalists ;
but often it was merely rich and poor, an unhealthy sign,
for the old democratic parties had frequently included
both. The Assemblies lost ground ; power might pass to
the Council, but was often exercised by the magistrates as
a board ; it illustrates their growing importance that a
city making an alliance or entering a League often altered
its magistracies to conform to those of the League or the
ally. Two magistracies steadily grew greater : the *agoranomos*, who saw to the corn supply, and the *gymnasiarchos*,
who superintended education. In some cities of Asia the
priestly *stephanephoros*, after whom the year was named,
became the chief magistrate ; only a wealthy man could
hold the office, for the duties included entertaining the
citizens. It was put up to sale, the city thus doubly bene-

fiting, and it shows the reality of civic patriotism, even in
the late period, that men were found to pay for the privilege of paying still further ; but in times of trouble there
was sometimes no purchaser, and the local god bought in
the office and named the year.  From the second century
priesthoods too were regularly sold, and entailed expenditure, but here the purchaser received some return ; he
might escape the burden of the gymnasiarchy or trierarchy,
or the obligation to provide money or choruses for the
festivals, while at Miletus in the first century the priest of
the Roman People even received a modest salary.  The
*gymnasiarchos* and *agoranomos* might also have to spend
largely themselves ; and the result of the changes above
indicated was that ultimately a poor man could no longer
hold one of the city offices, unless, as sometimes happened,
some king or wealthy citizen had endowed it.  When the
Roman Republic became dominant these tendencies were
carried still further ; Rome replaced the democracies by
timocracies, new boards of magistrates appeared, like the
politarchs in the Macedonian and Thessalian cities, and
sometimes a minute oligarchy held power, like the fifty
' Lords of Miletus '.  Rome might claim that she was only
carrying out to its logical conclusion the powers of the
*demiourgoi* and the *apocletoi* in the Achaean and Aetolian
Leagues (*post*).

One typical measure, much used by the kings, was
synoecism, the making of two or more cities or communities into one ;  Antigonus I formed Antigoneia Troas out
of seven cities, and Cassander synoecised twenty-six communities into Thessalonica.  The cities synoecised might
be obliterated, but often only part of the population was
moved, and the old cities survived as ' villages ' (*i.e.* demes)
of the new great city.  The most extraordinary synoecism
known was Demetrias, the city on the Gulf of Pagasae
which Demetrius founded as his southern capital.  It adjoined Pagasae, with a separate wall, making one city with
two quarters.  Nothing was destroyed to make it, but
Pagasae and every city of Magnesia from Cape Sepias to

Tempe on the Macedonian frontier became villages of
Demetrias, which thus embraced the whole Magnesian territory and formed a projection of Macedonia southwards.
When Rome deprived Philip V of Magnesia she broke this
synoecism up.

The city was not the only typical Greek state-form ; for
almost every country of Northern Greece was organised
under some traditional form of cantonal commune, called
indifferently a *koinon* (Community or League) or a Folk,
always with a religious centre. The growing feeling of
impotence in the third century among the smaller cities
in face of the monarchies led, in Greece itself, to a great
extension of the Federal principle, and the big Hellenistic
Leagues almost came to constitute a middle term between
city and monarchy ; they tended to come under single
heads, and Aratus enjoyed an authority in the Achaean
League very like one-man rule. They rendered much service ; they gave greater security and bargaining power as
against the monarchies, while they kept their members'
disputes within limits and prevented them fighting each
other. It is unfortunate that Greeks only possessed one
word for almost every form of public and private association ; they would have applied *koinon* equally to the League
of Nations, the Swiss Republic, a Cambridge College, a
Trade Union, and the village cricket club ; and it is too
late now, in translating it, to avoid various improper uses
of the word League.

Before coming to the Federal State proper (*Bundesstaat*),
one body must be noticed which was a confederation of
separate sovereign states (*Staatenbund*). The Panhellenic
League of Corinth, formed by Philip II, and continued by
Alexander under new treaties, was in its way a great conception, and afforded the only chance ever offered of the
realisation of that old dream, the unification of the Greek
world, if Greeks would have so regarded it. It was an
alliance between Alexander and the individual Greek states,
Sparta standing out, with a congress of delegates meeting
at Corinth ; the members remained sovereign states, and

their internal affairs were to be free from interference unless there was social revolution in any city (p. 104), but Alexander was President and Commander-in-Chief, and in practice their foreign policy was his. This however was not inevitable ; had the greater cities cared to work the League wholeheartedly in unison they were strong enough to prevent any encroachment on their liberties and make their voices heard in foreign politics. The strong point of the League was that it gave the small cities proportionate rights with the large ones, and some cities regarded it as a charter of liberty ; but in some cities it was unfortunately based on governments that were unpopular, and to many Greeks it was only a symbol of foreign domination ; the moment Alexander died it broke up. Its revival by Demetrius in 303 had a better chance, for his League was based on democratic governments which heartily supported him ; but this League also broke up after Ipsus. It was revived a third time by Antigonus Doson, the members now being, not single cities,—there were scarcely any single city-states left except Athens and Sparta,—but the Leagues of Achaea, Boeotia, Phocis, Thessaly, Epirus, Acarnania, *and* Macedonia ; for, as already noticed, the Macedonian king alone was no longer, in form, the Macedonian state. Doson's League had no pretensions to be Panhellenic (p. 18) ; but the League states were strong enough to force the Social War upon Philip V against his will, which illustrates what the old League of Corinth might have done had it desired. This League was the last attempt made by Macedonia to unite Greece. But Greece *was* ultimately unified in a single Panhellenic confederation ; it was done by the Emperor Hadrian three centuries after it had ceased to have any meaning, an ironical epitaph on the unity which Greece could never achieve for herself.

Turning to Federalism proper, we find three main classes : the League that was created by, or was the instrument of, some king ; the League which grew out of a cantonal commune ; and the League of cities. Of the first category Thessaly was the principal instance ; until Philip V lost

the country in 197 each successive Macedonian king from
Philip II onwards ruled Thessaly as part of Macedonia by
becoming head for life of its League ; similarly the Epirote
kings sometimes ruled Acarnania by holding the headship
of her League.    Epirus itself exhibits a long and complicated conflict between the principles of federalism and
monarchy ;  by 300 its three stems, Molossians, Chaonians,
and Thesprotians, had constituted themselves the federal
' Epirote Alliance ' under the headship of the Molossian
king, whom the Molossians could depose if they desired ;
in Pyrrhus' hands the monarchy had become practically
an autocracy ;  about 235 the people killed off Pyrrhus'
last descendants and became a federal republic.    Very
peculiar bodies were the Leagues founded by Antigonus I
during his struggle for power.  He would have liked to
have re-formed the League of Corinth, but as until 303
this was impossible, he created three sectional Leagues :
the Ionian, a revival of the old League ;  the Ilian, a League
of the Aeolian cities with Ilium as federal centre ;  and the
Islanders, the Ionian Cyclades with their federal centre at
Delos.    These Leagues were not sovereign states ;  they
had no Assembly, no civil head, no military or judicial
powers, and apparently no coinage ;  business was trans-
acted by a council of delegates, and extraordinary expenses
had to be met by the cities.    Their chief business was to
conduct their federal festivals and worship Antigonus ; they
were really channels by which he obtained influence over
their constituent free cities.

Of Leagues developed out of the cantonal communes of
different Folks there were several in Northern Greece ;  but
the principal example was Aetolia, the one country in
Greece which from first to last was never conquered by,
and never depended on, any king.    Aetolia possessed few
towns and no capital, the federal centre being the temple
of Apollo at Thermum ;  when after 321 she began to re-
organise her old commune, the League units were frequently
not towns but country districts grouped round some village or hill fort ;  but cities continued gradually to develop.

All political power belonged to the Assembly, which comprised every free Aetolian; it sprang simply from the army, the people under arms, and was its civil counterpart; it met twice a year, before and after the campaigning season. The head of the League was a general elected annually, who was President and Commander-in-Chief; re-election was only possible after some years' interval. The other officials were a cavalry leader, a secretary, an *agonothetes* to celebrate festivals, and seven stewards of finance. Aetolia was not an instance of constituent states delegating powers to a federal body; the League grew naturally out of the people's war organisation, but the cities had internal autonomy and their own citizenships.

As the Aetolian League expanded, any country that joined was dissolved into, and joined as, separate cities or units. If a new unit adjoined League territory, it entered into sympolity with Aetolia, that is, its people became for all purposes Aetolians, and attended the Assembly. But a city at a distance became an ally and entered into isopolity, an exchange of citizenships; its citizens became *potentially* Aetolians, but their potential Aetolian citizenship only became actual if they settled in, and (as they had the right to) became citizens of, some city of the Aetolian sympolity. We shall meet these potential citizenships again in other connections. The Aetolian League had a Council (*boule*) composed of members elected by the League units in proportion to military contingents; but this body had little power, and only decided current matters which could not wait till the next Assembly. As the League expanded, however, government by the Assembly, *i.e.* by mass meeting twice a year, became impossible, and Aetolia never hit on any form of representation; the result was that the Council threw up a small committee called *Apocletoi*, unknown to the constitution, who sat permanently with the General and really governed the country, though the Assembly kept the power of peace and war; between 280 and 220 Aetolia thus passed from being the most democratic to being about the least democratic State in Greece.

Aetolia was the first League to use its federal citizenship to enlarge its territory ; Achaea and Boeotia subsequently copied. By 220 the Aetolian sympolity stretched across Greece from sea to sea, embracing Western and Epicnemidian Locris, Malis, Doris, the Aenianes and Dolopes, part of Acarnania, part of Phocis, part of Thessaly, and Achaea Phthiotis ; members allied by isopolity were Cephallenia, Ambracia, Ceos, Chios, Vaxos in Crete, Phigaleia, and (in effect) Messenia ; later it even took in Lysimacheia, Cius, and Chalcedon. From about 290 to 189 it controlled Delphi, but Delphi never became a member.

Among Leagues of which, though representing some definite stem, the basis had been a union of cities and not a cantonal commune, Arcadia and Boeotia were old examples ; both suffered many vicissitudes of fortune, but the Boeotian League endured permanently and from time to time embraced Opuntian Locris and Megara, and the Arcadian, though sometimes mutilated, lasted till its cities joined the Achaean League. The Achaean was originally a League of the 12 Achaean cities, which broke up during the wars of the Successors ; it began to re-form in 280, and by 272 embraced the ten surviving Achaean cities, Helice and Bura having been destroyed by natural causes ; subsequently Olenus became an eleventh member. Its effective organisation, however, dated from 255, when a single general replaced the former two. The League was a sympolity like the Aetolian, other countries joining being similarly dissolved into their component parts ; the cities kept their citizenship, their constitutions (though some assimilated their magistracies to those of the League), their law courts, and so much internal autonomy that, unlike Aetolia, the local mints coined concurrently with the Federal mint ; no citizen of any city had private rights in another without a special grant. All foreign policy, however, was the League's, together with the army, the federal taxes, all weights and measures (which were made uniform),

F

and justice for offences against the League. The federal centre was the temple of Zeus Amarios at the capital Aigion. The general, who was President and Commander-in-Chief, could be re-elected every alternate year; and beside the secretary, treasurer, and admiral were ten *demiourgoi*, seemingly modelled on the Arcadian fifteen and corresponding to the original ten cities (though if each city originally had a right to one demiurge this was soon dropped), who with the general formed a governing board with considerable power.

It seems probable that Achaea had once had, like other states, a Council (*boule*) and an Assembly (*synodos*), the latter, however, limited by a property qualification, and that in the revived League the two coalesced to form the Achaean Council, which after the League expanded was certainly of great size, probably some thousands. This Council held two meetings a year at Aigion, in April and September, these meetings retaining the old name, *synodos*; some believe there were four regular meetings, but the others known seem to be extraordinary sessions in war time. The *synodos* dealt with all League policy and business except new treaties and alliances, and peace and war; these had to be referred to a *syncletos*, a meeting of all citizens over thirty. The *syncletos* was not an Assembly; it could only decide on matters referred to it by the *synodos*, and was a mass referendum, votes being taken by cities to prevent the meeting being swamped by the people of the city where it met; the *synodos* voted in the same way. A similar mass meeting was held every winter to elect the new officials, who entered office in May; subsequently, perhaps in 213, both election and entry were transferred to autumn.

Our judgment upon the League's constitution, then—a constitution which has been highly praised—must largely depend upon what the Council or *synodos* was. It was composed of delegations from the several cities in proportion to population, each chosen by its city. Some such form of delegation was known on the Councils of various

Greek states, but never in the Assemblies ; so far then as the system could be called representation, the Achaean League had advanced much further than any other Greek state, owing to its Council having in effect almost become the League Assembly ; but how far this was due to design is unknown.   Unhappily the crucial matters—whether the delegations were chosen by election or lot, and what chance of representation there was for minorities—are also unknown.   Greece never evolved any true system of representation, but that of the Achaean League, so far as it went, came nearest.  The League's greatest defect was that its constitution weighted the scales in favour of the well-to-do, while, in spite of its many good points, it was in one thing definitely behind Aetolia ; the limitation of the *syncletos* to citizens over 30 meant that half the men who would have to fight had no voice in the declaration of war, whereas Aetolia seemingly had no such limitation. This may help to explain why in war Aetolia was so much more efficient.

The later history of the *koinon* type of state, so far as not given in Chapter I, may be briefly indicated here.   In 189 Rome curtailed the Aetolian League and deprived it of Delphi, and after 168 she broke the League up altogether ; all the members, even to little stems like the Oetaeans, became separate Leagues, and these, with the Leagues formed in 197 (p. 22), now accounted for the whole of northern Greece.  The only feature of note among them is that the Thessalian League possessed, as the Island League had once possessed, the strange power of granting citizenship in its constituent cities.  The Achaean League, from 224 to 198 a satellite of Macedonia, became independent again in 197, so far as an ally of Rome could be ; but though in 191 it embraced all Peloponnese, it never recovered the position it had held in 228 (p. 17).  But the Federal principle still represented a possible element of power which Rome could not tolerate, and after 146 she dissolved the Achaean and its allied Leagues.  *Koina* of a kind were subsequently allowed to re-form ;  beside those of northern Greece, Leagues of Achaea, Arcadia, Argolis, and the Eleutherolacones are known in the Peloponnese ; but they were religious bodies, without political significance. Similar non-political *koina* formed, or were formed, in Asia Minor ; those of Bithynia and Pontus date from Pompey, that of Asia was in existence under Antony ; there were several others later. Their affinities go back to the Leagues created by Antigonus I ; they did in one way represent their provinces, for they could complain to Rome of the provincial governor, but their real business was to conduct the official worship of the Emperor. The only *koinon* known which retained true political functions in Augustus' reign was an old League of the 23 towns of Lycia.

Of the contending state-forms of the Hellenistic period it was thus monarchy which survived, though the Macedonian monarchies perished. Caesar contemplated a Graeco-Roman kingdom of the Hellenistic pattern ; Antony actually erected one. But the real heir of the Hellenistic kings was Augustus ; for, though his principate was in form Roman and not Hellenistic, his empire was joined by many threads to the Macedonian kingdoms. But this subject belongs to the history of Rome.

# CHAPTER III

## THE GREEK CITIES: SOCIAL-ECONOMIC CONDITIONS

Man as a political animal, a fraction of the *polis* or self-governing city state, had ended with Aristotle; with Alexander begins man as an individual. This individual needed to consider both the regulation of his own life and also his relations with the other individuals who with him composed the 'inhabited world'; to meet the former need there arose the philosophies of conduct (Chap. X), to meet the latter certain new ideas of human brotherhood. These originated on the day—one of the critical moments of history—when, at a banquet at Opis, Alexander prayed for a union of hearts (*homonoia*) and a joint commonwealth of Macedonians and Persians; he was the first to transcend national boundaries and to envisage, however imperfectly, a brotherhood of man in which there should be neither Greek nor barbarian. The Stoic philosophy was quick to grasp the concept, and Zeno's earliest work, his *Republic*, exhibited a resplendent hope which has never quite left men since; he dreamt of a world which should no longer be separate states, but one great City under one divine law, where all were citizens and members one of another, bound together, not by human laws, but by their own willing consent, or (as he phrased it) by Love. This is sometimes called cosmopolitanism, a word coined by the Cynics to signify that they belonged to no state; but other Greeks did not use it, and it has acquired such unpleasant associations that it is well to avoid it, for it does not at all express what the Stoics meant; it implied a shirking of

69

national duties which no Stoic would have tolerated, for
the wise man (they said) would do his duty by his own
country,[1] and they seem to have understood that if their
brotherhood were ever realised it must be through the
national state and not by its denial. Even the practical
world was influenced, in spite of itself, by Zeno's dream,
through the insistence of Zeno's school on certain notions
of equality and brotherhood and by the fact that the
'inhabited world' or *oecumene* now began to be treated
as a whole ; the stranger could no longer be *ipso facto* an
enemy, and Homonoia received perhaps more tributes
than any other Hellenistic concept. Certain ideas of the
interrelation of states, apart from actual treaties, began
to emerge ; and the germs of modern International Law
go back to third century Stoicism.

Between these ideas of individualism and brotherhood
the Greek had to work out his own salvation afresh. The
first thing to notice is a certain enlargement of the feeling
of humanity. The time was full of extraordinary contradictions,—which is perhaps to say that the Greek was
human,—and this feeling grew up in the midst of inter-
minable dissensions and wars. The Greek was as quarrel-
some as ever ; the change was, that he began to doubt
whether he ought to be. Isocrates in 370 had desired to
unite all Greeks for an attack on Persia ; Agelaus in 217
desired to unite them for defence against Rome ; the difference is eloquent. One result was an enormous growth of
arbitration. Arbitration had for long been employed,
though sparingly, in Greece, and Argos and Sparta had
once made a treaty to arbitrate all disputes ; but in and
after the third century arbitrations between cities, usually
boundary arbitrations, became exceedingly common ; generally the arbitrators were a commission from another city,
but Alexander and many of his successors also arbitrated
between cities without employing their powers, as did later
the Roman Senate. This perpetual boundary litigation,
the reason of which was the ever-present dread of starvation

[1] πολιτεύσεται ὁ σοφός.

and the consequent desire to get a larger share of the limited
arable land, was not ideal, but it was better than the alternative ; every award was a war strangled, and if awards
were not always observed, that only meant more awards ;
and even cities of no great repute, like some of the Cretan,
made permanent treaties of arbitration.

For a while, too, it looked as if war itself might modify
its character, for the great Macedonians, notably Alexander,
Demetrius, and Antigonus Gonatas, had managed to introduce a little chivalry into the business. It had once been
universal law that you might, on taking a city, kill the men
and sell the women and children ; by Alexander's time
this had been modified into a general sale, and he himself
sold the people of four cities,—Thebes and Gaza with no
excuse save the law, Tyre and Cyropolis with (as the world
went) every excuse as regarded the *men*. But his Successors seemingly dropped the horrible practice altogether ;
you now took a city to make it profitable to yourself, not
to make it a desert. It began to look as if the old rule
were dead ; and when in 279 the Gauls invaded Greece,
the Greek cities complained bitterly of the ' cruelty ' of
the natural man again obtruding itself.

Then came Mantinea : in 223 Antigonus Doson permitted
Aratus and the Achaeans to gratify their vengeance on
that city by selling the people. There had been great
provocation ; but we can still hear echoes of the storm of
protest which the proceeding evoked. As regarded the
rulers of the earth, Mantinea was the end of the hope of
better things ; by the second century, in the hands of
the Romans and Philip V, war came back to what it had
always been, and the Achaean Philopoemen's treatment
of Sparta was little better than Philip's brutality at Cius
and Maroneia. But some Greek cities, and many Greeks,
held to kindlier courses ; when Miletus and Magnesia in
the second century ended their struggle with a convention
to exchange prisoners head for head, Magnesia returned
her surplus prisoners without ransom. Lycurgus had once
passed a humane law at Athens forbidding Athenians to

purchase free Greek captives; some cities now did better, and undertook by treaty that if one of their citizens purchased a citizen of the other city he should liberate him against repayment of the price.  The known cases of individuals who managed, often at personal risk, to release or ransom captives, whether taken in war or by pirates, are numerous; and though the ransomed captive legally became slave to his ransomer till the ransom was repaid, repayment was often waived.  Among instances of altruism let me mention the names of two brothers of Aegiale, Hegesippus and Philopappus, who gave themselves as hostages to a pirate crew to save a number of women; for their reward was only a crown of green leaves and the record which by chance has saved their names from oblivion.

There was something too of humanity in the movement for safeguarding certain places against war.  A 'holy place'—a temple and its precinct—was immune from war, though the only penalty on the transgressor was the wrath of the gods; the whole island of Delos, Apollo's birthplace, was such a 'holy place', probably from time immemorial. Various cities now sought to get themselves and their territories made 'holy', *i.e.* immune from war, by the consent of the Greek world and the Hellenistic kings; Smyrna came first, about 240, and was followed by Magnesia on the Maeander, Alabanda, Teos, Miletus, and others; other dedications, never carried out, were recommended by oracles.  The influence of Delphi and the Amphiktyons counted for much in the movement, and gave it a religious basis.  There was a concurrent movement for making places inviolable (*asyla*), *i.e.* immune from reprisals (*syla*) or private war—the right of the claimant, whether individual or city, to carry off persons or goods without a state of war, a right which lay behind much of the privateering of the time.  Once every stranger had always been subject to reprisals; but the right had been steadily cut into, partly perhaps for its hampering effect upon trade, and many temples had long been asylums.  This quality was conferred on many other temples during the Hellenistic period, but it also became extended to whole cities and their territory ; the island of Tenos was first, about 270, and was followed by all the Greek cities which became ' holy ' and various others, ultimately by Delphi itself.

To call the title ' holy and inviolable ' an empty name is to misunderstand the time. The movement was a serious attempt to limit war ; did Seleucus II take the trouble he did to procure an empty name for Smyrna, his most loyal ally ? Even in Syria in the first century it retained some significance (p. 130), and only became an empty name in the Roman imperial period. But what *practical* effect holiness had is doubtful, for it did not alter the political quality of a city or circumscribe its political activities. It acted once, however, in a very curious way : Antiochus III, unable to take Xanthus, declared the city ' holy ' so as to save his face when he retired. *Asylia* did produce an effect ; it assisted to limit that self-help which was the negation of public order. For it extended far beyond certain cities and temples ; the Dionysiac artists were made inviolable so that the public could be sure of its shows, while every proxeny decree conferred *asylia* on the recipient, and the Greek world became a network of people who were inviolable by the subjects of this or that state. One need not suppose that an Aetolian privateersman raided a village with a list of inviolable Aetolian proxeni in his hand ; but Aetolia tried to meet that difficulty by giving certificates of exemption to friendly cities and undertaking to make good damage done to individuals. That under the Empire *asylia* became abused, and merely meant that certain cities were crowded with untouchable riff-raff, compelling Rome's interference, has no bearing on its merits as originally instituted.

Quite apart from Federalism, many things were now tending to draw the cities closer together and break down their old isolation. One was the very great number of grants of honorary citizenship to a man and his descendants which now occur ; every city came to possess friends in many others who were its citizens. The belief that a man could not be a citizen of two cities requires modification ; he could be a citizen of any number, but possibly, in the third and second centuries, he could only at one time be an *active* citizen of one city, his other citizenships being potential only. If Corinth granted honorary citizenship to a citizen of Argos, the Argive had the right, if he settled in Corinth, to take up that citizenship and become for all purposes a Corinthian ; but unless he did so his Corinthian citizenship was potential. What is unknown is whether, if he took up his Corinthian citizenship, he still remained an active citizen of Argos. But in the first century a man could unquestionably exercise two active citizenships—the natural development of events ; for in Bithynia Pompey forbade such multiple citizenship, but failed to stop it ; Dio was a citizen of Prusa, Nicomedia, and Apamea, and when Trajan desired to abolish multiple citizenship he found it was so common in Bithynia that he could not do so without shattering the whole communal system, and could only prohibit it for the future. Citizenship apart, every city now had many friends elsewhere who, if they visited her, were not mere aliens ; they had front seats at the games and dined in the town hall. Inter-city intercourse was taking on a different complexion.

But the matter went much further than individuals ; cities had begun to give their citizenship to the whole citizen body of another city, the process known as isopolity (p. 64). Early in the third century Athens gave Priene her citizenship ; later there were mutual grants of citizenship between many cities—Athens and Rhodes, Athens and Miletus, Messene and Phigaleia, Paros and Allaria, Miletus and a whole group, Cius, Phygela, Mylasa, Seleuceia-Tralles ; all Cyreneans were citizens of Tenos, all Teians of several Cretan cities. This worked as the honorary citizenships worked ; it was a potential citizenship, which any grantee could take up as of right if he desired. Beside citizenship, other rights were similarly granted. Athens gave proxeny to whole classes of men in some Thessalian cities ; all

Messenians and Pellaeans became proxeni of Delphi, all
Delphians of Sardes, all Acragantines of the Molossian
League. Individual grants of proxeny became so numerous that some cities ceased to set up the decrees ; in the
third century Epidaurus, a small city, averaged four a
year, and merely entered names on a list, as Anaphe was
already doing ; Delphi did the same from 197 ; about
264 Histiaea gave 32 in one year. Proxeny was a coveted
honour, for it not only conferred immunity from seizure
but gave the right to own land in the grantor city ; this
right was largely exercised, for Rome's first step after the
conquest of Achaea, with a view to weakening the Peloponnese, was to forbid ownership of land in two cities, though
she subsequently withdrew the prohibition. Whole cities
—Messene, Chersonesos, Alexandria, Smyrna, Sardes—
were given prior rights of consulting the Delphic oracle ;
Ithaca gave all Magnesians front seats at her local games,
the Odysseia ; many cities, to encourage trade, gave freedom from import and export duties to other cities as wholes.
All these things tended to bind the cities together ; Poseidippus in the third century could say " There are many
cities, but they are one Hellas ". One wonders how far
the process might have gone had not Rome intervened.

To what extent honorary citizenships were taken up
cannot be said. Few literary men, at any rate, worked in
their own cities ; they went where work, friends, perhaps
libraries, took them. Honours were conferred on many
poets and philosophers who gave recitations and lectures
in other cities, often of a kind calculated to interest the
local patriotism of the city visited, and doubtless this
class, when they settled elsewhere, habitually took up
their citizenships ; Menander of Thyrreion was called a
Cassopean, Metrodorus of Scepsis a Chalcedonian ; Apollonius of Alexandria and Deinocrates of Macedonia were
called Rhodians, Aristarchus of Samothrace an Alexandrian ;
many other cases are known. One may probably therefore assume a certain interchange of citizens between the
cities. On the other hand, League constitutions were usually

so framed that no citizen could acquire personal rights in another city without an express grant.

Another matter which drew the world together was the development of a common language. The educated everywhere began to use Attic; and out of Attic, modified by local usages, arose Hellenistic Greek, the ' common speech ', familiar as the Greek of the New Testament. For awhile a second ' common speech ' began to form out of the Doric dialects, and has left one great monument, Theocritus; but it could not hold its ground. Local dialects persisted in some countries till the first century; but ultimately the ' common speech ' conquered every Greek city, for, as it became the general medium of communication between peoples of different dialects, it finally compelled abandonment of the dialect. With the ' common speech ' appeared also what lawyers call ' common form '; the decrees of the cities all followed the same lines. In fact, the vast mass of honorary decrees passed during this period also constituted a bond between the cities, for normally, whenever one city honoured a citizen of another, commissioners took a copy of the decree to the city whose member was honoured; there they asked leave to set it up, and were entertained at a dinner and made a speech emphasising the solidarity and good feeling between the two cities. The enormous number of new festivals had the same effect; for, though the performers were only professionals going their round, the games themselves were a religious act and the cities sent religious envoys. The precincts of the city temples were crowded with *stelae* (standing slabs of stone) on which were engraved the city's decrees and records; this was the city's record office (though some also kept records on tablets stored in the Town Hall), and any visitor could there read the honours paid to his own compatriots. In the third century the honorary decree is often a valuable political document or even a political manifesto, but by the first century, when independent politics were passing away, it had degenerated; it grew in prolixity in proportion to the unimportance of

its contents, and might record the most trivial details of
the man's private life, even the number of guests at his
wedding ; for he now paid for it himself, and liked value
for his money.

Perhaps the most important thing of all was the judicial
commissions ;   not those which arbitrated a political
quarrel between two cities, but those which settled lawsuits within the city itself.   For before 300 the old system
of trying cases by a jury composed of a large body of citizens
was fast breaking down, as it deserved ; it was about the
worst legal system ever invented, for the juries' decisions
were habitually influenced by politics, mass passion, and
prejudice.   It was largely replaced throughout the Hellenistic period by a system under which a commission of one
or more judges (dicasts) came from another city and heard
all cases entered for trial.   It was not an ideal system, for
it did not function regularly ; seemingly you often asked
another city to help you only when things got pretty bad,
and it entailed much delay in justice—sometimes when a
commission did come it found no cases had been tried for
years ; and as prompt justice is only less important than
impartial justice, this doubtless led to much self-help,
with the usual undesirable accompaniments.   But when a
commission did come, it did well, for it stood outside the
passions of local factions ; and, judging by the remaining
records, commissions may in some places have come often
enough to avoid undue delay.   Their procedure was uniform ; they first settled all cases they could by persuasion
or informal arbitration ; the residue they either decided
in legal form themselves or sent to a jury.   In a recorded
instance at Calymna the dicasts sent by Iasos found over
350 cases awaiting them, and of these they settled over
340, 10 only being sent to a jury.   As the cases which had
to be judged strictly were judged by the local law (reinforced by royal rescripts where the city was under some
king's suzerainty) and not by that of the commissioners'
city, it meant that by the second century there must have
grown up in the Greek cities a body of true lawyers, a thing

previously unknown,—men who had studied the laws of
many cities beside their own ; Theophrastus' studies in
jurisprudence also helped to build up a sounder view of
the functions of law.  Moreover, as most cases everywhere
were settled informally, there must also have grown up a
body of rules for doing this, in which we may perhaps
see the rudiments of an interstate system of equity ;  equity
in England also began informally enough.  It sounds
strange to hear judges praised for being ' impartial and
just ' or for making no distinction between rich and poor,
things we take for granted.  But impartiality was something quite new in Greece, for the juries had weighted the
scales heavily in favour of the poor or of the debtor.
Some cities gained a name for impartiality ;  it seems as
if the principal industry of Priene was settling her neighbours' lawsuits.

The kings had an honourable record in the matter, and
possibly the first idea of these judicial commissions originated with Antigonus I.  Sometimes, where the city was
in some king's sphere, a king's governor, instead of appoint-
ing a commission, acted as judge himself, thus anticipating
the Roman governors of a later period ;  Cleon, Attalid
governor in Aegina, was highly praised by the city for being
" a just judge towards all, shewing no private motives,
determined to act neither unfairly nor arbitrarily, but en-
deavouring in most cases to bring the parties to agree " ;
that is, he acted precisely as a commission would have
acted.  The kings themselves were constantly being called
on to settle internal disturbances, which might mean anything from squabbles over mortgages to incipient revolution,
and they or their governors frequently sent judicial commissions for the purpose.

Of the cases handled by the dicasts, many arose under
a *symbolon, i.e.* a convention between two cities for the
settlement of private disputes between their citizens,
made to prevent either side being treated as strangers in
the courts of the other ; though the *symbolon* long antedates Hellenism, its increasing frequency marks a certain

advance, and it has been thought that it, as well as Stoicism, helped to give rise to the later idea of a Law of Nations. But of all classes of lawsuits, debtor and creditor cases were far the commonest, and were at the bottom of most of the internal dissensions in the cities. The juries had never been honest over cases of debt ; and the document from Calymna already referred to explains that dicasts tried to avoid leaving cases to a jury because the decision, taken by vote, of these quasi-political bodies was a fruitful source of new dissensions. And all our information about the judicial commissions emphasises one point : they strove, often successfully, to restore *homonoia*, concord, in the city. Taken in bulk, the surviving dicast decrees are a paean in praise of *homonoia*, that thing for which men longed but which they could not achieve. It was not lip-service ; we know well enough that a State may have trouble when that is the last thing which the bulk of its people desire. Every form of authority—kings, envoys, governors, generals of Leagues—was perpetually urging the people to live in concord ; the most praised women of the time, a Phila or an Apollonis, were those who tried to promote it ; even the gods intervened, and Apollo exhorts Iasos to *homonoia*. Homonoia herself was worshipped as a goddess at Priene. She was one of the great conceptions of the Hellenistic age, but she remained a pious aspiration only. Not until Rome had crushed all internal feuds was concord achieved ; then, in the Imperial period, cities freely celebrated Homonoia on their coinage, and she was frequently worshipped when all meaning in her worship had for Greeks passed away.

All these things might in time have led to more co-operation among the cities than was ever actually achieved. For in many things which needed common action they failed completely. One was a common calendar. The historian Timaeus introduced the clumsy reckoning by Olympiads (p. 228), but the cities continued each its own dating by its magistrates, and did not even all begin their years at the same time ; Athens began about July, Sparta about

October, Delos in January, Miletus ultimately about April; the confusion thus caused is terrible. The only city calendars whose translation into Julian years is reasonably certain are the Delian and Milesian; the arrangement of the important third century Athenian and Delphic calendars is still highly conjectural. Worse than this was the failure to provide decent roads and secure communications. Brigandage was common, sometimes organised under an archklepht; when Heracleides toured Greece *c.* 205 he noted that *one* road—that from Oropus to Tanagra—was safe. Piracy was worse than brigandage, and better organised. Here the kings gave no help; Demetrius and Antigonus Gonatas, Ptolemy II and Antiochus III, were all on excellent terms with the pirate captains, whom they found useful allies. Many so-called pirates were privateersmen. The real pirates—exiles, broken men, unemployed mercenaries, escaped slaves—lived in small strongholds round the Aegean; one such band for a time held Phygela in Ephesus' territory. Many attacks on the islands are known, but in the third century these were often only single-ship raids to catch a few slaves; for the pirates had one whole-hearted foe, Rhodes, and so long as Rhodes' power lasted she kept the evil within bounds. Her worst difficulty was Crete. In a Cretan city the old men, grown respectable with years, governed in proper form, while the younger men went out on their lawless occasions under some adventurous leader; Rhodes' efforts were directed to getting their city governments to restrain them. That is why, unlike the kings, she seldom interfered in the endless civil wars in the island; from her point of view they were useful, as they kept adventurers at home. But after 168 Rome's policy of weakening all strong states without putting anything in their place bore its fruit; Rhodes became unable to hold the scourge under, while Rome, after annexing Pergamum in 130, allowed the wild country of western Cilicia, formerly under Attalid rule, to become derelict; there the pirates drew together and founded a regular state. Cilicia cost Rome, as Rome deserved, two wars to put down ; and even Pompey's great effort—noteworthy for his answer to his captains' remonstrances in a gale, " We need not live but we *must* put to sea ", which the Hansa League afterwards took as its motto—only cleared the seas for the moment.

We have now considered the workings of internationalism among the cities ; we must turn to certain things which affected the individual, whether as a citizen or simply as a man, conscious (as people have been conscious at each great new advance in civilisation) of the increased importance of his individual life. With the weakening of the city tie came an enormous growth of non-political private associations and clubs. There had been a few such clubs in fourth-century Athens,[1] but Demetrius of Phalerum (317–307) had forbidden the formation of new ones ; and the great outburst of associations all over the Greek world dates from 300 onwards. Most were very small ; apart from the Dionysiac artists, a membership of 100 was quite unusual. They were primarily social and religious bodies grouped round the worship of some god ; possibly the *thiasoi* were more purely religious, while the *eranoi*, where the subscriptions were of importance,—one had an entrance fee of 30 drachmae,—were primarily social bodies. About 200, family associations appear, founded by some individual to perpetuate the family memory, the priesthood being hereditary among his descendants. Every club had its temple, however tiny, but finance was a perpetual difficulty ; many let their temples for secular purposes when not in use, like the Egretes at Athens, who in leasing theirs reserved one day a year for their annual festival. Epicteta's club at Thera, one of the wealthiest, had an annual revenue from its founder of 210 dr., and one at Athens once ended a year with 1,770 dr. in hand ; but these were exceptions, and the clubs came more and more to depend on some wealthy member who would bear expenses and was honoured with a statue, for which he paid himself—exactly what was happening in the cities (p. 93).

[1] The fifth-century oligarchic clubs were another matter.

G

These clubs were in no sense Friendly Societies; they might help a member in trouble, or see to his funeral, probably an excuse for a dinner; but there it ended. Associations of men named from their trades began to appear, but the professional trade guild was practically unknown to Hellenism, unless possibly in Egypt; true trade guilds only evolved under the Roman Empire, and finally Justinian's Code took account of their rules, as did English common law of the custom of merchants. Usually a club had no political meaning; but in the last struggle of the Achaean League against Rome clubs of 'patriots' appeared, i.e. men united to uphold the constitution of their fathers. The club modelled itself on the city organisation; it had officials with similar names and passed resolutions like city decrees; and it became so much the standard model that the most diverse forms of activity —the philosophic schools, the Museum at Alexandria, the Dionysiac artists, Ptolemy's garrison troops, the poets domiciled at Athens, the physicians trained at Cos, the Old Boys from this or that gymnasium—all adopted the same form of organisation. The number of clubs was great; in 146 the small city of Troezen possessed 23; obviously they met a want, and prevented the individual feeling lost in a vast new world. That their life seems to us tiresome and unutterably boring is true, but is hardly worth saying; there is no evidence either that the Greek was bored with his life or that the men of 2,000 years hence would not be equally bored with ours. The club's most important function in Greek life was to form the natural avenue for foreigners and foreign worships entering a city; purely Greek clubs occur at Athens and Rhodes, but normally they were either foreign or mixed, the latter assisting to break down racial barriers; thus one at Cnidus, besides Greeks, contained a Thracian, a Phoenician, a Pisidian, a Phrygian, and a Libyan. Slaves were sometimes members, but seemingly the first known slave club only occurs late in the period, in Egypt.

Some advance was made in education during the period;

the gymnasiarch, who supervised it, finally became almost the most important magistrate. Some cities, like Miletus, recognised that education should be, as Plato had suggested, the business of the state ; but to carry that out they too often depended on donations from kings and wealthy individuals, both for buildings and endowment; even Rhodes accepted a donation in this behalf from Eumenes II. In the more progressive cities elementary schools became well established ; in Ionia they embraced girls as well as boys, and at Teos and Chios the two were educated together, as had long been customary at Sparta. No qualification, seemingly, was required of teachers, but the magistrates tried to get men of character. Girls' education was apparently carried no further ; boys passed on to the ephebate. This had been remodelled at Athens by Lycurgus about 335 ; it embraced the 19th and 20th years, was compulsory, and though based on military training made some provision for education also ; but the names of the instructors, *cosmetes* (teacher of order) and *sophronistes* (teacher of self-control), show that Lycurgus' aim was rather the foundation of moral character. The ephebe system became practically universal in Greek cities, but Athens soon dropped, and other cities never adopted, compulsion ; it was voluntary education. Its centre was the gymnasium, which came to play in the Hellenistic city the part played in England by the public schools ; those who had been through the gymnasium constituted a kind of informal aristocracy, and in the new cities of Asia the gymnasium typified Greek life ; a place which could set one up was fairly on the road to become a city. A well-equipped city, like Pergamum, would have three gymnasia, for boys, ephebes, and the ' young men ' who had passed through the ephebate. The athletic training was thorough ; about the intellectual we are ill informed, but probably it did not go further than grammar, poetry (with music), and some rhetoric ; anyone who wanted higher education,—philosophy or science—had to go afterwards and work under some recognised teacher for himself. Some gymnasia however possessed libraries. The office of gymnasiarch was burdensome ; he often spent largely himself, both for necessary outlay and for special prizes or festivals. Indeed much time was wasted by all the scholars marching in procession to the sacrifices, both at the regular city festivals and on special occasions, like kings' visits or birthdays ; a Coan calendar gives, in a month, 8 days of festivals and 4 of examinations. Great men would ask for a holiday for the schools, but it generally only meant another procession ; one wonders if boys appreciated a holiday chiefly composed of compulsory chapel better than their work of racing and wrestling. In the school-rooms excavated at Pergamum and Priene the walls are covered from floor to roof with names, like Upper School at Eton. The ephebes, like their elders, formed associations, imitating the city organisation in little ; and the Old Boys' association or *gerousia*—those who had passed through the city gymnasium—ultimately under the Roman Empire became a sort of municipal senate. Even the little schoolgirls passed resolutions in proper form in honour of distinguished visitors.

The great Macedonian princesses of the two generations after Alexander (p. 51) exercised much influence on the position of Greek women. If Macedonia produced perhaps the most competent group of men the world had yet seen, the women were in all respects the men's counterparts ; they played a large part in affairs, received envoys and obtained concessions for them from their husbands, built temples, founded cities, engaged mercenaries, commanded armies, held fortresses, and acted on occasion as regents or even co-rulers ; the influence of a woman like Arsinoe Philadelphus, beautiful, able, masterful, on the men who served her was evidently enormous. These queens had their men's desire for culture ; Aratus dedicated poems to Phila, Poseidippus of Pella to Arsinoe, Callimachus to Berenice, wife of Ptolemy III ; Arsinoe corresponded with the physicist Strato, and Stratonice, the wife of Antiochus I, increased the art-collection at Delos. Hardly less notable

were some queens of Greek blood; Apollonis of Cyzicus,
who married Attalus I of Pergamum and was the mother
of famous sons, was spoken of as Romans spoke of the
' mother of the Gracchi ', a model of womanly qualities;
Cleomenes' sister Chilonis at Sparta would have honoured
any society. One Greek woman, Pythodoris, daughter of
a citizen of Tralles, attained to considerable power, and
ruled a wild kingdom stretching from Cerasus to Colchis;
but she was also Antony's granddaughter.

From the Macedonian courts, (relative) freedom broadened
down to the Greek home; and those women who desired
emancipation—probably a minority—were able to obtain
it in considerable measure. Demetrius of Phalerum had
passed laws at Athens to keep woman in her place, but
they were repealed when he fell; and though magistrates
called *gynaeconomi*—supervisors of women—appear in some
cities, the only thing they are known to have supervised
was girls' education. Stoicism, which subsequently inspired the better definition of marriage in the Roman
jurists, also helped to raise women's status. Women could
now get all the education they wanted; many philosophers
numbered women among their hearers, like Epicurus' pupil
Leontion, who married his friend Metrodorus. Poetesses
began to appear again in the third century, and Aristodama
of Smyrna toured Greece with her brother as business
manager, giving recitals and receiving many honours; a
woman scholar, and at least one painter, are known. Some
writers obviously wrote for female readers. Women now
received citizenship and proxeny from other cities for the
same services as men; and the women magistrates of the
Roman period date back at any rate to the first century
B.C., when a woman, Phile, held the highest office at Priene
and built a new aqueduct and reservoir. The relations
between the sexes became less cramped and more natural.
Women ran chariots at the games, founded clubs, and took
part in club life, though naturally to a less extent than
men; there were clubs for women only at Athens and
Alexandria. A girl of good family, Hipparchia, a disciple

of the Cynic Crates, married him and enthusiastically
adopted the life 'according to nature' of a wandering
beggar proper to his philosophy; few have carried emancipation further. But most of these things clearly relate
only to a minority. Freedom was not automatic, but had
to be grasped; education for the mass was rudimentary,
and even in the first century there were women, rich enough
to own slaves, who could neither read nor write; Greece
suffered from the sexes being on different levels of culture.
And far beyond these things was that terrible evil in the
woman's life, that often she was not allowed to rear the
children she bore. To what extent she may have acquiesced
in this secular precaution against hunger it is useless to
speculate; she has left no record.

For no prosperity among the upper classes could alter
the fundamental fact of life in Greece: the country had
only a limited amount of arable land, and could not of
itself support one man beyond a fixed number, long since
reached. Imported food had to be paid for; and as there
was no mineral wealth except Laurium, now fast failing,
and as every city round the Mediterranean could do its
own sea-carriage, food could only be paid for by exporting
manufactures or by transit duties. Corinth grew wealthy
on its transit trade; but the primitive Greek system of
manufacture, though it might enrich a few individuals,
was of little account to states as a whole. Consequently
the whole of old Greece lived always under the shadow
of the fear of too many mouths to feed. In the late fourth
and early third centuries this was met by mercenary service
and emigration to Asia. Fourth century writers were still
concerned with overpopulation, and about 300 there was
still a considerable surplus; but, though the country
remained fully peopled, the surplus gradually vanished.
Polybius says that Greeks in the middle of the second century
were refusing to rear more than one, or at most two, children; and there is plenty of evidence to bear him out.

The prevalence of infanticide in Greece has been strenuously asserted from the literary texts, and as strenuously

denied ; but for the late third and the second centuries
the inscriptions are conclusive. The evidence, so far as
I have collected it, can only be summarised briefly here.
Of some thousand families from Greece who received
Milesian citizenship c. 228–200, details of 79, with their
children, remain ; these brought 118 sons and 28 daughters,
many being minors ; [1] no natural causes can account for
those proportions. Of these families, 32 had one child
and 31 two ; and they shew a certain striving after two
sons. The inscriptions at large bear this out. Two sons
are fairly common, with a sprinkling of three ; at Eretria,
third century, certainly one family in 12 had more than
one son, which is lower than the Miletus immigrants, but
agrees with the evidence from Delphi ; at Pharsalus possibly one in seven ; and one must allow for some sons
having emigrated. But more than one daughter was
practically never reared, bearing out Poseidippus' statement
that " even a rich man always exposes a daughter ". Of
600 families from Delphic inscriptions, second century, just
1 per cent. reared 2 daughters ; the Miletus evidence agrees,
and throughout the whole mass of inscriptions cases of
sisters can be numbered on one's fingers, with one strange
local exception : a second century list of women subscribers
from Paros perhaps shews 20 sisters (8 families) out of 62
names, but the islands were prosperous and untouched by
war, and in population questions must be classed with
Asia, not Greece. Some allowance must be made for loss
of fertility ; thus at Rhodes adoptions were so common
that we get (c. 100) seven adopted sons in a list of 40 magistrates, and on her deme Telos a case of three in four ;
people do not kill their own children to adopt others.
Telos too boasts a family of seven, the only known Hellenistic
family over five, except the eight children of Cleopatra
Thea by three marriages ; but the prevalence of artificial
restriction is shown by the revival of families of four and

[1] Compare with this 61 families collected by Jardé from the
fourth-century orators at Athens and showing 87 sons and 44
daughters ; the disproportion is growing.

five at Athens during her afterbloom of prosperity in the
late second century.

The general conclusion from *c.* 230 onwards seems certain :
the one child family was commonest, but there was a
certain desire for two sons (to allow for a death in war) ;
families of four or five were very rare ; more than one
daughter was very seldom reared ; and infanticide on a
considerable scale, particularly of girls, is not in doubt.
Now it takes an average of three children per fertile marriage
to keep a population stationary ; the home-born Greek
population *must* therefore have declined considerably by
100 B.C. Greece had overdone the precautions against her
secular fear ; yet, except among Jews, no voice was raised
against infanticide on moral grounds till under the Empire
the Stoics Musonius and Epictetus spoke their minds.
Philip V after Cynoscephalae, for military reasons, took
steps to check it in Macedonia and encourage large families,
and raised Macedonia's armed strength nearly 50 per cent.
in a generation ; and under the Antonines Thebes made
the practice illegal, perhaps the only people except the
Jews who ever did till Christianity intervened.

Certainly there was no actual depopulation in Greece
till the Roman civil wars. Single cities, of course, might
fail for many reasons ; Larisa under Philip V was half
depopulated by war and the exile of Aetolian partisans,
and Heraclea-Latmos and Thyrreion in Acarnania contracted their ring-walls ; but then Thyrrheion, a little city,
had been holding a ring-wall larger than the Theban. These
things mean nothing ; Aristotle quotes temporary cases of
the sort as common enough ; and in the third century
cities who wanted new citizens—Larisa, Dyme, Miletus
(to settle Myus)—had no difficulty in getting enough Greeks
from other places. But by 100 enfranchisement or in-
corporation of aliens must have been taking place on a
considerable scale in Greece, as it did in Asia (p. 125) ;
no other explanation of the facts seems possible, for the
decline of the true Greek population is certain. Evidence
is not easy to get, as aliens took Greek names ; but Italians

were now commonly accepted as ephebes, and if one foreign people were accepted, others were not excluded. It is notable that Pergamum in 133 and Ephesus *c.* 85 gave metic status to the slaves then liberated ; and Philip V's idea that the solution of the future might lie in enfranchising freedmen may be correct, for the Greek cities became full of freedmen. Certainly in the first century Greece contained a large alien population, enfranchised or not, and what was happening in Asia and Egypt was happening on a smaller scale in Greece ; the Orontes flowed into the Ilissus before it flowed into the Tiber, and Juvenal's esurient Greekling had often little that was Greek about him but his name and speech. This change in the nature of the population can be detected fairly early at Corinth, which in the third century could only muster one quarter the hoplite force of the fifth, though the city had grown ; at Delos from 166 onwards it is self-evident. The process can also be seen at work in the breaking down of class and race distinctions. By the first century, when a wealthy man gave a feast to his fellow-citizens, he often invited the metics, the freedmen, and even the slaves ; sacrifices were sometimes now offered for the health, not of the citizens, but of all the inhabitants of the city ; and clubs occur like that of Nicocles in Laconia, whose members were the men and women of his family, some city magistrates, many artisans both free and freedmen, and a slave-girl.

One form of slavery in Hellenism stood apart from others, the mines (p. 204) ; they were a hell on earth which neither Stoicism nor Delphi could touch, and kings and cities were equally guilty. But ordinary domestic slavery was often not unkindly ; the slave might be better born and educated than the master, and more than one philosopher who shook the world was, or had been, a slave. Athens, which tolerated the horrors of Laurium, had for long—another strange contradiction—strictly limited the punishments allowable in the case of other slaves, and the Public Health law of Pergamum followed her example.

Stoicism worked for a better treatment of slaves, and gradually changed the atmosphere; slaves were to be pitied rather than punished, and all through the third century manumission of slaves by will, especially in philosophic circles, became increasingly common. But the real innovation came about 200, when under the influence of Delphi, always ready during the Aetolian domination to champion the cause of humanity, it became possible for the slave to purchase his freedom through the machinery of a fictitious sale to some god; the movement was aided by the mundane consideration that cheap free labour was rendering industrial slavery unprofitable. Some slaves earned money at their craft, and manumission soon became very common,—at Larisa 36 slaves were freed in one year, at Halos, a small town, over 40 in two,—and freedmen came to constitute a definite class in the cities, differing slightly in status from metics. But even manumission had its shadow side. That the freed slave-woman often engaged to stay on with her mistress during the latter's life, to work off her purchase-money, was not unfair; but sometimes she was bound to provide and train a child for her mistress to take her place. She might perhaps secure a foundling, but her usual course was obvious, and the clause was a compulsion to immorality; even were she married, the necessity to give her child as a slave was a horrible thing.

Of the number of slaves in Greece, or their proportion to the free population, nothing is known; but in other respects the manumissions at Delphi and Naupactus have thrown some light on the slave population of Northern Greece. Among purchased slaves the proportions of men and women were equal; but among house-born, judging by those liberated, women so preponderated that seemingly the girl baby born of a slave-mother had a better chance of life than if her mother were free. Purchased slaves were far more numerous than house-born; the commonest nationalities were Greek, Thracian, and Syrian, though every people is represented, from the Bastarnae to Arabia.

The standard price of a slave was 3 to 4 minae for either sex ; but among purchased slaves some nationalities fetched more. Macedonia easily heads the list with an average of $5\frac{3}{4}$ minae for men and $5\frac{1}{4}$ for women, bearing out what Polybius says of the qualities of that great race. Among men, Thracians with $5\frac{2}{5}$ and Romans and Italians (some of Hannibal's prisoners) with $5\frac{1}{4}$ shew up well, but their women only fetched the standard price ; Galatian men with $4\frac{1}{2}$ also stand out, but among women the Greeks with $4\frac{2}{5}$ come next to the Macedonians. There is a curious difference in sex price as well as in sex proportions between house-born and purchased slaves ; among purchased, 96 men whose nationalities are known average $3\frac{1}{3}$ minae and 98 women just under 4, but among house-born, while 101 women average just over 4, 47 men average $5\frac{1}{3}$ ; taken as a whole, the house-born slave, trained from infancy, was the more valuable. The highest recorded price is 25 minae for a Phrygian woman ; the few high prices known generally resulted from some special skill.

The most urgent question in Greece was the corn supply. The price of imported wheat at Athens in Demosthenes' time had normally averaged 5 drachmae the *medimnos* (bushel). As Alexander's circulation of the Persian treasure drove down the value of the drachma, wheat naturally rose in price ; about 300, with the drachma (6 obols) worth 3 obols, wheat, neglecting the seasonal variation, must have averaged some 10 dr. the bushel ; it fell gradually as money rose, but was still $5\frac{1}{3}$ dr. about 200. There was plenty of wheat in the world (p. 204) ; export of corn was well organised by the Ptolemies, and Athens, Corinth, Delos, many islands, Ionia, and perhaps other cities, relied primarily on imported corn ; but usually a city depended on its own harvest, though it might sometimes have to supplement it. A failure of a city's crop meant, therefore, anything from short rations to famine ; local famines throughout the period are common, land communication being very bad. Normally some magistracy, the *agora-nomos* or *sitophylaces*, looked after the corn dealers and

saw that the city was fed at a reasonable price. But
when prices rose in a shortage this system regularly broke
down, unless the *agoranomos* bought corn himself or could
persuade some wealthy merchant to sell it under cost
price ; the great number of men who thus paid the difference
themselves furnishes a remarkable testimony to the sound
public spirit in the cities. But this was only a palliative ;
and in the great famine of 329–325, which extended to
all Greece and Epirus and was aggravated by the corner
in Egyptian wheat engineered by Cleomenes, Alexander's
governor in Egypt, the State at Athens stepped in, raised
a subscription, and appointed a commission, which bought
corn as best it could and retailed it at the normal price,
the people also being rationed ; bread tickets are not a
modern discovery. These special commissions, and the
'measuring out' of corn, became thenceforth a regular
system in shortages. But it was an imperfect system ;
subscription was voluntary, and might be inadequate ;
and the poor could not always pay for their ration.

It was perhaps Samos—alarmed by her series of famines
about 246, when the money raised was twice lost by the
merchants employed and the city was only saved by a
private citizen, Bulagoras—who took the final step and
formed a permanent corn-fund ; enough was raised somehow from the rich and invested for the yearly interest to
suffice to supply the city with corn. Samos' example was
largely followed ; a system of state supply obtained at
Priene and Magnesia, and permanent corn-funds are known
at Miletus, Teos, Demetrias, Delos, Aegina, and Thuria ;
possibly they became almost universal. Even under
rationing these funds meant that the rich (who provided
the original capital) were feeding the poor, as the rich at
Rhodes were voluntarily doing by their food liturgies,
under which each wealthy man looked after a certain
number of poor. But Samos and Thuria went beyond this ;
at Samos the corn was distributed free every year to all
citizens, at Thuria (*c.* 100) to the poor only, the rich apparently paying increased prices. As kings and wealthy

men often also gave a largesse in corn, and as at Arcesine and Minoa in the second century (and this was hardly unique) wealthy men also began to distribute free tickets of admission to the local festivals, we see that the demoralising *panem et circenses*, free food and free games, were merely copied by Rome from later Hellenism.

In an age full of contradictions, none is more startling than the contrast between the miserable state of wages (p. 103) and the amazing liberality of the wealthy.[1] They would not pay; but they would give. What they gave was, however, invariably given to the State, the citizens (or the inhabitants) treated as a whole. Many a city seemed able to call on some wealthy man to rescue it whenever it chose: to give, or lend without interest, large sums to meet some special expenditure; to go on embassies without pay and champion the city against kings or Roman tax-gatherers; to build the bridge, the gymnasium, the temple, if funds ran short; to endow a new festival or a new school, fill the burdensome liturgies, provide oil for the athletes, prizes for the school-boys, banquets for the citizens and their wives; finally to be honoured with a statue, for which he himself paid. Men like Protogenes at Olbia, Menas at Sestos, Moschion at Priene, almost seem to carry the city on their shoulders. This constant reliance on some rich man stepping into the breach seems to indicate that the cities were not on an economic basis; but few ages can have shewn more public spirit, even if sometimes it was perhaps the equivalent of purchasing a title. " He impaired his own livelihood for the public good " was Epidaurus' testimony to one Aristobulus, while Pergamum said of Diodorus " His care for the common weal prevented him taking thought for his own ". And such public spirit was not confined to the wealthy. Nothing leaves a more pleasing impression than the numerous decrees of thanks passed to physicians. The municipal doctors were not a wealthy class—the one salary known is £40 a year; but

[1] That is, wealthy on Greek standards. Wealth and luxury, in Greek history, are relative terms only.

often they forewent their salaries during epidemics, and nevertheless, like Damiades of Sparta, " made no difference between rich and poor, free and slaves ". When all the Coan doctors were down with an epidemic Xenotimus came voluntarily to the city's aid, and Apollonius of Miletus fought the plague in the islands without reward ; there was a high standard of devotion in the profession. Philosophers, too, frequently remitted the fees for their lectures to those unable to pay. There really seem to have been quite a number of people who thought other things more important than money.

Yet, amid all the philanthropic feeling and public spirit of the time, philanthropy in our sense—the organised aid of the poor by the rich—was almost unknown. For the poor, as such, no provision existed ; the idea of democracy and equality was so strong that anything done must be done for all alike ; there was nothing corresponding to our mass of privately organised charities and hospitals. When we have mentioned the food liturgies at Rhodes, Athens' dole to men crippled, Polybius' statement that Opheltas in Boeotia helped the poor from State funds, and Heracleides' that the prosperous people of Tanagra were good to their poor,—" it is easy ", he adds drily, " to be good when you have enough to eat ",—we have about exhausted the list, unless we include the cases where organised bodies like demesmen supported the daughter of a deceased member. Distributions of meat from the sacrifices, on which stress has been laid, cannot have been common, unless conceivably at Athens ; the priests generally kept their perquisites, for which after all they had often paid, and anyhow meat scarcely came within the purview of the poor at all. The Myconos catalogue of c. 200, supplementary to one lost, mentions one distribution in four months, a dinner to wives of citizens and women initiated only. A Coan list, covering a few days, twice mentions meat which went ' to the city ', but it does not follow it was distributed ; Paul seems clear that much normally found its way into the shops. It might have been expected that the Stoics

and Cynics, with their sense of human brotherhood, would
have taken up philanthropy; but neither did. To Stoics,
poverty, like slavery, affected only the body, and what
affected only the body was a matter of indifference; the
poorest slave could be a king in his own soul, so they
concentrated on the soul and let the body be,—the reason
why they never advocated abolition. The Cynics glorified
the poverty they themselves practised; if absence of
possessions did not actually constitute virtue, it was the
indispensable condition of acquiring virtue; apparently
they did not distinguish between the involuntary poverty
of the labourer and the voluntary renunciation of the
philosopher. The one expression of philanthropy in literature—Cercidas' poem (p. 226)—was apparently evoked by
Cleomenes' revolution.

The prosperity of the Hellenistic age has often been
alluded to in this chapter; the matter must now be looked
at more closely. Prior to Sulla, and with local fluctuations,
it was without question a prosperous time for the upper
classes: the enormous expansion of trade (Chap. VII)
tells its own story, as does the growth of clubs, of new
festivals (p. 97), of table luxury with its accompanying
literature, of luxury in women's dress, especially silk and
gold woven cloth (p. 206), of better-planned cities, improved private houses, and more elaborate furniture
(Chap. IX). A distinction must however be drawn between
Greece itself and Asia (with the islands). Not all of Greece
felt the rising tide; Corinth and Aetolia, Ambracia and
Pagasae grew richer, but Athens, as regards wealth, fell
back till the late second century revival, as did Sparta for
other reasons. Northern Greece was generally prosperous,
as is shewn by the number of slaves and the manner in
which cities hardly heard of before now come into prominence; and the state of things at Messene c. 100–91
has been rather a revelation,[1] for Messenia was an agricultural country, unimportant and out of the trade streams.

[1] A. Wilhelm in *Jahresheft d. oesterr. arch. Instituts* XVII, 1914,
pp. 1 *sqq.*, combined with Dittenberger *Syll.*³ 736.

The average fortune of Messenian citizens at the time, according to Professor Wilhelm's calculation, was about one-fifth of a talent, as against one-fourth at Athens in Demosthenes' time, and the 2 per cent. land-tax produced about 2·5 drachmae a head, as against 2·75 fr. in France in 1908, the purchasing power of the drachma being of course far greater than that of the franc ; the women often spent over 100 dr. on a dress, and affected the expensive transparent silks ; silver plate was common, and fines ran up to 2,000 dr. Another point, easy to follow, is the growth in the scale of penalties for breach of arbitration awards ; in the fifth century the highest known is 5 talents, but in the second we get 20 (Cyclades), 30 and 50 (Asia Minor), and 60 (Locris). As to individuals, the richest man in Demosthenes' Greece, the Athenian Diphilos, possessed 160 talents : the richest c. 200, Alexander the Isian in Aetolia, had 200. We are justified in saying that, while Greece did not grow in prosperity like Asia, it enjoyed a very tolerable measure of it down to Sulla.

For Asia and the islands the evidence, quite apart from the growth of the cities and the expansion of trade, is overwhelming. Athens had drawn 15 talents a year tribute from Byzantium and 1 to 2 talents apiece from her Carian cities ; c. 200 Byzantium paid 80 talents a year to the Gauls, and subsequently Rhodes drew 120 talents a year from her Carian possessions, chiefly Caunos and Stratonicea. The scale of girls' dowries at Myconos compared to those in fourth-century Athens, the size of the subscriptions raised at Cos c. 200, the scale of fines in Epicteta's club at Thera compared to Athenian practice, the new custom, orginating in the clubs of Cos and Thera, of honouring members with crowns of gold instead of leaves, all tell an unmistakable story. In Asia Minor, whatever happened politically, prosperity and wealth grew steadily down to 88, perhaps down to the Civil Wars. That king's ministers should make great fortunes was natural, but by the first century private citizens too were sometimes wealthy out of all proportion to anything known in Greece ; one

Hieron at Laodicea on the Lycus possessed over 2,000 talents, and at one time Pompey's friend Pythodorus of Tralles was worth over 4,000 talents, including his land. But the best evidence is the amount Rome found to plunder in Asia. In 63 the publican Falcidius, having bought the taxes of Tralles for 900,000 sesterces (say 39 talents), offered a bribe of 50 talents to get them for a second year at the same figure, *i.e.* he had made *at least* 100 talents in one year out of one second-class city,—and the whole Macedonian land-tax had only produced some 200 talents annually. This is more eloquent than the vast fortunes extracted from Asia by Pompey and Crassus. In 86 Mithridates took 2,000 talents from Chios ; in 70 the Senate demanded 4,000 talents from Crete. Cassius took 500 talents from Rhodes and 8,090 more from individual Rhodians. Sulla in 84 took 20,000 talents from the province of Asia, called 5 years' arrears of taxes ; Brutus took 16,000 as a year's tax ; and finally Antony took 200,000, called nine years' taxes in advance, a greater sum than the treasure amassed by the Persian kings over two centuries from half the continent. One need not elaborate the story ; the days when the Hellenistic world was called ' poverty stricken ' are, or should be, long past.

This wealth was reflected in people's amusements ; not merely the multiplication of games, but the increased cost of celebration, the performers being now professionals. A complete list of the new Hellenistic festivals would fill a page. Between Alexander's death and 189 a great number, with games and sacrifices, entailing corresponding expense, were founded by the cities everywhere, while five annual festivals, at Thespiae, Cos, Delphi, Magnesia, and Miletus, were turned into ' crowned ' games, great quadrennial celebrations. Beside these were the mass of festivals founded by various kings, hardly inferior in number ; the greatest of these was the Ptolemaieia at Alexandria, the only festival whose honours ranked equal to those of the Olympia, though several were reckoned equal to the Pythia. In the second century several cities founded

H

festivals called Romaia in honour of Rome—at least 13 are known, that at Delphi in 189 being the first; while as late as 100 the Boeotian Ptoia became quadrennial, and Tanagra founded her Serapieia. Then came Sulla; and there were no more foundations till Augustus' peace. Naturally the performers at these festivals, the Dionysiac artists, grew enormously in importance. Their oldest association, the Athenian, dates from soon after Alexander; its privileges were secured to it by the Amphictyons soon after 279. The Isthmian association, with its centre at Corinth and special relations with Thespiae, formed soon afterwards; by the second century it embraced the whole of old Greece except Athens, and had sections in many cities. The destruction of Corinth in 146 hit it hard; internal strife among the sections followed, some joined the Athenian association, and the Isthmian body never recovered. A third association early formed in Asia, with its centre at Teos; it subsequently amalgamated with the players of the Pergamene court theatre, the association of Dionysus Kathegemon, and the whole body became dependent on the Attalids. In their palmy days the Dionysiac artists were almost an independent state, sending and receiving ambassadors; on them were lavished honours, privileges, immunity, safe-conducts; they were subsidised by kings and cities, and the Athenian association had the right to wear the purple; it would seem that it was better to amuse people than to govern them.

The rate of interest is some guide to the capital wealth of a country; but in Greece it is not a certain guide, for there were few of the modern facilities for the circulation of capital. Private banks were normally small, and the chief sources of capital available for traders or farmers to borrow were either some endowment, the capital of which was lent out at interest to obtain an annual revenue for the object of the endowment, or temple funds; but the *liquid* funds of a temple were generally small, and the temple at Delos for centuries lent at 10 per cent. regardless of changes in the value of money. However, the interest

curve may be given so far as known. In Alexander's
reign the usual rate was 12 per cent., omitting the risky
maritime loans, which ran much higher. By about 300
the rate had fallen to 10 per cent., reflecting the fall in the
value of the drachma consequent upon the circulation of
the Persian treasure, and 10 per cent. remained usual
throughout the third century, though $8\frac{1}{6}$ and 6 (this last
apparently a political favour) also occur ; in the first half
of the second century we meet 7 and $6\frac{2}{3}$, both business
transactions. After the middle of the century the rate
rises again ; $8\frac{1}{3}$ occurs, and by Sulla's time it has got back
to the old 12 per cent. After Sulla, interest is an index
of nothing but Roman rapacity ; Lucullus stemmed the
rise in Asia for a time by fixing 12 per cent. as a maximum,
but in the Civil Wars extraordinary rates, up to 48 per
cent., were extorted by Romans. So far as it goes, interest
indicates continuous prosperity down to 146 anyhow, with
money (as the world went) plentiful and cheap. The
drachma had become stable again before 200, for the farm
tenants at Thespiae have the option then of renewing at
the same rent, while at Delos c. 300 they could only renew
at a rent 10 per cent. higher ; but whether it ever quite
got back to the value of Alexander's time—wheat at 5
drachmae—is uncertain ; there are indications that down
to c. 100 wheat remained at somewhat over 5 drachmae.

A certain development in banking took place, but too
much must not be made of Greek banking, which never
attained the importance of the Roman. Private banks,
beside money-changing, took money on deposit and made
loans, and possibly the cheque system was understood.
The so-called ' state ' banks in some Greek cities, where
not a mere monopoly of money-changing farmed out to
some individual, were really an adjunct of the Treasury ;
they received and paid out the revenue, kept the city
accounts, and might advance money for an unforeseen
disbursement, recouping themselves later ; they did thus
save the city the trouble of borrowing abroad, which otherwise it often had to do.

For most of the city borrowing met with was mere
machinery ; it had no more to do with poverty than
municipal borrowing to-day. The reason was simple. A
city had no budget ; [1] certain receipts were merely ear-
marked to certain expenses ; an unforeseen expense, however small, meant a new tax or a subscription, which took
time, and the city borrowed the amount for convenience
and repaid at leisure. There was sometimes deliberate
procrastination over repayment, but again this had nothing
to do with poverty. One instance may be given. About
220–200, says Polybius, there was plenty of money in
Boeotia ; but Heracleides says debts were almost irre-
coverable. Now during this period Orchomenus borrowed
twice ; over Nicareta's loan the city procrastinated to the
utmost, while Eubulus' was paid off before the appointed
day ; obviously the governing considerations were personal
or political, not economic. The city of Delos understood
systematic borrowing, and was regularly financed from the
temple funds, perpetually borrowing and repaying. Officially, of course, almost every city was poor, for the city
Treasury rarely had any reserves ; but that did not mean
that the citizens were poor,—Cambridge men are not
necessarily poor because the University is. It meant
however that one city could seldom lend to another ; but
its *citizens* could and did, by a subscription in the city's
name. The cities really lived from hand to mouth. For
this reason Ephesus once raised money to arm some friends
by selling a dozen citizenships as a favour ; Thasos *c.* 285
sold four or five at a great price, 2000 drachmae apiece ;
in the Social War Tritaea sold some to raise mercenaries ;
these things had no more to do with poverty than the sale
of memberships by the M.C.C. to build its present pavilion.
A particular city of course might lose credit ; Oropus
once had to entice lenders by the promise of civic honours.

---

[1] ' City accounts ' are referred to at Miletus and Halicarnassus,
but are hardly likely to be rudimentary budgets. Delos sometimes kept a fund, called ἀδιάτακτα, available for unforeseen
expenses.

And the wealthiest might be thrown out of gear by war ; thus in 201 the actions of Philip V in Caria prevented Miletus getting in her revenue, and she had to borrow from her citizens in order to carry on, repaying by means of life annuities. But cities thus damaged soon recovered, as simple economic forms do.

The worst trouble of this immature financial system was the difficulty of carrying out public works. Co-operative works—even decent roads—were almost impossible unless kings took the lead, as they did when the world co-operated to restore Thebes in 316 and Rhodes after the earthquake of 225 ; and even city works were difficult unless a city had some special resource. Eretria did get a marsh drained by giving the contractor substantial privileges ; but Delos paid for her new harbour from the new trade Rome presented to her, and Miletus' superb market-places, where not built for her by the Seleucids, must have been made possible by the fact that the city itself owned wool factories, like a king.

It was not that the cities did not tax themselves. Direct taxes were repugnant to Greeks ; the traditional 10 per cent. of the harvest was Asiatic. Still, necessity sometimes compelled them to overcome their repugnance : Athens had long had a tax, the *eisphora*, on the sum total of a man's property, and in the Hellenistic period this was adopted by some cities, notably Miletus. Others, as Crannon and Delos, did take 10 per cent. of the harvest, or, as Delos and Cos, 10 per cent. of house rents. But generally money was raised indirectly, and very many indirect taxes are known. A tax of 2 per cent. on all exports and imports, a pasture tax on the number of animals reared, harbour dues, and taxes on stalls in the market, were general ; Cyzicus taxed sales of slaves and horses ; Cos had a special export duty on its wine, and taxed bread, flour, vegetables, salt fish, and many other things ; Teos in the third century taxed ploughing oxen, timber mules, timber cutting, sheep and pigs, garments woven from Milesian wool (possibly the raw material also)

purple dyeing, gardens, and bees. In some cases such
taxation was perhaps partly due to the city having to raise
taxes (tribute) for some king ; the city did not get the
whole benefit. But, even if it did, there was, throughout
the whole vexatious system, no proper means of making
private wealth available to the state except where the
*eisphora* obtained, and even the *eisphora* was imperfect,
for men were taxed on a simple declaration of their property,
and often under-declared. Farming-out of taxes was known,
but was unimportant till the coming of the Roman tax-
farmer, the hated publican.

We have sketched the prosperity of the Greek world ;
we must now turn to the reverse side, the condition of
the small man and the working class. Apart from some
Asiatic cities like Miletus, industry in Greece had not kept
pace with trade ; and the little man who employed a dozen
hands could not compete with the great serf and slave
factories of Alexandria and Pergamum. As to farming,
it has been thought that the real fall in farm rents at Delos
after 250 means that agriculture was failing ; but it only
means that *on Delos* men found transit trade more lucrative, for the perpetual desire of men throughout the third
and second centuries for a division of land suggests that
farming was much as usual, though in several countries
—Laconia, Aetolia, Thessaly—land at different times
became overburdened with debt. The great cities naturally
tended to form a proletariat class, but of *consumers* ; the
free industries of Hellenism were small and scattered, and
there was no class-conscious proletariat of *producers*.
But evidence on the whole subject is lamentably defective,
except in one quarter : we do know the condition of the
working man on Delos *c.* 300–250, and where a particular
trade like cutting inscriptions can be traced later, conditions do not improve ; and as men came to Delos from
other islands, one must suppose the outlook in the other
islands, prosperous as they were, was worse.

The depreciation of money about 300 led to a corresponding rise in prices ; wheat about doubled, oil rose

3½ times, common wine 2½ times. The average rent of
a house at Delos, under 20 drachmae in the fourth century,
was 100 dr. by the second, though here local overcrowding
played a part ; but food prices everywhere had not got
back to the level of Demosthenes' time by 250, and possibly not by 200. Against this, wages at Delos had actually
fallen compared with Demosthenes' Athens, probably the
result of untempered competition. The line of bare sub-
sistence, the pauper and slave rate, with wheat at 5 drachmae, was 2 obols a day per year for one man and a drachma
(6 obols) for a family ; but at Delos a skilled artisan was
only making, *at best*, 4 obols a day per year, and the unskilled 2 obols, sometimes less, even while wheat might be
anything up to 10 dr. ; that is, unskilled free labour,
which could be replaced by slaves, could not rise above
the slave rate and occasionally fell below it. Consequently,
as compared with the fourth century, the gap between
rich and poor grew wider ; and that was the most unhealthy phenomenon in Hellenism. The bearing of this
on the population question is obvious ; for the poor, rearing
children was most difficult. That the year included many
non-working (festival) days is immaterial ; men must eat
on Sundays. These wages may explain why some cities
were driven to free corn, *i.e.* pauperisation.

Of course there was social unrest. There were no trade
organisations, and in a slave society strikes were almost
impossible. (The strikes in Egypt, p. 158, are not in
point.) The bakers at Paros once came out because their
wages were withheld—apparently no uncommon event ;
the *agoranomos* promptly intervened, saw that they were
paid, and got them back. No other strike is recorded till
those in Roman Asia in the second century A.D., when
trade guilds were beginning to form, while the first recorded strike for better conditions was not till the fifth
century A.D. If things became quite unbearable, the only
known resource was a rising or a revolution.

The fourth century was already obsessed by the fear
of social revolution,—one reason why the well-to-do turned

to Macedonia as champion of the existing order. In the treaties between Alexander and the cities of the League of Corinth it was provided that Macedonia and the League should repress, in any League city, any movement for abolition of debt, division of land, confiscation of personal property, or liberation of slaves to assist the revolution ; the constitution of Demetrius' revived League of 303 contained similar provisions. The revolution therefore had now a general programme under four heads. The poor desired the land, but with the small men of every type the driving force was debt ; simple communities may be patient of rude conditions of life, but they always hate the creditor. The temple accounts of Delos, which show many very small loans and many bad debts, throw some light on the debt question.

From quite another angle, philosophy made its contribution to the subject ; the Stoic insistence on equality and brotherhood sank into men's souls, and inspired visions of something better than the existing order. Some took refuge from civilisation in drawing fancy pictures of virtuous barbarians living according to Nature, prototypes of Tacitus' *Germania* ; and Utopias began to appear. Plato and Aristotle had indeed drawn Ideal States, but not states of much use to working men ; and the first Utopia, Zeno's (p. 69), was too splendid and too remote for human nature to grasp. But Euhemerus (*c.* 300) and Iambulus (third century) created true modern Utopias, located on islands in the Indian Ocean ; and in Iambulus' great Sun-state Stoic Communism appears full-grown. The people were equal in all respects, even in wisdom ; they lived in social bodies or ' systems ' in which all worked equally and equally shared the produce ; they escaped ' slavery to the means of production ' because the island fortunately bore crops, partly by itself, all the year round ; each in turn filled every duty from servant to governor, the governor of each system being the oldest member, who had to die at a certain age (a provision taken from a tradition at Ceos) ; there was thus no place for wealth, ambition, or learning, the foes of equality, or for class war, because there were no classes ; above all things the people prized Homonoia and were united in concord and love. What Iambulus and his fellows really aimed at was the abolition of that class war whose horrors many Greeks had seen ; and indeed, even while revolutionary philosophers and conservative governments were alike honouring Concord, some practical devotees of that goddess were always ready to massacre their fellows in her name.

Except possibly for a slave rising in Chios, the first outbreak recorded in the third century was a proletarian revolt at Cassandreia in 279, engineered by one Apollodorus, who made himself tyrant, tortured the wealthy, and gave part of their property to his followers ; he shewed that a mercenary force made this easy of accomplishment, and had a powerful career till Antigonus Gonatas suppressed him. Four disturbances in the islands followed, one certainly between rich and poor, which the kings got settled without open revolt. But the great revolutions of the third century were the two at Sparta, which was in an unhealthy state because a few had monopolised all the land. Agis IV (*acc.* 244) attempted to cancel debts and divide up the land by peaceful reform, and failed ; his stronger successor Cleomenes III, aided by the Stoic Sphaerus, Zeno's pupil, carried the reform through by force, abolished debts, and nationalised the land, which he divided into 4,000 lots for Spartiates and 15,000 for Perioeci, filling up the Spartiate body from Perioeci and metics. Neither king touched the Helot question, for both believed that, far from being revolutionaries, they were restoring the old Sparta of Lycurgus ; but Greece thought that Cleomenes was carrying out the programme of the revolution, and in his ensuing war with the Achaean League he had the poor in every city on his side ; at one city, Cynaetha, the revolution went through and the land was divided. Had he foregone his military ambitions, which aimed at the headship of the Peloponnese, he could have made his reform at Sparta a permanent success ; but the well-to-do rulers of the League in desperation called on Macedonia for help, and Antigonus Doson took Sparta (222) and restored the old state of things. Revolution broke out again at Sparta in 207 under the lead of Nabis (p. 20) ; he carried out all the four points of the revolutionary programme, freeing many Helots, though he too never dealt radically with the Helot question ; every Greek revolution, except perhaps the Pergamene, conveys a sense of unreality, as it never included slaves. Nabis plundered the wealthy, but—so he said—solely for the State ; perhaps the State now paid for the common meals (this, if many Helots were freed, would have been unavoidable), and there are indications that Nabis was not as cruel as his enemies have drawn him. Rome, having overthrown Macedonia, ultimately intervened in Macedonia's stead and clipped Nabis' wings ; and though she did not interfere with the revolution in Sparta itself, the wealthy in Greece were henceforth ready to welcome her as their champion.

About 200 there was trouble between debtors and creditors in the Aetolian League ; the successful general Scopas tried to cancel debts, failed before the opposition of the wealthy, and went into exile to Egypt, the trouble continuing for years. There was also chronic trouble in Thessaly ; and Eumenes II accused Perseus before the Senate of intending to use the Thessalian debtors to murder Rome's wealthy friends, a changed rôle indeed for a Macedonian king. But no great outbreak is known between 200 and 132, whether from lack of information or because prices had reached a better relation to wages. Certainly in 146, in the last struggle with Rome, the Achaean League decreed a moratorium and the freeing and arming of 12,000 slaves ; but this was hardly revolution, though the debtors' rising in Dyme after the Roman conquest, when the town archives were burnt, may have been. Mithridates however did attempt later to use social revolution as a weapon against Rome (p. 39), while Ephesus employed much the same weapon to counter him. The great slave rising in Sicily affected the Aegean ; the slaves rose on Delos

(130), but were suppressed; they rose in the mines of Macedonia; they rose at Laurium, captured Sunium, and for some time ravaged Attica; they apparently rose at Pergamum. Some have recently talked of a Red International *c.* 130-63, and of Sulla and Pompey delivering the world from Bolshevism; but Bolshevism is a very strict social-economic theory, and these slave-risings were a blind product of the misery of mass slavery in mines or royal factories or (in Italy) on the great estates. Slaves rose to get liberty, debtors to get property; as to Mithridates, he would have utilised anything that promised vengeance on Rome. There was only one movement, apart from those at Sparta, which was working on a theory or which can be called socialistic; and the Pergamene, if we had details, might be more interesting than the Spartan, since for the first time a new constructive idea emerged. When Aristonicus in 132 raised the banner of revolt against Rome (p. 37), he threw in his lot with the slave rising, and was joined by the Stoic Blossius of Cumae, the outspoken friend of Tiberius Gracchus, who played the part of Sphaerus at Sparta; and the two proposed to set up Iambulus' Sun-State upon earth. The effect on their mixed following—Asiatic mercenaries, city volunteers, Mysian highlanders, broken men and slaves—was such that they destroyed a Roman consul and a consular army, which even Macedonia had never done. It was indeed a great dream. But Rome finally conquered Aristonicus and shattered the hope of a Sun-State; and under Roman rule there was no further place for dreams.

# CHAPTER IV

## ASIA

The interest of Seleucid history lies in the attempt of the dynasty to Hellenise parts of Asia through Greek cities and settlements. The Seleucid realm itself fluctuated greatly. Seleucus, from 312 ruler of Babylon, conquered the east and lost India before 303, but gained Northern Syria and Mesopotamia in 301, Cilicia in 296, and all Asia Minor but the native kingdoms and certain cities in 281 ; his son and grandson ruled an empire stretching from the Aegean and the Mediterranean to Turkestan and Afghanistan. Between 250 and 227, with the gradual establishment of the Graeco-Bactrian and Parthian kingdoms, everything east of Media—Susiana—Persis—Carmania was lost ; but in 198 Antiochus III took the rest of Syria from Egypt. In 189, following his defeat by Rome, this king lost Asia Minor (except Eastern Cilicia) ; but the Seleucids still ruled a great empire, till the death of Antiochus Sidetes in 129 entailed the final loss of Babylonia and Judaea, and reduced them to a local dynasty in Northern Syria. Unfortunately we know all too little about Northern Syria, the real homeland of the dynasty ; much of our information has to be drawn from Asia Minor.

The Seleucid empire possessed three separate nerve-centres, Ionia, Northern Syria, and Babylonia ; all else was secondary, and if Antioch, the North Syrian capital, stood in the best position for reaching the other centres, Sardes and Seleuceia on the Tigris were also capitals little inferior in importance. Many waves of conquerors had passed over Western Asia, all leaving some deposit behind ;

beside the cultures of Babylon and Persia there stood races of primitive barbarism, while the coast was in the hands of the Greek cities of Asia Minor and the great mercantile towns of Phoenicia. Persia had imposed some semblance of unity on the country, outside the Greek cities, and in some respects the Seleucid administration was rooted in the Achaemenid, as that had perhaps been in the Assyrian ; there is a sort of historical continuity, though the rulers and the dominant culture might change. One feature of Seleucid rule was the resurrection of Babylonia, whose ancient culture was to the Seleucids what that of Egypt was to the Ptolemies. Cuneiform literature revived ; beside scientific astronomical work (Chap. IX) and business documents, chronicles of current events were written, and myths were versified ; one carries on Marduk's story from the end of the Creation Epic. Rituals, incantations, and omen literature, especially the latter, were frequently copied and studied, as were Sumerian hymns and their Babylonian translations ; many commentaries and syllabaries are known, with a new form of the latter, apparently for Greek use ; the last cuneiform document extant dates from 6 B.C. This activity points to a religious revival, which was fostered by the early kings ; Antiochus I carried to completion Alexander's project of restoring E-Sagila, Bel's temple at Babylon which Xerxes had destroyed, and re-founded Nebo's temple at Borsippa, while Bel's priest Berossus dedicated to him his work on Babylonian history ; and under Seleucus a priest of Uruk, possibly at his request, found at Susa and copied the old ritual of the gods of Uruk, whose worship was re-established. The priests of Uruk also collected a temple library. Mr. Sidney Smith has suggested to me that the Seleucids favoured Babylonian religion as a bulwark against Zoroastrianism, the creed of Persian nationalism ; and indeed the principal weakness which broke up the empire was its failure to secure the co-operation of the Iranian element, which Alexander had recognised as vital.

The Seleucids themselves, like the Achaemenids and

Alexander, regarded their empire as embracing the three categories of subject dynasts, peoples, and cities ; and a survey of that empire at its fullest extent, omitting the farther east, may be briefly given. The Seleucid satrapies in Asia Minor, which were governed by generals in the usual form, were Hellespontine Phrygia, Phrygia, Lydia, Caria, Cilicia, and southern Cappadocia (Cappadocia Seleucis) with Cataonia ; Lycia was Egyptian, and the coasts of southern Ionia, Caria, Pamphylia, and western Cilicia were taken by Egypt before 272 ; Egypt's hold fluctuated, but the Seleucids were never fully masters of the coastline till 197. From the Black Sea the empire was cut off entirely by three states : the native kingdoms of Pontus or Northern Cappadocia (including much of Paphlagonia) and Bithynia, and between them the powerful Greek city of Heraclea, whose territory included several other towns,—Tios, Cierus, Amastris. Bithynia and Pontus were penetrating northern Phrygia, and soon after 275 they settled their allies, the invading Gauls, in that country (Galatia) ; later in the century southern Cappadocia made itself a native kingdom under Ariarathes. From 262 the Pergamene dynasts began to carve out a little principality in Aeolis. Pisidia—the table-land of the Taurus—was unsubdued ; it was ruled by petty dynasts, but the semi-Greek city of Selge was strong enough to resist all attempts, Seleucid or other, on its independence. Later in the century dynasts are found established outside Pisidia, as Olympichus in Caria, the Macedonian house of Lysias about Philomelium in Phrygia, and (from 189) the native line of Moagetes at populous Cibyra. All that the Seleucids were ever sure of was Hellespontine Phrygia, Lydia, inner Caria, southern Phrygia, eastern Cilicia, and the great through route from Sardes to Antioch ; and after Seleucus' death they never pressed their power upon the smaller native dynasties, their aim, rather, being good relations secured by treaties and intermarriage. Beside the Gauls, their one consistent enemy was Pergamum.

In Syria they generally held the country north of the

Lebanon, with Damascus, and Aradus in Phoenicia, though the boundary between Seleucid and Egyptian Syria fluctuated; northward of Syria and Mesopotamia their only permanent province was probably Commagene, though rulers in Armenia were intermittently tributary. Outside Asia Minor they seemingly broke up some of the big satrapies, as had perhaps been Alexander's purpose; but their arrangements are difficult to determine. Mesopotamia probably became three satrapies,—Mesopotamia, Cyrrhestice, and Parapotamia along the Euphrates; the Gulf province, Chaldea, was separated from Babylonia, and after Babylonia was lost the then general of the Gulf province, Hyspasines, made it an independent state (Mesene) and refounded its capital Antioch (perhaps Mohammerah) as Charax, subsequently an important trade centre. The thickly-peopled Northern Syria became four satrapies, with four later for southern Syria, probably Damascus and the Lebanon with Phoenicia, Samaria and Galilee with the coast, Transjordania, and Idumaea, the arrangement perhaps fluctuating; Judaea was a tributary priest-state under Seleucid suzerainty. Some 25–28 satrapies can be made out, including the farther east; Appian's statement that there were 72 is a confusion with the hyparchies, for each satrapy was for administrative purposes divided into several districts under hyparchs, subordinate to the general, which possibly represented the Persian chiliarchies. The financial administration of each satrapy was under an *economus*, superior to the hyparchs but subordinate to the general; in each hyparchy the *economus* had a subordinate called ' over the revenues '. There was also an official called *dioecetes*, who on Egyptian analogy may have been the head of the whole financial administration, representing the post created by Alexander for Harpalus. Like Antigonus I, the Seleucids imitated, though sparingly, Alexander's plan of using Persians as provincial governors; and later, like Alexander, they revived the Persian office of vizier, now called minister for affairs. They maintained the Persian postal service.

There was a land registry in each hyparchy, which
gave the boundaries of villages and properties; from
these were compiled the register of the satrapy, which
was kept at the capital of the satrapy by a registrar in a
bureau called 'the royal records'; from the satrapal
registries were compiled the central register which the
king used. The central and satrapal registries did not
give the detailed boundaries, and the central register, in
view of the distances involved, was not always up to date.
It was the same system as the Egyptian, with the hyparchy
as the unit instead of the village; it seems obvious that,
considering the scale, the Seleucids, had they wished,
could never have drawn the taxation net so close as did
the Ptolemies. The administration introduced the Greek
system of leases and sometimes leased King's land; and
in some Seleucid cities, possibly in all, deeds of sale were
registered.

The relation of the Seleucid kings to the land, in Asia
Minor and Northern Syria, was rooted far back in history.
Possibly all or most of the land had originally been owned
by a number of priest-states, and prior to Alexander the
history of the country had consisted in a steady encroachment upon these states by the various conquerors, who
brought their own religions. Omitting independent hill-
folk, as the Pisidians, the land as Alexander found it fell
into three categories, King's land, Temple land, and city
land, the land of the established Greek cities; but the
Seleucids claimed the temple lands as over-lords, and in
the Seleucid period the real distinction was between King's
land and city land; the King's land must have included
the bulk of the country and certainly all mines and forests
not on city land. Of the King's land, part was in hand and
part had been granted out to large landowners, natives
and Persians. Some of these landed families might long
antedate Persian rule, just as some lasted into Roman
times; but the king was their feudal superior, and the
actual property in the land was in him. These landowners, like mediaeval barons, lived in castles on their

estates—fortified quadrangles built round a courtyard,—
kept a body of retainers, collected the taxes from their
land, and remitted them to the Treasury.

The actual inhabitants of the agricultural land everywhere were the native peasantry living in villages, a class
which rarely changes, whatever conquerors may come and
go.  Where the King's land was in hand, the peasantry,
the ' king's people ', cultivated it and paid their taxes
to the officials.  Where the land was in grant to a landowner, the peasants of the villages on the estate, though
they paid their taxes through him, were still officially the
king's people, not his.  The peasants were not quasi-serfs,
as in Egypt, but full serfs, bought and sold with the land ;
they could not leave their ' own place ' and they had no
village organisation ;   their taxes were paid individually
and not through their villages, but as between the king
and the landowner it was doubtless better for the peasant
when his taxes were collected by a responsible official.
But when a Greek city had acquired land and with it
peasantry, conditions had often been modified, whether
by deliberate freeing of serfs or by natural evolution is
uncertain ;   the peasants *might* sometimes still be serfs,
as in Alexander's time at Zelea, but generally they became
free hereditary ' settlers ' (*catoeci*), paying taxes to the
city, and their villages sometimes began to acquire a kind
of corporate life ;   they were in a different category from
the slave-cultivators in *e.g.* Laconia.  The Greek city then
was a boon to the Asiatic peasant and tended to raise his
status.

The Seleucids did not free the serfs ;   but they had
special judges for the king's peasants, thus wisely keeping
law and administration separate, and they initiated three
schemes which progressively diminished the area of serfdom and might in time have abolished it altogether.  First
came the Greek cities they founded, which turned King's
land into city land on a great scale.  Secondly, they were
ready, unlike the Ptolemies, to give or sell King's land
out and out, on condition that the grantee joined his land

I

to some city and made of it city-land; naturally the
cities were willing enough to increase their territories.
Thirdly, they set to work to abolish the feudal landowners,
which entailed the abolition of what had practically been
private ownership of serfs. Eumenes of Cardia and Antigonus I had begun to transfer feudal estates to Greeks
or Macedonians, and under the Seleucids, who were wholeheartedly on the side of the cities, feudal estates, transferred to new owners, also tended to become city-land;
it seems to have been mainly outside their sphere, in
Pisidia, Cappadocia, Pontus, that the great feudal estates
lasted into Roman times. Wherever land became city-
land, the peasant might, and doubtless generally did,
cease to be a serf. This must have also affected the peasants
on the remaining King's land, for under the earlier Roman
Empire these peasants were approximating to settlers
with corporate organisation; possibly for a time they were
even better off economically than those on city land. But
under the later Roman Empire they fell back, and by
Justinian's time even private ownership of serfs had again
appeared in Asia.

The ancient temple states, great and small, were extremely
numerous, and some still possessed a large amount of
land. They dated back to a pre-Aryan social system based
on matriarchy, utterly foreign to Greek or Persian ideas;
originally they probably all worshipped the great fertility
goddess of Asia and the companion god who was alike her
son and consort. Probably to this ancient religion belongs
the custom of the marriage of a full brother and sister
which has been traced in so many ruling families of western
Asia—the house of Maussollus in Caria is a well-known
instance,—and which even led to the Seleucid, and later
the Nabataean, queens being officially styled ' sister '
(p. 50); another trace of it, which lasted long, is that
in some Greek inscriptions from Phrygia the wife's name
precedes her husband's. Some of these sanctuaries had
been invaded by alien deities, who nevertheless succumbed
to the old organisation; and by Hellenistic times the

accumulated influence of Indo-European ideas—Phrygian, Persian, Greek—had sometimes raised the god to the first place at the expense of the goddess, and some names had been hellenised (p. 283). The ruler of the temple state, an hereditary high priest, had often learnt to trace his descent from some hero of the Greek mythological cycle. But the *system* had never changed ; the priest ruled the lands of the temple state and the peasantry on them, the ' god's peasants ', and to him they paid their taxes. The temple village itself contained a number of men devoted to the god, sometimes eunuchs ; but the feature that so struck Greeks was the crowd of female temple slaves, sacred prostitutes who ministered to the fertility worship of the goddess. They were usually the daughters of the god's peasants, who served awhile in the temple before becoming peasants' wives ; for land and people lived by the power of the goddess, and to give a daughter to assist to spread her influence was only an act of right feeling towards society ; women boasted their descent from a line of temple prostitutes. The temple often acted as the local bank, and its village was the scene of a great annual fair.

The best known temple states and their deities may be noticed. In Cappadocia, Ma of Comana (the ' place of hymns ') with 6,000 temple slaves, men and women ; Zeus of Venasa with 3,000 ; and Artemis Perasia of Castabala —Hieropolis, whose priestesses could walk barefoot over hot charcoal. In Pontus, Ma of Comana Pontica, with 6,000 temple slaves and a strict taboo on pigs and pigs' flesh ; Anaïtis of Zela ; and Mēn Pharnakou (with Selene) of Cabeira, by whom the Pontic kings officially swore. In Phrygia, Cybele-Agdistis and Attis at Pessinus, Leto and Lairbenos near Dionysopolis, Mēn Karou near Attoudda, the Dindymene Mother in Cyzicus' territory, and Zeus of Aizani. Also the two temples of Mēn Askænos (Mannes of Ouramna) and Selene near Pisidian Antioch ; the Zizimene Mother in Lycaonia ; Mēn Tiamou or Tyrannus and Mother Anaïtis in Lydia ; Zeus of Olba in Cilicia ;

and the various places called Hieropolis, ' city of the temple,' which if Greek influence was strong became Hierapolis ' sacred city '—a fundamental distinction. Artemis of Ephesus herself was only the fertility goddess whose old temple had been annexed to a Greek city ; for long that temple, with its high priest, the Megabyzus or King Bee, and its swarm of consecrated girls, who at Ephesus were virgins and were possibly known as ' bees ', remained a state within the state till Lysimachus gave the temple administration to a Greek board, and removed the bee from Ephesus' coinage. Similar priest-states existed in Northern Syria, as at Bambyce and Emesa, and extended into Albania and Iberia under the Caucasus, home of so many broken fragments of older races. (See further Chap. X.)

Though the earlier Seleucids were ready to respect the religious feelings of their subjects [1] and restored or enlarged the temples at Bambyce and Olba, they fought the temporal power of the priest-kings as they fought feudalism. Their policy aimed at leaving undisturbed to the temple state its priest, temple, and temple village, with enough land for the temple's service, and secularising the rest of the temple estate ; Antioch towards Pisidia, for example, was probably carved out of the once vast estate of Mēn Askænos. The priest-states however were able to prevent the policy being fully carried out, and in the days of their decline the Seleucids again enlarged the territories of some Syrian temples and gave them the right of asylum, a parallel to what happened in Egypt. In the troubled period before Augustus some of the hereditary priesthoods vanished, and a Pompey or an Anthony made priests at his pleasure ; at Olba Antony gave the priest-state to a woman ; Zela, Cabeira, and later Comana Pontica became Graeco-Roman cities, and the Roman Empire continued to cut down temple lands to the minimum necessary. But some of the great priestly families lasted into

[1] The first exception was Antiochus III, at Ecbatana and in Elymais.

Christian times, and gave distinguished bishops to the Church.

The treasure amassed by the Achaemenids shews that western Asia was already passing from economy in kind to a money basis, and the Seleucid cities must have quickened the process, though probably it proceeded more slowly than in Egypt, and in many rural districts economy in kind must have been the rule. An extant list of Seleucid taxes mentions harbour dues, import duties, taxes on markets, on sales, on some businesses, on cattle and gardens, with a poll tax on the King's peasants ; while mines and forests also provided revenue. There is of course a general likeness here to the Egyptian taxes (Chap. V), though it is not known how heavy the Seleucid taxes were, except that gardens (and therefore presumably vineyards) paid a tenth of the produce, much less than in Egypt ; but so far as our scanty knowledge goes, the difference from the Egyptian system was great. No royal monopolies are known except mines ; none of the perpetual discontent which characterised the Egyptian peasantry and workers is heard of ; and the all-important land-tax on the King's land was raised quite differently. The Seleucids continued the practice, immemorial in Asia and Egypt, of taking a tenth of the harvest ; they were thus partners with the peasantry, sharing losses in a bad year, a matter of which Antony boasted when he desired to extend the system to Greek cities. Possibly it was customary to claim also a second tenth for land lying fallow under the usual system of biennial rotation ; the question is obscure, but even so the peasant would keep four-fifths of his crop, a far higher share than in Egypt.[1] Possibly part of the land tax was paid in money, but enough was rendered in kind to make the king a great corn-merchant. How the corn was dealt with is unknown, except that the taxes of each satrapy flowed into its capital ; the money would be remitted to the central Treasury (*Basilikon*), but distance and trans-

[1] The unexplained figures in 1 Maccabees x. 29 conflict with all the other evidence and must be treated as untrustworthy.

port would prevent the corn being so treated ; there must have been several centres. The peasantry had to perform some forced labour.

All estimates of Seleucid revenue are conjectural. The value of the land tax varied with the price of corn, and there are no recorded corn-prices for the country districts and few for the coastal cities ; also corn was not necessarily the same price in Syria or Babylonia as in Miletus or Samos. Judging by what happened elsewhere, there must have been a great rise in price culminating about 300, followed by a long decline ; in the early second century the kings were straitened for money, and though this was partly due to the indemnity to Rome it shews there was little accumulated treasure. But later in the second century a fresh rise is probable, seeing that wheat in Egypt was 60 per cent. higher in the first century than in the third (though this was partly due to less energetic cultivation) ; conformably to this, the dynasty from and after Antiochus Epiphanes was apparently better off again (relatively), in spite of its great losses of territory, though trade partly accounted for this. But, generally speaking, the Seleucids never acquired anything approaching such wealth as the Ptolemies drew from Egypt ; they must for one thing have spent far more on the country in proportion to their income.

In considering the Seleucid foundations, clear ideas are needed of what founding a city meant. In Greek theory, a collection of houses was only a city (*polis*) if it possessed municipal self-government and certain organs of corporate life. The indispensable minimum was a division of the citizens into tribes, a Council chosen from those tribes, responsible magistrates elected or chosen by lot, and its own city-land, laws, and finances ; generally, though not necessarily, there was also a city-wall, a primary Assembly, and local subdivisions of the city territory (demes). A collection of houses without these marks was a village ; size had nothing to do with it, and to Greeks Babylon, Memphis, Jerusalem were, properly speaking, villages,

though they had made one exception among barbarians :
they recognised the highly-organised Phoenician towns as
cities, and Aristotle included among his Greek city-consti-
tutions that of Carthage. But after Alexander the old
antithesis ' either city or village ' no longer applied ; new
and intermediate forms grew up, and new terms are found,
such as *politeuma* [1] (corporation) and *catoecia* (settlement),
to describe communities with some quasi-autonomous
organisation falling short of that of the city, the members
of the latter organisation being *catoeci* (settlers) ; the
*politeuma*, like the city, had a religious centre, might
possess a council and magistrates, and supplied a means
of incorporating in the city a body of aliens without making
them citizens. Careful writers also, like Isidore and
Strabo, use ' village-city ' for a large native town with no
organisation a Greek could understand ; what a native
subject town was like before it became hellenised is usually
unknown. In fact, the village began to shade off into the
city by gradations, and one cannot always say if a particular place was a city or not, though the coinage sometimes helps. If one wants to understand the hellenisation
of Asia it is necessary to bear these dry distinctions in mind.

Alexander had envisaged the fusion of Europe and Asia,
and it is probable that the Alexandrias he founded, which
in any case were largely military settlements, were not
full Greek cities, but were a new type of town designed to
promote that fusion, composed of one or more quasi-
autonomous *politeumata* or corporations, the Greek being
the most important ; they were certainly subject to royal
governors, while the old Greek cities were not, and the
Greeks settled in them refused to regard his system as
Hellenic ' life and training '. If we may judge from Doura
(Salihîyeh) on the Euphrates, founded by Nicanor, general
of Antigonus I, at a time when Antigonus was imitating
Alexander, where the ruins reveal an early Hellenistic

---

[1] This *word*, in this sense, perhaps has occurred as yet only in
Egypt's sphere ; but the *thing* was common enough in Asia, though
possibly *κατοικία* was the word usually employed.

city, the land of these towns remained King's land, and
their citizens received lots of land, though at Doura the
lots formed part of larger divisions called *Hekades*, whose
meaning is unknown. Seleucus and his dynasty, on the
other hand, aimed at hellenising Asia ; the Graeco-Macedonian, with his superior civilisation, was to be the dominant race, and their empire was to rest on a vast network
of cities and settlements more or less Greek ; the Greek
city seemed to them to afford the only chance of erecting
a stable state amid the multitudes of Asiatics. Which
of their foundations were technically ' cities ' cannot always
be ascertained, but probably Macedonian or dynastic names
always signified full Greek organisation and city rights,
and possibly Alexander's foundations became full cities
also ; and doubtless when a native town acquired a dynastic
name it meant that it was ' refounded ' as a full Greek
city, entailing substantial re-modelling. The work of the
individual Seleucids cannot always be distinguished ; but,
roughly, the city organisation in Northern Syria and
Babylonia-Susiana was primarily due to Seleucus, in Iran
to Antiochus I, in Asia Minor to Antiochus I and Antiochus
II, with a noteworthy extension everywhere later due to
Antiochus Epiphanes. The vastness of the work the
Seleucids did in the time is one of the most amazing things
in history ; and a complete list of their cities and settlements, were one possible, would fill pages.

Northern Syria, already full of Antigonus' veterans,
became under Seleucus a second Macedonia ; here was a
new Pieria and Cyrrhestice, and across the Euphrates a
new Mygdonia ; and here were Seleucus' four great cities,
capitals of the four north Syrian satrapies. Antioch, the
capital of the empire, on the then navigable Orontes,
had ultimately four quarters, each with its own wall, within
the city wall ; Seleucus built the first quarter, Seleucus II
the third, Antiochus Epiphanes the last. Antioch was
never a centre of learning ; though a great trade emporium,
its repute was always that of a pleasure city, and its park,
Daphne, became notorious ; Poseidonius, himself a native

of the neighbouring Apamea, castigates the luxury of the
Syrian Greeks. Near the mouth of the Orontes was the
harbour city, the strong Seleuceia in Pieria, burial-place
of the dynasty, rising gloriously from the sea in terrace
after terrace up its great cliff, and worshipping a conical
stone come down from an older world. Farther south
lay Laodicea on the Sea (Latakiyeh), and on the middle
Orontes, in a steaming plain, Apamea, the Seleucid arsenal,
which replaced Antigonus' Pella ; here were the quarters
of the elephants, and great studs of horses. Beside these
four, the country became thick with settlement, down to
Laodicea of the Lebanon and Heliopolis (Baalbek), near
the Orontes' source ; thicker still were the cities to the
eastward, grouped about Beroea (Aleppo) on the Chalus,
on the road from Antioch to Hierapolis-Bambyce, and
about Chalcis further south ; northward, an Antioch in
Cyrrhestice. A long line of cities fringed the Euphrates ;
among them, Doura was refounded as Europus, Thapsacus
as Amphipolis ; further north an Apamea guarded the boat-
bridge at Zeugma, which superseded Thapsacus as the
usual crossing. In northern Mesopotamia, among others,
were two famous cities, Antioch-Nisibis in Mygdonia and
Antioch-Edessa in the Urfa valley. In the second century
Hamath became Epiphaneia, Berytus Laodicea, and an
Antioch appears on the sea of Galilee ; and for a moment
Jerusalem was named Antioch (p. 170).

In Babylonia and Susiana Seleucus was working on
Alexander's ideas with regard to the Persian Gulf, as
Lysimachus perhaps did for the Black Sea. The greatest
city here was Seleucus' first foundation, Seleuceia on the
Tigris, some distance below Baghdad ; Susa became
Seleuceia on the Eulaeus ; there was another Seleuceia
in the Susian plain and one on the Persian Gulf ; an
Apamea in Mesene ; above Baghdad an Apamea, an
Antioch, and another Doura ; toward the Susian hills the
important Artemita. Alexandria on the Persian Gulf, the
later Charax (p. 111), was refounded as an Antioch by
Epiphanes. Babyon itself was ruined by Antigonus I,

and in 275 Antiochus I moved the remaining civil population, leaving merely the temple ; Epiphanes probably
refounded it as a Greek city, to be ruined again by the
Parthians. Uruk (Warka) also became hellenised as
Orchoi.

In Iran, there was a large group of foundations in Media,
partly to bridle the hill tribes, among them Europus-
Rhagae near Teheran and Apamea at the Caspian Gates ;
in Parthia, Hecatompylos and four other towns ; in Persis,
an Antioch and a Laodicea, though the native feeling was
strong and the native priest-kings, ancestors of the Sas-
sanian dynasty, still ruled at Persepolis. The great massacre of Greeks in the revolt after Alexander's death must
have half ruined Alexander's eastern foundations ; Antiochus I refounded Heraclea in Khorasan as Achaiis, restored
Alexandria-Herat, refounded Alexandreschate-Chodjend on
the Jaxartes as an Antioch, and rebuilt Alexandria-Merv
as Antiochia Margiana. The refounding of Ecbatana as
Epiphaneia belongs to Epiphanes.

In Asia Minor the through route between Syria and
Ionia was well cared for. Where the roads from Melitene
through the Cappadocian Mazaka and from Tarsus through
Iconium joined rose Laodicea ' the Burnt ', so called from
the furnaces of the quicksilver mines at Zizima ; westward
stood the great Apamea-Celaenae, called ' the Ark ', a
name of unknown meaning which led it later to put Noah's
Ark on its coins ; further westward on the Lycus, where
the roads to Ephesus and Sardes diverged, another Laodicea.
These were the main knots of traffic. From Laodicea the
Burnt a road ran south which reached the sea at Seleuceia
(Selefkia) on the Calycadnus, and another north by Philomelium and Synnada to Nicea and Nicodemia in Bithynia.
From Apamea roads ran to Antioch, Apollonia, and Seleuceia ' the iron ', outpost cities toward independent Pisidia ;
from Laodicea on the Lycus a road went south through
native Cibyra to the Pamphylian coast. At this Laodicea
the main road branched : one road went to Sardes and
continued northward to Seleucid Thyateira, whence a

road ran to Pergamum and another north by Stratonicea
on the Caïcus to Cyzicus ; the other road went to Ephesus,
passing through Antioch on the Maeander, Antioch-Nysa,
and Antioch-Tralles, whence a branch ran south by Antioch-
Alabanda to Stratonicea in Caria. Under Epiphanes
many Cilician towns were remodelled, and 50 Greek cities
were known there later ; Mallos, Tarsus, Adana became
Antiochs and Mopsuestia Seleuceia, and Tarsus presently
became an important university town.

Beside cities, the Seleucids founded in Asia Minor a
number of military settlements, some fortified, which later
boasted their Macedonian origin ; many ultimately became
cities, as Nacrasa by 159. The settlers (cleruchs), mercenaries of many races, called themselves "the Macedonians of" so and so and presumably were organised
as a *politeuma* or *catoecia* ; they received lots of land,
normally larger if less fertile than the lots of the Egyptian
cleruchs (p. 150), and were probably utilised to bring
uncultivated land into cultivation, though this is only
mentioned under the Attalids. The general opinion is
that the lots of Seleucid cleruchs, unlike those in Egypt
and Pergamum, were not taxed, but the evidence is hardly
satisfactory. There must have been many similar settlements in Syria, and possibly Antigonus I had already made
such, *e.g.* Carrhae in Mesopotamia and Docimeum in
Phrygia. The lots remained King's land, but by the second
century they could be divided, sold, and even inherited
by a woman. These colonies were usually attached to
some village and bore native names, but they could be
attached to a city,—there was one at Magnesia under
Sipylos, partly within the wall ; possibly some of the new
cities comprised cleruch land. Their purpose was primarily
military, the cleruchs being liable to military service ;
and one chain which ran across Asia Minor from the Caïcus
to the Maeander—Nacrasa, Thyateira, Hyrcanis, Cadoi,
Blaundos, the Myso-Macedonians, Pelte—was clearly intended to protect Ionia against the Galatians. In Asia
Minor there were also many non-military settlements

(*catoeciai*) in villages, with similar corporate organisation ;
but whether some were Greek, corresponding to the evolution of ' private land ' in Egypt, or whether they only
represented the development of the native village, is unknown.

For the characteristic feature of the Seleucid period was
the steady upward growth of these various political forms,
a growth which proceeded without interruption far into
Roman times ;   the amorphous native village tended to
become an organised settlement, the settlement and the
native subject town tended to become hellenised cities ;
Isidore, who uses terms carefully, gives many ' cities ' in
inner Asia with native names, and some occur in Syria.
The organised villages ultimately grouped themselves,
probably with some imitation of Greek forms, into associations or Leagues, whose roots go back to Hellenistic
times ;   such associations were the Caystriani, Hyrgaleis,
Heptakometai, Pentedemitai, and very many others,
some of which ultimately coined, a right usually confined
to cities.   Of course the development of the village into
the hellenised city was not absolutely new, and the process
was at work in Greece also, *e.g.* in third century Aetolia ;
but an Aetolian village differed considerably from one of
Phrygian serfs, and what was unparalleled under the
Seleucids was the scale of operations.   Given time enough,
the ultimate result, in Asia Minor and Northern Syria,
would have been a kingdom composed entirely of cities
with contiguous territories and enjoying domestic autonomy, the whole under the suzerainty of a god-king who
managed the main lines of policy.   Whether the early
Seleucids actually envisaged this is unknown ;   but certainly
Rome did, and the way Rome at the start tried to rush
matters suggests that the idea was Hellenistic.   For when
Pompey, having struck down Mithridates, found himself
able to make what settlement he chose, he tried in some
places to carry through this idea by one stroke of the pen ;
thus he divided Pontus into eleven city districts, and of
the eleven cities only Sinope, Amisus, and Amaseia were

Greek, the rest being native towns or villages turned into Graeco-Roman cities, like Eupatoria-Magnopolis and Cabeira-Diospolis ; similarly he made twelve city districts of Bithynia. But the Roman Empire was content with a slower and more natural growth, which naturally was not uniform ; a city might decay and become a village again.

One instance may be given of the complexity which Hellenistic state-forms might assume in Asia. In Caria was an old religious League of native villages who worshipped Zeus Chrysaoreus. One village, Alabanda, was refounded as an Antioch, and, though a Greek city, remained a member of this Carian League. An important new city, Stratonicea, had some of these villages assigned to it as city land ; they became its demes, and through them it also became a member of the League. One of these demes, a community which itself worshipped Zeus Panamaros, became far enough advanced in organisation to pass decrees and confer its ' citizenship ', *i.e.* demesmanship, on strangers ; among others, it conferred ' citizenship ' on certain citizens of Stratonicea, the city of which, in Greek eyes, it formed part. No wonder Strabo abandoned the attempt to find a name in Greek phraseology for this old Carian League as he knew it, and took refuge in calling it a ' system '.

The part played by Asiatics in the new cities, as a prelude to their hellenisation, is obscure, and conditions must have varied. Some new cities *appear* to be purely Greek, as Antioch in Persis, or the city, conjectured to be the refounded Babylon, to which belong certain inscriptions from Babylonia shewing a gymnasium with Greek names of members ; but Greek names mean little, for Phoenicians were adopting such soon after 300, and many Asiatics must have done the same. Then some cities, old and new, admitted selected Asiatics to citizenship even in the third century (there were old precedents, for there was much Carian and Libyan blood in the citizen bodies of Miletus and Cyrene) ; thus Aspendus enrolled some mixed Asiatic mercenaries in her tribes, Smyrna enfranchised a body of

Persian troops, Stratonicea had Carian demes. Sardes, which in the third century had only its native organisation, was in the second a Greek city ; it seems inconceivable that it had not many Lydian citizens, just as Selge, which invented for itself a Greek foundation legend, certainly had many Pisidian, and the hellenised Lycian towns many Lycian ; Antioch-Tarsus too must have had many native citizens, while Pergamum in 133 enfranchised Asiatics wholesale (p. 136).

But where there was a great body of natives, other forms can also be detected. Seleuceia on the Tigris kept its Hellenic character to the end, but also drained Babylon's population ; it replaced Opis, a large native town, and it was in some way a double city, for on its coins two turreted city-goddesses take hands. Now its total population is given, ultimately, as 600,000, while the wall was only $4\frac{1}{8}$ miles round, less than Corinth (5 miles), Thebes ($5\frac{3}{8}$), or Megalopolis ($5\frac{3}{4}$) ; obviously therefore the wall circumscribed the Greek city only, and outside the wall was a great native population ; doubtless Opis became its ' village ', and the second city-goddess might be Opis as representing Seleuceia's Babylonian population.[1] The organisation of this population is unknown, though it cannot have been part of the Greek city ; but its presence would explain why Seleuceians are persistently called Babylonians. Similarly at Apollonia towards Pisidia the Thracian and Lycian towns remained distinct. Antioch again differed ; Seleucus' city was purely Greek, but in Antioch later there was a large Syrian element, and this must be the explanation of the mysterious second quarter, which had no royal founder (p. 120) : Syrians settled outside the wall, and were subsequently taken in and enclosed by the second wall ; possibly they formed a *politeuma* of their own, like the non-Greek *politeumata* at Alexandria (p. 147). Antioch-Edessa, called ' semi-barbarian ', may have been of this

[1] The two goddesses might *conceivably* represent the Semitic "double Fortune" (see Cumont, *Études Syriennes*, p. 263), but there are difficulties.

type. In fact, many cities may have solved the native question by means of *politeumata*, as they solved the Jewish (p. 175) ; Antioch towards Pisidia, a Greek city, required the foundation near it of a separate sanctuary of Mēn Askænos, which points to a large native quarter from the start. Lastly, there were native towns, like Sirynca in Hyrcania, where a few Greeks settled among the natives, probably for trading purposes, and no question of Greek political forms arose.

But though we know too little of the political forms under which Asia became partly hellenised, there were other forces at work beside the political. Greek law made its way, aided probably by the policy, perhaps originally Alexander's, which placed under Greek law foreign *politeumata* in the cities ; a Graeco-Syrian law developed of which Rome had to take account, and whose history in Asia has been traced for many centuries ; and Greek legal forms penetrated far. As the city-law of Alexandria, though Greek, is not apparently Greek of any one city, so the succession law recently recovered from Doura on the Euphrates is Athenian with other elements ; but most striking are the first century documents—Greek leases, written in Greek, made between men with Iranian names —found at Avroman, for these come, not from any city, but from a remote village in Persian Kurdistan. By A.D. Nabataean epitaphs were translating Greek forms. Greek speech too was used by very many Asiatics, as it was in native Cibyra, and not only in the cities ; there are many Greek loan-words in Syriac and Aramaic, and Greek expelled the native languages entirely from Lydia and western Phrygia. But powerful instrument as Greek was, its success had its limits ; eastern Phrygia, Lycia, Lycaonia, Syria retained their native languages in the country districts, as naturally did inner Asia ; even at Tyre Phoenician was still spoken at the Christian era. Mercenaries settled in Asia had from the start taken native wives ; certainly by the first century intermarriage and the mixture of peoples in daily life and trade was doing its work, and,

precisely as in Egypt at the time, the term ' Greek ' sometimes denoted culture, not blood ; the " Greek woman, a
Syrophoenician by race " of Mark vii, 26 was such a ' cul-
ture-Greek ', perhaps with Greek political rights in her
city. After the great European immigration in the third
century came to an end, first a balance was established,
and then the Greek began to lose ground, partly through
mixing his blood with Asiatic stocks. There were exceptions, cities which kept themselves predominantly Greek,
but what happened elsewhere is again illustrated by Doura,
(which was never in Rome's sphere).

The nomenclature there, in the early second century,
was Greek. But soon after A.D., though certain families
retained names entirely Greek, there was an extraordinary
mixture of forms, Babylonian, Persian, Syrian : men's
names like Samisilabos (Shamash is my father), Rhagea-
dados, Baphaladados and Zebidadados (compounds of
Adad), Rhageibelos (the repose of Bel), Daniel and Barna-
bas, and women's names formed from Asiatic deities, preferably from Nanaia, the Babylonian goddess of the city,
as Maththanath (gift of Anaïtis), Bathnanaia (daughter of
Nanaia), Mekatnanaia, Baribonnaia, Rhigoutai (the name
of Esther's Sabbath handmaid), and the goddess-name of
Flaubert's heroine Salammbo, who at last appears as a
woman, Salamboua, just as Greek inscriptions have now
revealed Shelley's Asia as a woman's name. Free admixture of blood had taken place, and the Greek used was becoming ungrammatical and losing its inflections ; one Greek
immigrant found it convenient to take an Asiatic name.
Families occur in which, while the brothers' names were
still Greek, the sisters' names were Asiatic ; that is, some
Greek settlers were marrying native wives, the sons, as
was customary, being named from the father's tongue, the
daughters from the mother's. In the same way Syrian
Greeks before 100 were marrying Syrian women—Taosa,
Ribu, Rumatha ; and some Syrian cities took Atargatis or
Astarte as city-goddess. But seemingly Doura did *not*
adopt the full brother-and-sister marriage of the country,

as was ultimately done by Greeks in Egypt; the two
sister-marriages noted occur in families with Greek names
and are with half-sisters on the father's side, which some
Greek laws permitted.

The general lines of the relations of the old Greek cities
to the kings have already been given (Chap. II). Probably
under Seleucus and Antiochus I they were subject allies,
paying taxes, though there is little information, for the
'Galatian' tax levied by Antiochus I to pay the tribute
to the Gauls was a special matter; but some cities, like
Erythrae, were seemingly tax-free. Certainly the early
Seleucids courted the cities, and were seemingly popular;
Antiochus II, a king whom inscriptions reveal in a favourable light, restored complete freedom to the Ionian cities,
an act to which they always looked back as to a charter.
When Antiochus III recovered the Asia Minor coast from
Egypt he put forward a new theory : all the cities were,
notionally, his subjects, and freedom was an act of grace
on his part. Some in fact again paid taxes, but after he
lost Asia Minor in 188 the position of the cities depended
on Rome and Pergamum. One native city, Aradus, received very exceptional privileges from Seleucus II, including the right to harbour political refugees.

The new Seleucid cities certainly paid taxes, for so much
King's land went to supply them with city land that the
Treasury could never have stood the drain of land tax
involved had it not received an equivalent; and many
were under city governors (*epistatai*), who are mentioned
in Nacrasa, some Syrian cities, Seleuceia on the Tigris, and
the city supposed to be Babylon. Obviously, wherever
there was a large native population, some authority beyond the city magistrates was desirable ; but at Antioch
in Persis, if there was an *epistates*, he did not control the
Assembly, and the city dated by some local priesthood and
not by the Seleucid era. But when the dynasty began to
decline, the Syrian cities gradually succeeded in securing
a large measure of independence. By 148/7 the four great
North Syrian cities had autonomy enough to form the

K

coinage alliance of the 'sister peoples'. In the civil wars of the dynasty, the Syrian cities figure as political factors, supporting this or that contestant; and, as the price of help, very many from 140 onwards secured from some king the title 'holy and inviolable' (p. 73), which meant immunity from attacks by him and the right to shelter offenders against him, and began to coin, often using eras from which they dated their freedom.

Probably the greatest Seleucid achievement, after their colonisation, was the introduction of a true calendar. It was not quite the first, for some Phoenician cities had already begun to use a fixed era; but it was the first comprehensive one, and marked a great advance on reckoning by eponymous magistrates or the years of a king's reign —a barbarism still employed in dating the Statutes of Great Britain. Dates were reckoned in plain figures from the Seleucid era, but unfortunately that era was not uniform; in Babylonia the year One began with 1 Nisan (March-April) 311, Seleucus' first New Year festival after he recovered Babylon, but in Syria with the beginning of the then current Macedonian year, 1 Dios (October) 312. There was thus some five months difference between the two eras. The Seleucid calendar was widely adopted in Asia, even by Jews, and lasted long; Doura dated by it even after A.D., and it still (it is said) survives among Syrian Christians.

\* \* \* \* \*

Poor as is our information regarding the Seleucids, it is perhaps poorer as regards the kingdom of Pergamum, which, starting from small beginnings, ruled Asia Minor within the Taurus from 228 to 223 and from 188 to 133; but indications point to a kingdom of the Ptolemaic pattern, an organised machine for the accumulation of wealth, which from the point of view of Hellenism stood on a lower level than the Seleucid. The political position made of the Attalids consistent enemies of the Seleucids and friends of Egypt; Egypt therefore they naturally imitated, but, as

they could not claim divinity as the basis of their rule
(p. 46) and were not national kings, they posed instead
as democratic rulers ; their palace was only a big house,
they never used the royal ' we ', and they sometimes called
themselves citizens of Pergamum.  Possibly their idea was
to be First Citizens, a sort of anticipation of Augustus.
But the fact that the Attalids made a businesslike and
competent affair of their dominion, and that Romans and
pro-Roman Greeks speak well of Rome's loyal supporters,
cannot conceal the real undercurrent of Greek feeling about
them ; to nationally-minded Greeks Eumenes II was Judas,
the arch-traitor to Hellenism, the man who instigated Rome
to break the Seleucid dynasty, which stood for Hellenistic
evolution.  The people of Antioch might laugh at their
Antiochus, and he might demean himself to play practical
jokes upon them ; but the grammarian Daphitas in bitter
earnest likened the upstart Attalids, lording it over Greek
cities in their purple, to the purple weals on the back of
a whipped slave, and was crucified accordingly.  No Greek
ever spoke thus of the Seleucids.

Where Pergamum ruled, the Seleucid policy of steadily
diminishing King's land and the area of serfdom was abolished ; the Attalids seemingly not only conserved their
King's land but extended it by appropriating the temple
estates and making the temples dependent on some city ;
they were aided in this by the fact that, while there were
many old temple states in Aeolis, none were really powerful.  Like the Ptolemies, they must have gifted the (re-
vocable) user of estates on King's land to officials, for
Attalus III found many such estates to confiscate, or rather
resume.  They made some foundations, however, of which
two were certainly full cities : Attaleia in Pamphylia, their
seaport toward Egypt, where the Laodicea-Cibyra road
reached the sea, and Philadelphia in the volcanic district
of Lydia, which became a considerable place later ; it was
called ' Little Athens ', and was built with a view to resist-
ing the earthquakes which often shook it.  They enlarged
Elaea as Pergamum's port, and built another harbour,

Hellenopólis, on the propontis. They founded some military colonies of the usual type, the first two being Philetaireia under Mount Ida and Attaleia on the Hermus ; several other names of Attalid foundations are known, but whether cities or military colonies cannot be said. The Attalids depended on a mercenary army, though they utilised the Mysian highlanders both for war and colonies. In their enlarged kingdom they governed the satrapies by generals in the usual form, and had a minister ' for affairs ' or vizier like the Seleucids.

Their relations to the Greek cities in their kingdom were clearly exposed at the peace conference after the defeat of Antiochus III, when Rome gave to Eumenes II Seleucid Asia Minor : while Rhodes pleaded for the freedom of the Greek cities, Eumenes asked for them as his subjects. Rome compromised and gave him as subjects all those that had been tributary to Attalus I or had aided Antiochus, and declared the rest free ; among those subject were Ephesus, Teos, and Tralles, while some of the cities which were declared free—Samos, Priene, Magnesia, Lampsacus are known—entered into ' friendship and alliance ' with Rome, which circumscribed their actions in another direction. But a considerable number of cities, including Miletus and Smyrna, were really free ; and Apollonia towards Pisidia dated an era from 189. Naturally there was discontent among the subject cities, and it is known how Eumenes dealt with one Greek city, probably the Seleucid Apollonia on the Rhyndacus in Hellespontine Phrygia : he abolished its autonomy, confiscated its temples, and placed it under the general of the satrapy. Later on he restored its domestic autonomy and temples, but the city remained tributary and subject to the general ; Teos was also tributary, and doubtless therefore, as later writers state, all the non-free Greek cities, for Teos had the advantage of being the headquarters in Asia of the Dionysiac artists, whom the Attalids favoured. Some cities—Ephesus and Amblada are named—were apparently taxed at a lump sum, assessed on a property valuation, which they raised

from their citizens as they chose. But at Apollonia the
citizens were taxed directly and not through the city ;
there seem to have been many taxes, and perhaps the long
list which Teos herself imposed on her citizens (p. 101)
was connected in some way with the Attalid taxation ;
but we cannot obtain a clear idea of the system. Against
this, however, the kings gave from the Treasury subven-
tions to some cities, as Teos and Apollonia, which were
paid annually to the city stewards and could be used both
for the civil and religious expenses of the city.

The non-free Greek cities, then, under the Attalids had
little of autonomy but the form, and even that was pre-
carious and could be withdrawn at the king's pleasure ;
the city was subject in some way to the provincial
general, and was taxed, while its acceptance of royal sub-
sidies gave the king the right to interfere in its internal
financial administration. There were other arbitrary inter-
ferences. Some Attalid confiscated the revenues produced
by the fisheries in the sacred lakes of Artemis at Ephesus,
a thing Ephesus never forgave ; and the kings claimed the
right, as Antigonus I at the end and Lysimachus had done,
to shift populations about as seemed to them expedient ;
part of Priapus' territory was given to Parium, Dardanus
was joined to Abydus, Gargara was half-swamped by a
sudden influx of Asiatics, the village of Gergitha was moved
from the Troad to the Caïcus. At Nacrasa and Aegina,
and doubtless elsewhere, there was an *epistates* (city governor), at Pergamum an inspector of the temple revenues.
Pergamum itself, though it had the forms of a Greek city,
was controlled by the king through his appointment of
the principal magistrates, the five city generals, who were
nominated by and took orders from him ; probably they
alone could bring matters before the Assembly and Council.
This enabled the Attalids to control the city's finances, as
the Ptolemies did with their cities in Asia Minor, though
on different lines.

Pergamene finance flourished and enabled the kings to
employ large armies, but little is known of how they

obtained the money. Their King's land, other than that in gift to officials or used for military settlements (cleruch land), they managed themselves, as was usual, but probably they employed the Egyptian system of taking a calculated amount from the peasants and not, as did the Seleucids, a proportion of the harvest ; for the general of Hellespontine Phrygia is found assuming that, if seed corn be needed, application must be made to the king, who therefore controlled all surplus wheat outside the cities. The favoured cleruchs in the military colonies, however, paid a tenth of the produce as taxes.    Aeolis and the Troad were good agricultural and cattle-raising districts ; the royal studs of horses were probably kept near Mount Ida, and Ida itself supplied timber and pitch. It was partly the need of Idaean pitch which held Egypt to the Attalids, while their cattle supplied the world with parchment. Their economic system is unknown, but doubtless it was highly developed, especially as regards natural products ; the kings were as interested in scientific agriculture as the early Ptolemies, and Attalus I wrote on Mount Ida and Attalus III on gardens.    It is noteworthy that, to describe the king's treasure, the Ptolemaic term *rhiscus* was used and not *gaza*, which was used by the Macedonian kings in Asia—Antigonus I, Lysimachus, and the Seleucids ; and presumably parchment and pitch, at any rate, must have been royal monopolies.    One feature of their system, however, differed from that of any other kingdom : their extended use of slave labour.    All, kings and cities alike, used slave labour in mines.    But whereas in Egypt the monopoly manufactures were carried on by quasi-serfs, the royal factories in Pergamum, which turned out parchment, textiles, and the famous ' Attalid cloth ' interwoven with gold thread, employed masses of slaves, largely women, under a ' superintendent of the royal factories ' ; and the Attalid state must really have been based, not on cities and settlements like the Seleucid, but on wealth produced by serf and slave labour.    But it did render two services to the world ; it shielded a large number of cities from

the Galatians, and it assembled at Pergamum a library
second only to the Alexandrian.

The Attalid kings gradually transformed the old hill-
fortress of Pergamum on its crescent ridge into a magnificent capital, not laid out on the usual rectangular plan,
but picturesque in a way that perhaps Seleuceia in Pieria
alone could approach. At its foot the houses of the common people were crowded together ; the Greek city climbed
the flanks of the hill, and along the summit towered the
splendid buildings of the kings. The main approach road
led to the propylaea which formed the entrance to the
three gymnasia, rising one above the other in terraces but-
tressed by great retaining walls ; the theatre opened on
the upper terrace, and above it the citadel wall enclosed
part of the ridge. Within this wall along the ridge from
north to south stood the palace, the library, and Athena's
temple ; next to this, but outside the wall, rose the huge
altar of Zeus Soter (p. 262), surrounded by a tiled court
which served as a market-place ; beyond this were Dionysus' temple and the lower market-place, where stood a
clock, Hermes with a cornucopia from which water flowed
at intervals. The Public Health law of the city, given by
some Attalid, is partially known. It provided for house-
owners scavenging the streets and repairing houses ruinous
or likely to become so ; if the owner did not do his duty,
the *astynomi* could fine him and do the work at his expense, and if they neglected to do so the city generals
could do it ; as the generals took orders from the king,
the king was the ultimate health authority. There was
provision for keeping the roads in good order ; all cisterns
were registered, and the penalties for fouling the town
water supply by washing clothes or watering animals were
severe. But for all its grandeur and its Greek city forms,
Pergamum was a semi-Asiatic town ; in Athena's temple
there was worshipped beside her Zeus Sabazios, a form of
the universal deity of Asia Minor whom Stratonice, the
wife of Eumenes II, had brought with her from her Cappadocian home ; and the lower city was crowded with

foreign traders, corporations of mercenaries, freedmen, and
the great mass of slave workers in the Crown factories.
Attalus III, by the will which bequeathed his kingdom to
Rome, also made Pergamum a free city ; and the citizens,
to forestall a slave revolt in imitation of the Sicilian, enfranchised all metics and mercenaries, including the Mysians
and Paphlagonians settled in the city's territory, and raised
freedmen and slaves, except some of the women, to the
status of metics,—a revolution in itself, and the most
wholesale enfranchisement of Asiatics actually recorded.

\*       \*       \*       \*       \*

The native kingdoms of Asia Minor were only super-
ficially hellenised.  Cappadocia, Pontus, Armenia retained
their old feudal systems ; and though Cappadocia, in imitation of the Seleucids, was divided into ten satrapies or
generalships, she dated by a Persian calendar.  These
Asiatic kings took Greek cult-names, used Greek speech
and titles at their courts and cultivated the Dionysiac
artists ; they employed Greek experts of every kind where
they could, and built towns with their own names—Ariar-
athea in Cappadocia, Eupatoria in Pontus, Arsamosata and
later Tigranocerta in Armenia ; but these were only king's
towns, and the kingdoms remained essentially Asiatic ;
Mithridates Eupator himself was only a barbarian varnished.  The Greek inscription on the tomb on Nimrud-dagh
of Pompey's friend Antiochus I of Commagene illustrates
this mixed Hellenism.  It is written in very florid Greek,
like Babu English, by one who did not understand the use
of the Greek article.  The king, who was really half a
Seleucid, traces his descent from Darius I and Alexander,
and treats Persia and Macedonia as the two ' roots ' of his
kingship ; he uses the Macedonian calendar, but attributes
his successes to piety and holiness, and the gods he worships are the Persian Ahura-mazda and Mithras with Greek
names attached.  He makes a foundation to secure for
ever their worship at his tomb, with worship of himself
as a hero—a Greek form—but the foundation resembles
nothing Greek : a number of villages were consecrated to

the service and also a body of hierodules (temple slaves) whose descendants should minister to the cult for ever,— the old Asiatic forms of the priest-state revived.

In Bithynia alone Hellenism went deeper; the native dynasty regarded itself as a rival and counterpoise to the Attalids, and founded many towns. Nicomedia ' the beautiful ' replaced the Greek Astacus, destroyed by Lysimachus, and became an important city in Roman times; Prusias I built Prusias on the Sea, which had the right of coining, to replace Cius, a Greek city destroyed by Philip V, and refounded Cierus as Prusias on the Hypius; he also on Hannibal's advice founded Prusa (Broussa),—possibly to replace another lost Greek city, Atussa,—whose port Myrleia later became hellenised as Apamea; the kingdom also included Lysimachus' Nicea. Nicea and Prusias must have had some autonomy, and the other towns may have possessed at least Greek city-forms, for it is noteworthy that all replaced older Greek cities.

One people in Asia Minor remained practically untouched by Hellenism till the Roman period, the Galatians. They were a foreign body camped in a strange land, living in strongholds whence they raided and plundered, and ruling over the native peasantry who cultivated their fields; they perhaps received accessions from Europe, and kept their language, tribal organisation, customs, and virtues—the bravery of the men, the fierce chastity of the women. As finally constituted, their three tribes fell each into four divisions or tetrarchies, each division governed by a tetrarch with a judge under him; the judges tried civil cases, but criminal jurisdiction, and perhaps policy, was in the hands of a council of 300 elders, who met at their holy place Drynemetos, perhaps a circular moot in a grove; from the tetrarchs were chosen those war-leaders who appear in Greek and Roman literature as ' kings '. With the temple-state of Pessinus, which lay within their territory, they did not interfere till after 166, when they occupied Pessinus and their religion gradually became Phrygianised. The correspondence of Eumenes II, when suzerain of Galatia

(183–166), with the priest-king of Pessinus, Attis, is illu-
minating ; Eumenes wrote to him as one king to another,
and Attis' friendship supported his influence in Galatia,
while Attis' brother had gone over to the Gauls, taken a
Galatian name, and was striving to win the priesthood for
himself, doubtless in Galatian interest and with Galatian
support. Eumenes II built a temple and porticoes at
Pessinus and finally broke what remained of Galatian
power, and after the massacre of their aristocracy by
Mithridates the Gauls began to adopt the general civilisation of the country ; but even in the third century A.D.
their language was not yet extinct and they still worshipped a Celtic god as Zeus Boussourigios.

\*       \*       \*       \*       \*

This chapter may properly conclude with some indication of the importance of the old Greek cities of Asia,
cities which with their ancient traditions, large populations,
compact and busy life, growing wealth, magnificent public
buildings, and vast walls, scarcely felt themselves inferior
to a kingdom. Though none of these cities ever rivalled
fourth-century Athens in size, much less Syracuse, Miletus
in the second century, with her territory, perhaps had a
population of nearly 100,000, including slaves, while Ephesus
was larger and Rhodes cannot have been much smaller.
About 300 Miletus was still the greatest of the Ionian cities,
firmly based on her wool trade and building the largest
Greek temple in Asia ; but subsequently Ephesus and
Smyrna passed her. After 250 Smyrna was in the ascend-
ant ; her independence was complete, and a striking
account remains of her relations with and hearty support
of Seleucus II ; when in 244 he crossed the Taurus Smyrna
almost acted as his viceroy, for in his name she confirmed
grants of land made by his father, engaged him to make
new grants, and engaged his Treasury to make payments
to mercenaries. At Ephesus the concentration of the
eastern trade along the Apamea-Ephesus route, conjoined
with Lysimachus' removal of the city to the sea after the
old harbour silted up, brought about a great development ;

possibly Ephesus originated the cistophori which became
the typical coinage of the Pergamene kingdom, and spread
throughout Asia Minor.  In the second century the Attalids began to make her the port of their kingdom, but she
never forgave their confiscations, and in 132 she seized her
chance of revenge ;  her fleet defeated Aristonicus at sea,
and cleared Rome's way into Asia.  Thereon, though Pergamum was the formal capital of the Roman province of
Asia, Ephesus became in fact the chief city, with the
governor's seat and the provincial treasury.  She was the
natural gateway of the land, for she was more than a
Greek city ;  her far-famed temple of the Asiatic fertility
goddess, with its eunuchs and its consecrated girls, its pre-
historic asylum and its sacred fish, belonged to an older
world.

Passing northward, Magnesia on the Maeander could
stretch her arms from Ithaca to the Oxus ;  she helped to
defend Delphi against the Gauls, she gave to Bactrian
Hellenism its most powerful dynasty and thereby invaded
India, and she helped the Seleucid to create Antioch towards
Pisidia, Antioch in Persis, and doubtless, if we knew, other
cities ;  there was not much infanticide in third-century
Magnesia.  Her great temple of Artemis Leukophryene,
successor of the Dindymene Mother, was inferior in size
only to those at Ephesus and Didyma (p. 257), and was
said to be more beautiful than either.  In actual strength,
Heraclea Pontica about 280 probably surpassed any mainland city ;  she ruled a great territory, including other
cities, and once boasted herself stronger than Seleucus ;
but she could not hold her position in the later period.
This applies also to Sinope ;  it had looked for a moment
as if Lysimachus would make the Black Sea his lake and
Sinope would queen it over a vast new trade ;  but Lysimachus left no successor, and Sinope fell back to become
the capital of the Pontic kings.  But independent Cyzicus,
with her wonderful double harbour and competent fleet,
more than held her place, for through her the manufactures of Asia Minor passed to the Euxine.  Her policy

was consistent friendship, possibly alliance, with Pergamum, for she had a good road up the Macestus valley to Sardes, and was the northern outlet for Pergamene trade ; her relations with Pergamum resembled those of Rhodes with Egypt, and she gave to the dynasty its best queen, Apollonis (p. 85), whom she subsequently deified. Princes of many lines were sent to Cyzicus for their education. In 278 she was already strong enough to fight the Galatian Trocmi single-handed ; but two centuries later she could face and almost capture Mithridates at the height of his power. Under Augustus she ruled an extensive territory, including old cities like Zelea, and performed a more dangerous feat than fighting Mithridates : she flogged two Romans. She had good reason ; but she was lucky to escape with nothing worse than five years of taxation.

But no other city—so Strabo says—was the equal of Rhodes. In the historic siege of 304 she had successfully resisted the full power of Demetrius, and down to 166 she grew steadily in strength and resources ; her merchants and bankers desired peace, but she stood for two things, a balance of power and a free sea, and for these she would always fight the aggressor ; she helped Macedonia to pull down the overwhelming sea-power of Ptolemy II, Pergamum to check Philip V, Rome to defeat Antiochus III. Her government was a limited democracy, or perhaps rather an aristocracy, under which, as in eighteenth-century England, power rested with the leading families ; but they did their duty by the poor, and in spite of her cosmopolitan harbour population Rhodes never had internal troubles, and could in an emergency arm her slaves. The surrounding islands were her demes, and she claimed the strange power of vetoing honours they might grant. Magnificently situated, the trade between Egypt and the north, between Syria and the west, passed through her port ; in 170 her 2 per cent. import and export duty produced a million drachmae, and the mass of Rhodian amphorae handles found all over the world attest her trade. She was the centre of international banking and exchange, the

key city of Hellenistic commerce ; when in 225 she was
shattered by an earthquake and a commercial crisis threatened, the Hellenistic world demonstrated its commercial
solidarity by the lavish help in money and kind sent to
her by every Greek-speaking king and many cities.

By 200, when the Macedonian fleet had decayed, Rhodes
ruled the Aegean, re-formed the Island League under her
presidency like a king, and kept piracy under ; after 188
she ruled most of Caria and Lycia. When in 220 Byzantium put a toll on shipping passing the Bosphorus, Rhodes
at once took measures to free the Straits. Her fleet probably never exceeded some fifty ships at sea at once, but
its quality was the best in the world ; she had defeated
Egyptian and Syrian fleets single-handed, and her boast
ran that every Rhodian was worth a warship. At Myonnesus, where the Roman fleet encountered that of Antiochus III, it was the Rhodian squadron which pulled Rome
through ; had the day gone otherwise it was still Rhodes'
victory, for a Rhodian exile commanded for Antiochus.
Entry to some of her arsenals (so also at Cyzicus) was forbidden to the public under pain of death. The city was
adorned with works of art, including many paintings by
Protogenes and Parrhasius, the well-known Colossus (p.
261), and many other colossal statues, and in the second
century was a centre of Greek learning, a home of philosophy and rhetoric, rendered illustrious by the names of
Panaetius and Poseidonius ; she long remained a considerable University. Her code of maritime law was famous,
and was adopted by the Antonines ; possibly fragments of
it are imbedded in the Byzantine compilation called the
*Rhodian Sea Law*, and thence passed to Venice, the only
Greek law which may thus have reached the modern world.

# CHAPTER V

## EGYPT

The papyri which, during the last generation, have been recovered from Egypt give a picture of that country under the Ptolemies far more detailed in some respects than anything else in Greek antiquity and almost comparable to modern history. But it is a world in itself, whose interest lies primarily in the economic system of the Ptolemies, the most thorough-going system of State nationalisation known, unless conceivably the Peruvian ; on Hellenism in general Egypt throws comparatively little light, and but for the Museum and Library at Alexandria would hardly have affected the development of Greek civilisation. For the Greek in Egypt remained a stranger amid the dense mass of natives, who would ultimately have absorbed him but for Rome's intervention. The country was not indeed peopled up to the limit under Ptolemy I, as there was still uncultivated land ; but in the first century the population may have been some 9 millions, 10 millions being about the limit the country could support. Some Macedonians came with Ptolemy I and always held a privileged position, but were too few to matter ; and the rule of the early Ptolemies reposed on Greeks, who flooded into the country down to the middle of the third century, whether as mercenaries or settlers. With them came Thracians and western Asiatics, most of whom, except the Jews, soon became hellenised ; in 252 there was a Roman in Ptolemy's army.

For a time the Greeks ruled Egypt like a conquered country. This was not what Alexander had meant ; in his system, while Europeans managed finance and the army

142

of occupation, the civil government (under himself) was
entrusted to Egyptians ; the nomes (divisions of the
country) remained under native nomarchs, and he appointed
native governors instead of a Macedonian satrap. Even
Ptolemy I, while satrap, did not entirely discard Alexander's
idea, and gave more place to natives than they subsequently
possessed ; the change came when he initiated a policy of
over-sea conquest. His immediate successors aimed at the
empire of the Aegean and its coasts, and treated Egypt as
a money-making machine ; and under the first three
Ptolemies no native, after 312, ever bore arms. But by
the end of the third century the position had altered. In
217 the newly enrolled native troops won the battle of
Raphia for Ptolemy IV, and learnt their importance ; and,
Greek immigration having ceased, the Greek element
thenceforth lost ground to the Egyptian. It will be best
to give a sketch of Ptolemaic Egypt and its system as it
existed in the third century, and then notice the later
changes, particularly as revealed by the great series of
ordinances of Ptolemy Euergetes II.

The two main differences between the empires of the
Ptolemies and of the Seleucids [1] lay in their economic
systems and their attitude toward Greek city-life. The
Ptolemies were certain from the first that they could not
found a strong state in Egypt, as the Seleucids were doing
in Asia, on the basis of the Greek city ; and though Ptolemy
I would have been no Successor of Alexander's had he not
founded some city, in Egypt he only founded one, Ptolemais
in Upper Egypt, doubtless to counterbalance the centre of
priestly influence at Thebes. Ptolemais was in form an
autonomous Greek city, but its autonomy was presently
limited by the general of the Thebaid becoming its chief
magistrate, a measure which recalls the limited autonomy
of Pergamum or Thessalonica. Naucratis continued to

---

[1] The resemblances and divergences in the political, administrative and economic systems of the two empires show that both
systems derive from common sources, Macedonian and Persian, but
were developed very differently.

exist, but lost all importance in face of Alexandria ; and,
Alexandria apart, the only activity shewn by the Ptolemies
in regard to cities was in their foreign possessions. These
possessions were once very extensive, though they fluctuated from time to time. The Ptolemies held or controlled
the Cyclades, with some intermission, from 285 to 245 ;
Samos from 281 to 201 ; most of the coast of Asia Minor
from the Calycadnus in Cilicia to Ephesus from *c.* 273 (or
earlier) intermittently to 197, though many cities and
districts often changed hands in their wars with the
Seleucids ; much of the Hellespontine and Thracian coasts
with Lesbos and Samothrace from *c.* 241 to *c.* 202, including
even Abdera in Macedonia's sphere ; Southern Syria up to
the Lebanon and much of Phoenicia, with a fluctuating
boundary, till 198 ; Thera, Methana in the Argolid, and
Itanos in Crete, till 146 ; the Cyrenaica (except for its brief
independence *c.* 258–246) till 96 ; and Cyprus, their last
foreign possession, till 58. They renamed many cities ;
Methana, Patara in Lycia, some city in Ceos, all became
Arsinoe. But Arsinoe and Philadelphia in Cilicia may be
new foundations, and there were such in Syria, as Philoteria
on Lake Gennesareth ; while other native towns were refounded as Greek cities, Ake (Acre) becoming Ptolemais
and Rabbath-Ammon Philadelphia.

The Greek cities in their foreign possessions were frankly
subject towns and, as such, taxed, and the form of government was connected with the Egyptian form. One innovation of the Ptolemies in Egypt had been to abolish the
native nomarchs and govern the nomes by Greek or Macedonian generals, as though they were satrapies ; the foreign
possessions were also governed by generals, as was usual
in all Macedonian kingdoms, with *epistatai* (city governors)
over the cities. But the important thing was that the
internal affairs of these Greek cities were under the control,
not only of Ptolemy through the general and *epistates*, but
of the finance minister (*dioecetes*) at Alexandria ; for just
as in each nome there stood beside the general a subordinate
of the finance minister, an *economus*, so there was an

*economus* as well as a general in provinces like Caria, exercising authority in the Greek cities. No other monarchy went to this length, and it suggests an attempt to introduce the Egyptian economic system into the Greek world. How far this was really done is unfortunately unknown ; but the Greek Lesbos, beside money taxes, paid a tax in corn, which means that its city land was treated as though it were King's land ; at Halicarnassus there was seemingly a trierarchy to help maintain Egypt's navy ; and Ptolemy II attempted to replace the city coinages in Asia by his own. Syria was doubtless organised somewhat on the Egyptian model, but not nearly so thoroughly ; beside the priest-state of Judaea, native chiefs like the Tobiads in Ammon (p. 167) still existed under Ptolemaic suzerainty.

As regards public works in Egypt, Ptolemy I founded the Library and Museum (p. 216), and began great native temples at Dendera, Edfu, Kom Ombo, and Philae, on which his successors worked for a couple of centuries. Ptolemy II completed the Library, restored the canal which Darius I had constructed to connect the Red Sea with the Nile by way of the Bitter Lakes, and early in his reign began to drain Lake Moeris to create the Arsinoïte nome, the Fayum, thus recovering much fertile land which he made a centre of Greek settlement ; the original swamp was ultimately reduced to a lake about the size of Lake Karun to-day. The caravan route from Coptos on the Nile to Berenice on the Red Sea was equipped with wells and block-houses ; there was a swift official post modelled on the Persian, and a slower method of forwarding heavy parcels and persons, based on a system of requisitioning draught animals along the route ; Ptolemy II introduced the camel, and later a camel post ran from the south to Alexandria. The notable series of explorations along the Red Sea coast are mentioned elsewhere (Chap. VII). But the greatest achievement was probably the completion of Alexandria.

Alexandria, distinguished from the rest of Egypt as ' the city,' stood on the neck of land between the sea and Lake Mareotis, with harbours on both. Deinocrates had laid it

L

out on the rectangular plan usual in Hellenistic cities
(p. 253) and found even in Greek villages in the Fayum ;
but the roads actually uncovered are Roman, and the
Hellenistic city is known principally from Strabo, who
describes a great street 100 feet wide running east and west,
and crossed at right angles by a second. Several streets
bore the cult-names of Arsinoe II. Alexander had joined
the island of Pharos to the mainland by a mole seven
furlongs long called Heptastadion, which formed a double
harbour, a type known at Syracuse, Sinope, and Cyzicus ;
to the east of the mole was a natural basin, now neglected,
to the west an artificial port, Eunostos, formed by break-
waters, and connected with Lake Mareotis by a canal.
Each had a small closed inner harbour opening from it,—
from the eastern harbour Ptolemy's private port, and from
Eunostos the war harbour, Kibotos. The harbour on Lake
Mareotis took the Nile traffic and was said to clear a bigger
tonnage even than the sea-harbours ; there lay the gorgeous pleasure fleet of Ptolemy II, and later the splendid
villa mounted on a barge built for Ptolemy IV. On the
eastern harbour lay the Royal quarter, Brucheion, where
amid temples and spacious gardens stood the Palace, the
Museum and Library, the quarters of the Guard, the tombs
of the Ptolemies, and the gorgeous tomb built for Alexander's body by Ptolemy II when he brought it from
Memphis, a tomb still regarded as holy by the Roman
Emperors and to which Caracalla made a pilgrimage. Over
the whole kept watch the Pharos, the lighthouse erected
on the island by Sostratus of Cnidus for the safety of
mariners (p. 256).

Within the city were the buildings which housed the
central bureaux of the whole administration, the central
stores for corn, oil, and other products, the Hall of Justice,
and the Gymnasium ; beyond the east gate lay the stadium,
and the hippodrome for chariot races ; in the west, near
the native quarter, stood Parmeniscus' great temple of
Serapis ; an artificial hill dedicated to Pan gave a view of
the whole city. Shops and bazaars lined the central

thoroughfare, and by 100 the houses were probably several
storeys high ; lodging houses were known, managed by the
owner's slaves. A canal brought Nile water to the city,
distributed through conduits to fill a system of underground
cisterns, from which the inhabitants drew ; later on some
houses apparently could get their water by pumping. The
city overflowed its wall on both sides ; on the west lay the
native Egyptian quarter, on the east, beyond the suburb
of Eleusis, the gardens of the wealthy extended to Canopus,
Alexandria's playground. By 200 Alexandria was the
greatest city of the known world, though Rome passed her
later ; by Augustus' time the total population was perhaps
a million. In a recently discovered dialogue an enthusiast
claims that Alexandria *is* the world : the whole earth is
her city-land, and other cities only her villages. Something of her wealth and magnificence under Ptolemy II can
be gathered from Callixenus' account, preserved by Athenaeus, of that king's festival procession.

That this vast agglomeration of humanity could ever be
a " city " in the strict Greek sense was a physical impossi-
bility. Alexandria was a collection of *politeumata*,[1] based
on nationalities, the Greek *politeuma* being much the most
important ; outside these stood a few privileged Macedonians at one end and the mass of Egyptians at the other.
It had not even a city Council (though some think otherwise) ; and the argument that Alexander could not have
founded a city without a Council presupposes that what he
founded was a ' city,' a *polis*, whereas his foundations were
probably of a new mixed type. The Greek *politeuma* of
Alexandria, however, approximated more closely to the
*polis* type than any other actually known ; the Greeks were
called ' the citizens ', ' the Alexandrians ', and were divided
into tribes ; they supplied the magistrates, of Greek type,
who looked after building, public health, and so on, and
also Greek courts which administered a law compounded
of the ' city law '—the law of the Greek citizens—and royal
rescripts, and which seemingly had jurisdiction over all the

[1] See the discussion of town forms in Chap. IV.

inhabitants except (after the third century) the Jewish *politeuma* ; the land attached to Alexandria was the land ' of the Alexandrians,' *i.e.* of the Greek *politeuma*, and if a Council be ever discovered it is probable that it will be that *politeuma's* governing council, which must have existed. There were, however, many Greek inhabitants not members of the Greek *politeuma*, and the whole population was subject to Ptolemy's governor, who in the later period had military power ;   there were other royal officials, like the prefect of police, and possibly the *exegetes*, who was responsible for the food supply and can hardly have been a magistrate, for he wore the purple.   The interesting thing about the constitution is to see the personal ' city law ' of the Greeks, by its extension to non-Greeks, well on its way to become a true territorial law ;   this may have been part of Alexander's scheme for fusing different races, and certainly, after Graeco-Egyptian intermarriage began in the second century, Alexandria, apart from the Jews and a minority of Greeks, did ultimately fuse into a more or less homogeneous mass, turbulent, crazy for shows, sarcastic and sometimes hostile toward the dynasty, for which at the end it nevertheless fought and which it long regretted.

To describe the Ptolemaic system is to describe a body without a head, for all threads ran to Alexandria, and of the central bureaux there nothing is known ;   the extant information comes from the country.   Already under the Persians payment in money was displacing payment in kind, and the process gained momentum under the Ptolemies ;   but the latter form of economy still persisted, and capital was always relatively scarce in the country, interest being 24 per cent. to 36 per cent., rates unknown in Greece except upon maritime loans.   As regards the fellahin, the basis of the system was that each man had his ' own place ', which he could not leave except by official order or permission.   The germs of the monopoly system have been traced in the old temple monopolies of Pharaonic times and in the famous corner in wheat brought off by Alexander's financial superintendent Cleomenes when he was virtually in control of the country ; but the system as we know it appears as the creation of Ptolemy II, though conceivably his father originated it.

The king was the State ; and Ptolemy I after Perdiccas' death had claimed Egypt as ' spear-won ' territory, which by Macedonian custom passed to the king. He therefore claimed to own the entire soil of Egypt, except the lands of Naucratis, Alexandria, and Ptolemais : not only the old royal domains, but also the temple lands and the lands of the feudal nobility, whom the Ptolemies abolished. The entire land was divided into two categories only : King's land in the narrower sense, *i.e.* land in hand, and land in grant. King's land was farmed for Ptolemy by the ' royal peasants,' the ' king's people.' These formed a substantial part of the fellahin population of the villages, and their ancestors had cultivated King's land for untold centuries ; many were small peasants, but among them were farmers of some substance. Their customary tenure became partly translated into Greek forms : they were registered as lessees. But they had no written leases and the king did not undertake the corresponding duties of a lessor ; and as they could not leave their villages, were compelled to cultivate their land and could be compelled to cultivate more if ground fell vacant (for the State was built up on the maxim that the king's cultivation must be carried on), could have their animals requisitioned, gave compulsory labour on the dykes and canals, and could be turned out at any time, they differed little in fact from serfs. How much of Egypt was King's land is unknown ; certainly a very substantial part, and in the Fayum and the Delta perhaps the larger part.

Land in grant fell into four classes : (*a*) temple lands, (*b*) cleruch land, (*c*) gift land, and (*d*) the so-called private land. (*a*) The king, who was also an Egyptian god, cultivated the former temple lands himself, allotted what produce was required to the temple, and kept the rest. Probably extensive lands in the Thebaid belonged to this class. (*b*) The cleruchs (holders of a *kleros* or military allot-

ment) were military settlers, originally mercenaries of many
nationalities, Greeks predominating, grouped in settlements ; to place them on the land ensured a supply of
soldiers, and enabled the king to bring waste land into
cultivation, for their lots were often, though not always,
uncultivated ground, of which the user was sold to them
at a low price on terms that they should reclaim it ; they
could make it corn-land or garden-land as they wished
(vineyards being reckoned with garden-land), and paid
rent accordingly, for corn-land in corn, for garden-land in
money ; their rents were not heavy, as part of their rent
was their obligation to military service. If a cleruch died,
or failed to render his rent or military service, the king
could resume the land ; but by 218 the ' lot ' had become
heritable and passed to the cleruch's son, and later it became alienable, though probably the cleruch never acquired
the power of willing it beyond the circle of his own male
kin.  (c) Gift land meant an extensive estate, comprising
one or more villages with their lands, conferred on some
official, who became the superior of the village authorities ;
the object was to get the land fully developed through his
agency, but the king could resume the estate.  The Zeno
papyri have supplied much information about the estate
in the Fayum bestowed by Ptolemy II on his finance minister
Apollonius.  (d) Private land originally meant house,
garden, and vineyard ; even the house and garden of a
Royal peasant were ' private.'  Greeks sometimes called it
property, but it was, like every other Ptolemaic form, not
property but user ; apart from the Greek cities, the property
or legal estate in any land in Egypt never left the king.
But the kings presently began to give to civilians the perpetual user of land other than house and garden,—waste
land, or cleruch land that had escheated, or even King's
land that had become unoccupied ; and this land also was
reckoned ' private.'  It grew greatly in importance by the
first century, and even more under Roman rule ; as the
cleruchs furnished the military element to the State, so
the ' private ' occupiers probably staffed the smaller offices

of the bureaucracy.  One may compare the parallel forms in Seleucid Asia, where civil colonies are perhaps found alongside the military ones (p. 123).

The main Egyptian staple was wheat.  All corn-land, in whatsoever hand, paid a tax in corn direct to the king ; and on the King's land no part of the crop belonged to the peasant till he had taken out the king's quota, which was the larger share, and transported this to the king's barn in his village.  While in Asia the Seleucids were partners with the peasantry and shared losses (p. 117), in Egypt every parcel of ground contributed its allotted amount to the king as a first charge, loss falling on the cultivator alone ; this was one of the sources of Ptolemy's great wealth.  The royal peasants had not more than enough left to live on ; the king supplied next year's seed corn.  From the village barns the wheat passed to the central barn of the nome, and was thence taken down the Nile and stored in the King's Barn in Alexandria ; the wheat was a second Nile, a vast river fed by a thousand rills, pouring down to the capital.  Ptolemy was the greatest corn merchant the world had seen.

For the staples which were royal monopolies, like textiles and oil, the treatment differed.  As regards textiles, all flax, and perhaps all wool, had to be sold to the king at a fixed price ; he apparently decided each year how much flax should be sown, while on foreign wool there was a 20 per cent. import duty, which led to Apollonius experimenting with Milesian sheep (the merino of Greece) within the tariff wall.  The weavers seemingly lived in their villages, but the looms were not nationalised ; the weaver was not actually forced to work, but he was not free to leave his ' own place,' and the State apparently exacted a fixed amount of linen or cloth from him in proportion to the raw material delivered.  Textiles ceased to be an absolute monopoly c. 100, and the right of manufacture could then be let out.

But the great royal monopoly was oil.  The olive, though long since introduced into Egypt, was scarce and only used as a fruit, and oil was derived from sesame (the best), croton, linseed, safflower, and colocynth (gourd seeds). The king decided each year how much land should be planted with oil-producing plants; planting was compulsory, and the king took the whole produce at a fixed price; the oil was made in the state factories, the workers being serfs, compelled to work and tied to their ' own place ' unless shifted elsewhere by official orders; finally the oil was distributed through retailers at a fixed price. At the same time, the workers in the oil-factories received a share of profits amounting to about 4 per cent. on the selling price; but what this means, and whether it were really as enlightened a measure as some have supposed, cannot be said till we know what wages they got and how wages stood in Egypt generally in regard to prices. To prevent competition, there was a heavy import duty on foreign oil; in 259 Ptolemy II sold his oil in Egypt at 52 drachmae the metretes, and the import duty was 50 per cent., with a regulation that oil imported must be sold to himself at 46 drachmae. It worked thus. The shipper of Greek oil had to pay 26 Ptolemaic drachmae duty and also the Alexandrian harbour and other dues, about 2 drachmae, and sell at 46 Ptolemaic drachmae; that left him some 18 Ptolemaic drachmae the metretes to cover the cost price of the oil, the 2 per cent. export duty of the city he shipped from, the cost of the voyage, and his own profit; he therefore could not ship oil to Egypt unless its cost price were very far below 18 Ptolemaic drachmae, which was equivalent to about 15 Attic (Alexander) drachmae. But about 259 the retail price of free oil at Delos ranged from 21 to 17 Attic drachmae; that is, the Egyptian duty was calculated to prevent import altogether, and if nevertheless Apollonius did import olive oil, using his own ships, the great dioecetes could afford to pay for his fancies. But Ptolemy took no chances; if anyone, despite the duty, *did* take foreign oil up the Nile for his own use he paid another 12 per cent., and if he tried to sell it it was confiscated and he was fined 100 drachmae the metretes. Oil was a cast-iron monopoly, in which everything was nationalised,—production, fabrication, distribution ; and Ptolemy's profits ranged from 70 per cent. on sesame oil to 300 per cent. or more on colocynth.

Of many other things the king had either a monopoly or a share in the business. The manufacture of papyrus, the world's writing material, became a monopoly under Ptolemy II. In 333 a roll of papyrus cost in Greece 2 drachmae ; in 296, with Egypt opened up, a drachma bought several rolls ; but after 279, under the monopoly, a roll averaged nearly 2 drachmae again. Further monopolies were mines, quarries, saltworks, and natron pits (carbonate of soda, used as soap) ; possibly too the business of fulling cloth. Hemp was treated like flax. All imported spices had to be sold to the king at his own price. He had a 25 per cent. share in all fisheries and all honey, with corresponding 25 per cent. import duties to protect his interests. He owned part of the merchant fleet on the Nile, and perhaps leather factories ; Cleopatra ran a wool mill, possibly with her own maids. Banking was really a monopoly ; there was a State bank in Alexandria, and banks in the nome capitals and the villages, let out to private individuals, which beside banking and money-changing acted as branches of the State bank,[1] receiving the money taxes and making payments on Treasury account like the so-called state banks in Greek cities. Many businesses beside banking, *e.g.* brewing, bee-keeping, and breeding pigs, could only be carried on by purchasing an annual licence from the Treasury ; conceivably this applied to all businesses not monopolised. The king owned all pasture land, and had large herds of cattle ; the royal peasants, after reaping their corn, had to grow a green crop on which they fed the royal cattle, paying a tax for doing so. He also owned large flocks of pigs and geese, which were let out ; no tree could be cut in Egypt but by his leave, for it was rooted in his soil.

Last came the *apomoira*, a tax of one-sixth of the produce

[1] Some think they were really branches under officials.

of vineyards, paid in kind, and of orchards and gardens, paid in money. The *apomoira* had belonged to the temples, but in 266/5 Ptolemy II diverted it to the cult of the deified Arsinoe Philadelphus, which probably meant that part went to the Treasury. As in addition to the *apomoira* Ptolemy II took a 33½ per cent. tax on the produce of vineyards, orchards, and gardens, based on a three years average, a large part of the year's vintage was his, even though wine delivered in kind at once passed into trade through the financial officials ; the 33½ per cent. import duty on fine Greek wines corresponded to the tax, nicely calculated so as not to spoil Ptolemy's wine-business and yet admit those Ionian wines which Alexandria could not do without. What happened to the natural monopolies in the countries which Egypt ruled—the silphium of Cyrene, the balsam of Jericho, the bitumen of the Dead Sea—is unknown.

In addition there was a formidable list of money taxes and duties. A succession duty on estates ; a house duty of 5 per cent. on the rent ; a 10 per cent. tax on sales ; 2 per cent. on sales in a market ; 33½ per cent. on dovecots ; taxes on cattle and slaves ; a poll-tax on all native Egyptians except the priests. There was an octroi on goods passing from Upper to Lower Egypt, and from the country into the towns ; a 2 per cent. import and export duty at the Nile harbours ; and import and export duties, some very heavy, at Alexandria and the other seaports. There were taxes for a gold crown on the king's accession, taxes to maintain the fleet and the lighthouse, and taxes for local objects, as police, doctors, baths. The reform was introduced of separating the Treasury from the king's privy purse, the latter being under an official called the *Idios Logos* (' private account '), subordinate to the *dioecetes* ; among other things (judging from the regulations of Augustus' time) all exposed babies were Ptolemy's perquisite and were collected by the *Idios Logos* as saleable articles. The care taken over trifles was astounding ; the great Apollonius makes a few shillings by selling his roses, and re-uses Milesian oil jars. Unhappily the income of the Ptolemies is unknown ; [1] but the dynasty was generally regarded as much the richest thing in the world, and accumulated that 'Treasure of the Ptolemies' which so excited Roman covetousness.

To run a State on these lines full statistics were necessary ; and the system of registration was very thorough. Every village had its land register, kept up to date, which described every parcel of land in the village territory ; the capital of the nome had a register for the nome, compiled from the village registers ; at Alexandria there must have been a register for the whole country, compiled from the nome registers. There must have been a register of houses ; all draught oxen and working animals were registered ; if a man bought a licence to go fishing an agent followed him to register his catch. The official land register sufficed for the taxation of real property ; taxation of moveables was based on a system of declarations by the owners combined with official inspection. Censuses of the population were periodically taken. Supervision was as thorough as registration ; everything was inspected, and Ptolemy knew each day what each of his subjects was worth and what most of them were doing. There was probably no such thing as independent trade in the home market, unless in the Greek cities ; retail traders were only State agents for distribution, with their profits fixed. Even when the taxes collected in money were farmed out it was not a free operation, unless in the foreign possessions ; the tax-farmer was controlled by the State,—about the best thing the Ptolemies did,— and was only a piece of machinery for collecting the taxes ; but care was taken that he did collect them, for, if he did not pay the calculated amount, his property and that of his sureties could be confiscated. Not only the royal peasants but other farmers were ordered what crops to sow ; even Apollonius once received such an order, which could only have been given by Ptolemy II personally. All the ploughing oxen of the royal peasants were at the State's disposal,

[1] Jerome's figure, 14,800 talents under Ptolemy II, is worth little.

and at seed time and harvest were so distributed as to get the land cultivated to the best advantage. A good deal was done to improve agriculture; beside the stricter organisation, new seeds were experimented with and Arabian sheep were introduced; Apollonius too imported Milesian sheep and Sicilian pigs for his estate, and planted fir-trees to see if Egypt's dearth of timber were curable; by Augustus' time olives were plentiful in the Fayum.

The system necessitated a whole army of officials, administrative and financial. For administration, each nome was divided into *topoi* and each *topos* comprised so many villages; over each village and each *topos* were two native officials, and, theoretically, two in each nome, the nomarch and his scribe. But the general was really head of the nome, his functions being chiefly civil and legal, though his name remained a symbol of conquest. The *dioecetes* or finance minister, the second man in the kingdom, was head of the financial side, and appointed the smaller financial officials; from his bureau in Alexandria he exercised control over the two great centres there, the King's Barn for the corn and natural produce, the State Bank for the taxes in money. In the nome capitals and the villages were the nome and village barns in which the corn was collected on its way to Alexandria, with their appropriate officials, and the nome and village banks, through which the money taxes passed; these were looked after by the subordinate of the dioecetes in each nome, the *economus*, but later this office was doubled, one *economus* for the produce and one for the money. No trust was placed in the honesty of the financial officials; they not only had to find sureties, but to each was assigned a ' counter-scribe ' or checker; when a peasant brought his corn to the barn he got no receipt till the checker had verified the barn-master's weighing. If enough men did not volunteer, the smaller offices were filled compulsorily.

Ptolemy, as absolute monarch, was the fount of law, and his rescripts had legal force. But the ordinary administration of law had to take account of two different systems,

the Greek and the Egyptian ; for though Greeks had come
from many cities, their law had to be treated as a whole,
and in fact the ' city law ' of Alexandria shews a mixture
of elements from Athens and (possibly) Asia Minor. The
Ptolemies recognised the Greek principle that law was
personal, not territorial, and that the Egyptians must live
under their own law ; they had their old native judges,
the Laocritae, their native land-law was translated into
Greek, and later in the third century a special tribunal
was erected to judge disputes between Greeks and Egyptians,
taking account of both laws. For judging Greeks, panels
of judges called Chrematistae, usually three in a panel,
were created, each panel going circuit in its own district ;
appeals lay to the Chief Justice in Alexandria. Egyptian
law could be pleaded before the Chrematistae, and they
tended in time to oust the Laocritae. Naturally the two
laws began to influence each other, but on the whole the
Greek grew at the expense of the Egyptian. But much
more important was the part played by the administrative
officials, especially the general. A habit grew up of taking
to them all small matters (magistrate's cases) instead of
waiting for assizes, and in the second century the officials
were fast cutting into the judges' powers, apparently in
every sort of civil case ; their decisions were apparently
informal, not judicial, but people were content with the
speedier and easier way. The same thing then was happening in Egypt as with the judicial commissions in Greece
(p. 77) : informal jurisdiction gained ground on the regular
jurisdiction. Finally in Egypt the whole vast class of
royal peasants and monopoly workers were withdrawn
from the sphere of the regular courts and placed under the
jurisdiction of the financial officials and the *dioecetes*, who
gave severe sentences ; administration and law had become confounded, normally a very bad thing, and administration had usurped the law's powers.

Egyptian society in the third century was sharply
divided ; the upper stratum, which supplied the bureaucracy, comprised the Egyptian priestly caste, the cleruchs

(who were tending to form a military aristocracy), the civilian occupiers of ' private ' land, and the Greeks of the three cities ; the lower consisted of the vast mass of fellahin. The fellahin had no education, and orders, especially those relating to taxes, were often issued in demotic, the late-Egyptian speech of the time. They suffered from the very efficiency of the system under which they lived ; it had been tightened up till there were none of those loopholes for evasion which have so often tempered rigorous conditions in the East. Poor as their life was, they knew nothing better ; but it is obvious, from the numerous risings from 216 onwards, that there was much discontent. For wages, an artisan got 2–3 obols a day, a labourer (in 254) one obol for heavy work, less for light. Even on the wretched Greek standard (p. 103) such wages seem impossible ; but bread was cheap, and until some thorough study of wages and prices in Egypt has been made, comment seems useless. There was, however, no slavery in Egypt, apart from the household slaves of the Greeks ; native labour was too cheap and too thoroughly controlled for slavery to be worth while.

Perhaps the clearest light on the position of the fellahin is thrown by the numerous strikes, an old Egyptian custom. Riots in which the manager got badly beaten were not uncommon, but proper strikes also were numerous, both in the third century and later : strikes of miners, quarry-men, boatmen, workers of all sorts, royal peasants, retailers, police, even officials. Workmen's strikes were not strikes for better wages or conditions, for there were none to be got ; they were the product of blank despair, aggravated perhaps by some accident, as delay in sending seed-corn. The men had one weapon which officialdom feared ; they could throw the machine out of gear by leaving their ' own place '. A strike notice reads : " We are worn out ; we will run away " ; and they usually took refuge in some temple with the right of asylum. Asylum has been called the Egyptians' *Habeas Corpus* ; Ptolemy's power ended at the precinct wall, and the worried officials had no weapon

but persuasion or some little concession with which to get
the men back to their ' own place '. The first three Ptolemies reduced the number of temples that could give asylum ;
to abolish or violate the right even they did not dare. It
is the more noteworthy, and evidence of the hatred felt in
Egypt for Persian rule, that the Egyptian priests, with the
sanction of Ptolemy I, themselves denied the right to one
class, the descendants of Persians settled in Egypt. These
cannot have been numerous, but their exclusion gave rise
later to a strange legal fiction : creditors bringing actions
would describe the debtor, whatever he was, as ' descendant
of a Persian ', to prevent him taking sanctuary.

The power of the priestly caste, the only remains of the
old native aristocracy, was early broken ; the king took
the temple lands, the peasants on which became indistin-
guishable from the royal peasants, caused all priests to come
to Alexandria to celebrate his birthday, and deprived them
of their lucrative monopolies of oil and flax ; he did however allow the temples—and this was the only breach in
the State monopolies—to manufacture sufficient linen and
oil for their own use. The priestly caste had also to help
to fill the smaller administrative offices, service in which
was compulsory ; the priests could hold meetings (synods),
but only apparently to regulate religious matters, and to
confer honours on the king. But the kings at the same time
took care not to offend the strong religious susceptibilities
of the natives ; they distinguished gods from priests,
honoured and fostered the Egyptian religion, provided
endowments, and built native temples ; for Ptolemy, like
Pharaoh, was himself an Egyptian god, the Sun-god's son.

The Greeks came to Egypt to grow rich ; so far as they
could they transported to Egypt their own life, and for a
century did not mix with the Egyptians. They brought
their own gods, read Homer and Euripides, and formed
endless clubs. Their elementary education was neither
compulsory nor run by the State, one of the few things in
Egypt which was not ; we have school books and school
exercises in plenty, the subjects being reading and writing,

some grammar and mathematics, and Homer; but
illiteracy was not uncommon. Gymnasia were founded in
all the nome capitals (*metropoleis*) and even in villages
where Greeks were numerous, like Philadelphia in the
Fayum ; later one is found at Thebes and even as far south
as Ombi near the Cataracts. With the gymnasium came
the ephebe system. As to secondary education, many
authors were apparently read, but rhetoric was the principal
subject, for it led to the higher offices ; mathematics were
studied for land surveying and for working the complicated
equations between the Egyptian and Macedonian calendars,
so complicated that Apollonius' steward Zeno once confessed
he really did not know *what* day it was by Macedonian
reckoning. The formation of private associations extended
to the native Egyptians ; a long list of trade associations
is known, but it is not certain if they were more than
religious and social centres. The mercenaries formed
numerous clubs, some local, as the mercenaries in Cyprus,
others on an ethnic basis which called themselves *politeumata* as though they were part of the state,—those of the
Cretans, Idumaeans, Mysians, Boeotians, are known ; their
nationality of course soon became only a name. But the
Greeks themselves, scattered about Egypt and unable to
form cities, formed themselves into true *politeumata* ; each
might cover a considerable district,—we get " the Greeks
in the Delta ", " in the Thebaid ", " in the Arsinoite nome ",
—but the members imitated what of autonomous Greek
organisation they could. Private life is illustrated by
masses of extant correspondence, sometimes interesting ;
the letter written to Cleon, the hydraulic engineer who
drained Lake Moeris, by his wife Metrodora after his dis-
grace and fall is a credit to human nature. The letters
show a much greater degree of freedom among women than
was expected, and they also shew one of those strange
contradictions of which Hellenism is full—a large measure
of family affection and frequent exposure of children.

But the Ptolemies, for all their early successes, failed to
build a permanently powerful state on the exploitation of

a people ; once the influx of Greeks ceased their military power soon decayed, and in 168 only Rome's intervention saved Egypt from conquest by Antiochus Epiphanes. The Ptolemaic system depended absolutely on the competence and honesty of the officials ; it may have worked well in the strong hands of Ptolemy II, but under the weaker kings of the second century abuses began to multiply, till in the long civil war between Euergetes II and his sister Cleopatra II officialdom finally broke down. Euergetes' great series of decrees [1] about 118 give a vivid picture of the disorganisation : officials were collecting or extorting money for their own ends, and had seized the best of the King's land ; they forced the people to work for them without payment, quartered troops on those exempt, cheated the taxpayer with false weights and measures, and seized even royal peasants for debt, with their cattle and implements ; Egyptians were dragged before the Greek courts, and, worst of all, were imprisoned without trial by the officials themselves. Was the fault in the officials or in the system ? Probably both ; the system could only work decently if administered by men superior to the common failings of humanity. Doubtless the long civil war aggravated the mischief ; but, whatever the faults of Euergetes II, once that war was over he met the evil vigorously, even to the imposition of the death penalty, stopped imprisonment without proper trial, and re-established the power of the native judges, the Laocritae, on the basis that in contractual cases between Greek and Egyptian the forum should depend on the language of the contract, but that all suits between Egyptians should go before the Laocritae. He also introduced a number of measures for protecting the person and property of the tax-payer, and for repairing the damages of the war ; for equity and fair-mindedness his regulations stand high above most things of the second century. Their partial success is shewn by the fact that the dynasty lasted another century, and in spite of a succession of poor rulers remained strong

[1] Given in full *Tebtunis Papyri* I, No. 5.

M

enough to conduct further exploration southward and to make a tolerable fight against Caesar. But the system itself Euergetes did not question ; his aim was to restore its efficiency and to get it justly administered.

Raphia had aroused the national consciousness of the Egyptians, and in the second century the Greeks were on the defensive. The priestly decrees for Ptolemy IV after Raphia and for Ptolemy V (the Rosetta stone) show strong Egyptian colouring and give to the kings the titles of a native Pharaoh ; Ptolemy V was crowned in Egyptian fashion at Memphis, which became a second royal residence ; the native risings which began in 216 culminated in the great revolt under Ptolemy V, and continued spasmodically throughout the century. Euergetes II greatly extended the powers, privileges, and possessions of the priesthood in an attempt to conciliate the natives. This strange man was hated by the Greeks,—by the literary men because he temporarily broke up the Museum, by the Alexandrians because in the civil war he had let his troops loose on the hostile mob, by all because, as they thought, he favoured the Egyptians ; and they have blackened his memory accordingly. But he partially understood the position, realised the ambitions of Rome, and entertained the great idea of constructing a national Graeco-Egyptian monarchy ; beside his other reforms he remodelled the native army organisation, and made an Egyptian, Paōs, his ' kinsman ' and governor of the Thebaid. His aim, like that of Antiochus Epiphanes, was to strengthen his kingdom as against Rome on a new basis ; and by admitting Egyptians to participation he hoped to avoid the difficulties which had wrecked Antiochus' purely hellenising policy. But he in turn failed to create a national monarchy because it was incompatible with the economic system of Ptolemy II, and he did not attempt to revise that too lucrative system ; hence he was unable to win over the Egyptians, and revolts continued till in 85 Ptolemy Lathyros suppressed the last and partly destroyed Thebes.

Many things illustrate the native revival after 200, and

the Egyptianising policy of the kings. No more great
estates were conferred on Greek officials. Many new
asylums were made or old ones restored; between 93 and
57 four were created in one village, Theadelphia, and the
right became so abused that Rome curtailed it drastically,
though possibly it lasted till the Christian Church took it
over. Under Euergetes II the long struggle between the
calendars ended in the Macedonian having to conform to
the Egyptian. Ptolemy I had introduced a silver coinage,
strange to the Egyptians, and debts contracted in silver
could only be paid in copper by adding 10 per cent.; but
after 200 the ratio of silver to copper, 1 : 120, rose steadily
till in the first century it reached 1 : 500 ; *i.e.* the country
was flooded with copper coinage to please the natives.
After Raphia the Egyptian warrior-class, the *machimoi*, was
revived ; they were made cleruchs with smaller lots, and
the Greek cleruchs began to be called *catoeci* for distinction ;
later *catoeci* came to mean cleruchs of Greek *culture*;
finally *catoeci* and *machimoi* lost all racial meaning, and only
meant men who held larger or smaller lots. In 215 a
Greek and an Egyptian were joint tenants in a lease, and
after 200 mixture of blood began ; names ceased to be any
criterion of race, as some natives rose in the scale and took
Greek names, and some Greeks sank ; Greek and native
names occur in the same family. Some Greeks kept themselves aloof ; but a new mixed race formed intermediate
between Greeks and fellahin, and Hellene came to mean
a man with some Greek *culture*. The living Greek language
of the third-century papyri was replaced by the barbarous
Greek of the natives ; some Greeks too learnt Egyptian.
The Egyptianised Greek adopted native religion and
customs, even to embalming his dead ; in the first century
brother and sister marriage appeared among Greeks, and
became so common that Rome subsequently had to stop
it ; even those who had passed through the gymnasium
made offerings to Egyptian gods. Popular literature
began to prophesy the downfall of the hated Alexandria.
What the Ptolemies had brought to Egypt was not the

spirit of Greece, but only external forms; by the first
century Egypt was fast absorbing the foreign element in
her body, and Augustus, to save what remained of
Hellenism, had to return to Ptolemy I, nurse the Greek
element, foster the gymnasia, and again break the re-
acquired power of the priests.

Egypt was Ptolemy's estate; its interest is that it enables
us to study a thorough-going system of nationalisation,
and that it largely supplied the model for the bureaucracy
of Imperial Rome. The widespread belief that the earlier
Ptolemies were the fathers of their people, ready to fulfil
the requirements of philosophy, rests on no evidence at all
except on very occasional exhortations to the officials to
behave properly; while an unknown Stoic of the third
century, who has left an invaluable fragment on the theory
of the Hellenistic monarchy, condemned some king—he
certainly meant the reigning Ptolemy—who treated his
people's possessions as his own. While one gladly admits
that the ' profit-sharing ' of the oil workers may ultimately
turn out to mean something, one cannot forget that, contrary to the custom elsewhere, the whole loss of a bad crop
was thrown on the peasant, and some think the whole loss
of a low Nile also, though this is disputed. Naturally the
earlier Ptolemies aimed, not at acquiring money, but at
constructing a strong state; their condemnation is that
the money they acquired was in no sense used for the
benefit of those who made it. They improved the land;
they did not improve the condition of the people. There
was no desire to oppress the Egyptians; but there was
no desire to help them, beyond keeping them fit to work,
a thing done by every businesslike slaveowner. If the
Library and the Museum glorify the Ptolemies in the eyes
of world-history, that did not help their subjects; and
material wealth and wealth of material need not blind us
to the fact that their government, ethically considered,
stood well below that of the other two Macedonian dynasties. The Antigonids, with small resources, but national
rulers of a free people, were the shield of the Greek world

against northern barbarism and enabled the growth of the
rather wonderful culture of the third century ; the Seleucids,
overweighted and overworked, nevertheless strove, not
without success, to raise the civilisation level of half a continent. But the Ptolemies farmed their estate and filled
their Treasury.

# CHAPTER VI

## HELLENISM AND THE JEWS

The aim of this chapter is to sketch the workings of
Hellenism on the Jews, the rise and the fortunes of a
movement which brought the Greek world into contact
with the one race strong enough to resist the impact of its
victorious culture.

Few Greeks in the Hellenistic period ever managed to
learn very much about the Jews. Alexander, who had seen
the civilisations of Egypt and Babylon, conversed with
Indian ascetics, and brought to Europe the first knowledge
of the Iranian Avesta, never visited Jerusalem; his Staff
probably thought it another priest-state of the type familiar
to them in Asia Minor and Syria, and Theophrastus only
knew of the Jews as philosophic star-gazers who had invented human sacrifice. A little knowledge began under
Ptolemy I, whose contemporary Hecataeus of Abdera, in
a rather mixed account, did seize on two salient facts :
the Jew made no images of the gods, and by command of
his lawgiver Moses did not practise infanticide. From
the start the Greek felt that the Jew differed from other
men. But no Jew made his history available to Greeks
before Josephus, late in the first century A.D., and when
the Greek Alexander Polyhistor (c. 50 B.C.) attempted the
task he could only produce a burlesque ; even Strabo,
who knew so much, was utterly at sea over Jewish history
and had obviously never even heard of Jewish literature.
In some sense the Jews always formed a world apart.

The little hill-state of Judaea, where Ezra had originated
modern Judaism, contained only part of the race when

Ptolemy I acquired it in 301.  Gaza and the coastal plain
were not Jewish, and the Philistine towns became hellenised ;  Samaria was inhabited by a mixed race, who
worshipped Yahweh at Shechem after their own fashion ;
in Galilee and the Peraea Antigonus I had already made
Greek settlements, to be reinforced, especially east of the
Jordan, by those of the Ptolemies (p. 144).  The fighting
Idumaeans (Edomites), important to Egypt as mercenaries,
occupied southern Judaea as well as the land south of the
Dead Sea.  Judaea had no outlet to the great world.  But
many of Jewish race still lived east of the Euphrates,
chiefly in Babylonia ;  *Jonah* about 300 represents the
view-point of an Assyrian Jew, while *Tobit* gives a glimpse
of the colony in Media.  In Jewish tradition these eastern
Jews were the Ten Tribes, those in Judaea being Judah
and Benjamin ;  but in reality the tribal system, whatever
it originally represented, had lost all local meaning, and a
Jew of Judaea might belong by descent to any tribe ;
the Maccabees were of Levi, Anna the prophetess of Asher,
and the Aristeas-letter makes the High Priest send repre-
sentatives of all the twelve to Ptolemy II.

Down to 198 Judaea was under Ptolemaic rule, and little
is heard of its history except stories of quarrels between
two leading families, the Oniads, who held the High Priesthood, and the Tobiads, whose stronghold was near Heshbon
in Ammon and who may or may not have been partly of
Ammonite blood.  As regards literature, the third century
seems a blank.  The *Epistle of Jeremy* may date from 306,
and *Jonah* about 300 ; part of *Zechariah*, Chaps. ix–xiv,
may possibly be later than Alexander ;  then there seems
nothing else till *Ecclesiastes, c.* 200.  The revival of literature took place in the subsequent troubles of the Seleucid
period ;  and if absence of history and literature be a test
of happiness, Judaea may have been fairly happy under
the Ptolemies, though obviously by 200 the wealthy class
were discontented, largely perhaps under the burden of
the heavy Egyptian taxation.  A certain expansion of the
people was inevitably taking place, for as Jews reared all

their children they increased faster than other races, and
Jewish communities formed in Transjordania and subsequently in Galilee.  Doubtless the Ptolemies would try to
direct emigration to their own possessions ; but how far
the Egyptian Jews came from Judaea cannot be said.

The first three Ptolemies seemingly followed the usual
Hellenistic practice of not interfering with the religion of
their subjects ; but Ptolemy IV, an enthusiastic worshipper
of Dionysus, was perhaps deceived by the supposed equation
of Sabazios and Sabaoth into believing that the Jews
merely worshipped Dionysus under another name and
form, and as Dionysus was also equated with Serapis through
the Osiris element in the latter, he possibly dreamt of
establishing one religion in his empire, that of Dionysus,
which should unify its principal racial elements.  What
attempt, if any, he actually made to introduce Dionysus-
worship into Judaea is quite uncertain ; but he did incur
the hostility of a section, who worked hard to blacken his
memory, as can be seen in *III Maccabees*.  *Ecclesiastes*
gives a lamentable account, from the aristocratic side, of
the state of Judaea at the end of his reign :  the land was
full of the tears of the oppressed, and the dead happier
than the living ; his spies were so ubiquitous that a bird
of the air would carry the matter.  The Preacher himself
was evidently prepared to welcome Antiochus III, the
' king well-born '.  But Polybius says the common people
favoured Egypt ;  it means therefore that before 200—
how long before cannot be said—an aristocratic party had
fallen out with Ptolemy and were turning to his rival.
That party must now be considered.

Egyptian rule, and the neighbouring Hellenistic cities,
had accustomed the Jews to the Greek language and
nomenclature and other external phenomena of Greek
civilisation, and though Ezra's influence remained strong
in Judaea, elements of the governing class, those about
the High Priest, were favourable to Hellenism ;  they
claimed to be as good Jews as their fellows, but were willing
to adopt the outward forms of the dominant civilisation.

This was the party which supported the Seleucids, the strict Jews usually looking to Egypt ; with reason *Ecclesiastes* has been the hunting-ground of those scholars who have sought in Jewish literature traces of the Greek spirit. These hellenising Jews provoked bitter enmity among the pious ; they are 'the ungodly' so often referred to in subsequent Jewish writings, and Jewish Hellenism may be the ' strange woman ' of *Proverbs*, ' which flattereth with her lips ', but whose ' house inclineth unto death '. They were accused of neglecting circumcision and of exhibiting all the moral shortcomings commonly attributed in the Old Testament to backsliders ; it comes as an anticlimax when in 169 the two definite charges made against them were that they favoured Greek athletic exercises (which involved nudity) and wore Greek hats. In 198 Judaea changed masters ; Antiochus III wrested all southern Syria from Egypt, and, as was customary with new acquisitions, temporarily remitted various taxes. But the country did not settle down well under Seleucid rule, though it adopted, and retained, the Seleucid calendar ; the parties tended to try and play off Syria and Egypt against one another, and matters were not improved by the attempt of Heliodorus, minister of Seleucus IV, to seize the Temple treasure. A party of strict Jews, who tried and failed to reform some irregularities connected with the Temple, left Judaea under the leadership of one called ' the Star ' and went to Damascus, where they established a ' New Covenant ' of repentance. This was the general position when Antiochus Epiphanes turned his attention to Judaea.

Pious Jews could not speak too much evil of Antiochus, " the man clad in purple, fierce, unjust, fiery, lightningborn " of the Sibylline books, who persecuted their worship and drenched the land in blood ; *Daniel* shows how the ' Little Horn ' was hated, and he became the prototype of Antichrist. But it was the Jewish Hellenisers, not Antiochus, who began the trouble, and his first interference was in a domestic quarrel, though doubtless he would have done better to have stood aloof. The High Priest, Onias III, had gone to Antioch before Antiochus' accession to gain the king's ear over some matter in the unending feud with the Tobiad faction ; his brother Jason, a leader of the hellenising party, intrigued against him and persuaded Antiochus by promise of higher tribute to depose Onias and make him High Priest ; he also obtained leave for the Jews to set up a gymnasium in Jerusalem and call themselves Antiochenes, *i.e.* Jerusalem was renamed Antioch. But in 170 Antiochus, being dissatisfied, expelled Jason and gave the High Priesthood to Menelaus of the Tobiad faction, possibly himself a Tobiad, who offered yet higher tribute. Both Oniads and Tobiads were Hellenisers, and their quarrel had no religious import. In 169, while Antiochus was invading Egypt, Jason returned, took all Jerusalem but the citadel, where Menelaus found refuge, and slaughtered Menelaus' partisans. Clearly Jason had considerable support, and to Antiochus it looked as if, at a critical moment, Jerusalem had risen in his rear. On his way back from Egypt he entered the city ; Jason fled, his partisans were slaughtered by the Syrian troops, and Menelaus, restored to power, conducted Antiochus into the Temple and put the treasure into his hands. Antiochus entered the Holy of Holies, and strange stories were told later of what he saw there.

So far Antiochus had not touched the Jewish religion, and it must be remembered that, though he was important to the Jews, they were not equally important to him ; he was concerned at first with conquering Egypt, and subsequently with safeguarding Babylonia against Parthia ; Judaea to him was only one small vassal-state among others, whose affairs one generally left to one's provincial governors. But in 168 Rome warned him off from Egypt in a manner which violated every decency of international intercourse and outraged the whole of Hellenism in his person ; and the friend of Rome saw what he had to expect from her. He decided that his one chance was to make of his empire a united people in culture and religion, which

could alike only be Greek ; Judaea must bow to the common
need, like other places.  Menelaus may have told him there
would be no difficulty, and, as Dr. Bevan has pointed out,
tradition nowhere represents Antiochus as hostile to the
Jews themselves ; what he had in mind was Rome.  In
167 his general Apollonius occupied Jerusalem, levelled
the wall, and built and garrisoned a new citadel in the
' city of David ' ;  he was followed by a commissioner
with an order prohibiting the Jewish religion.  A Greek
altar, the ' Abomination of Desolation ', was placed upon
the Jewish altar in the Temple court, on which doubtless
pigs *were* sacrificed for the monthly purification ; and the
Temple became a temple of Zeus Olympius, whose mani-
festation on earth was Antiochus himself.  Yahweh's
temple in Shechem similarly became a temple of Zeus
Xenios, by request (it was said) of the Samaritans.

Many conformed, for the hellenising party supported
Antiochus, but many offered passive resistance ; that some
met death heroically as martyrs is certain, though the
highly coloured details are untrustworthy.  Active resistance was, in the tradition, started at Modin by Mattathiah
of the Hasmonaean family ;  he died in 166–5, and his
son Judas, called Maccabaeus (the Hammer), collected a
band of men like-minded, waged guerrilla war, and in 164
defeated 6,000 troops under Gorgias, sent by the governor
of Syria.  To Antiochus, Judas was merely an unimportant
rebel against lawful authority ;  he had already crossed the
Euphrates to attack Parthia, and in 163 he died.  Judas
took the Temple, but not the citadel, and restored the
worship of Yahweh ; and in December 164 a great thanks-
giving festival was held in Jerusalem.  In 162 Lysias,
regent for the infant Antiochus V, came in person, mastered
the country, and besieged Jerusalem, but the advance on
Antioch of his rival Philippus, Epiphanes' minister for
affairs, recalled him, and to win the Jews he gave them
back their religion, preserving only the Seleucid suzerainty ;
he also executed Menelaus.  This was the end of the war
of religion, for Antiochus' attempt at uniformity did not

survive his death ; but though Judas played the part of a patriot, what saved the worship of Yahweh was not his sword but Seleucid dissension.

The same dissension enabled the Maccabees to set up an independent state. The Roman Senate, always ready to damage the Seleucids, accepted Judas as an ally ; but when Demetrius I secured the Seleucid throne he reconquered Judaea. After Judas on the 15th of Adar (March) 160 had defeated and killed his general Nicanor,—a day long kept as a festival,—Nicanor's successor Bacchides, with whom was the new High Priest Alcimus, of the priestly house, defeated and killed Judas, garrisoned the country, and installed Alcimus, but did not meddle with religion ; Judas' brother Jonathan and his guerrillas made peace, and all seemed settled. Then the pretender Alexander Balas attacked Demetrius. Both bid for Jonathan's help, but Balas won him by offering him the High Priesthood ; and when in 150 Balas conquered Demetrius, Jonathan the High Priest, clever and unscrupulous, became nominally the Seleucid military governor of Judaea, but really an independent prince. In 147 he took Joppa and gave Judaea an outlet to the sea. After his death his brother Simon, favoured by fresh conflicts in Syria, expelled the garrison from the citadel of Jerusalem and in 142 made a peace with the weak Demetrius II which was reckoned the beginning of freedom ; the Jews made Simon hereditary High Priest and Governor, and Rome recognised him as such.

We must now turn to the history of the *Diaspora* (Dispersion); the Jews outside Judaea. In Egypt there had for long been Jewish settlements. From the seventh to the fifth century a body, originally mercenaries settled by some king, existed at Elephantine on the upper Nile ; they had a temple of Yahweh, whom they worshipped beside the goddesses Aschima and Anat (Anaïtis), were under an Egyptian governor, swore by Egyptian gods, and in the fifth century spoke Aramaic, the *lingua franca* of the Persian empire, and had an Aramaic folkbook which

contained the story of Achikar the Wise. Other Jews
settled in Egypt in Jeremiah's time, and there was an old
colony at Memphis. Subsequently Ptolemy I brought a
number to Alexandria, and there gave their upper class
the same position of privilege as Macedonians. All through
the third century Jews came to Egypt, generally settling
in Alexandria, but sometimes in the country, where under
Ptolemy III they already had two synagogues ; to the one
at Leontopolis Ptolemy III gave the right of asylum.
They took up land, and were often employed as tax-
collectors, but seldom did banking or money-lending and
hardly ever occur as traders ; one Jewish horse-dealer
named Daniel is mentioned. They mainly occupied one
quarter in Alexandria, and, as their numbers increased,
were organised separately (p. 175), and ceased to be ' Macedonians ' ; the Jew who under Augustus *called* himself a
Macedonian was a proselyte or an antiquary.

In the second century their settlements in Egypt were
numerous ; synagogues were built in several places, and
the village authorities distinguished sharply between Jews
and Greeks ; one Jewish-Egyptian marriage is known.
Under Ptolemy VI, Onias, son of the High Priest Onias III,
came to Egypt and was presented with a ruined temple in
Leontopolis, where about 160 he built a smaller model of
the Temple in Jerusalem as a religious centre for the Jews
of Egypt, and copied the Temple service ; it lasted till
A.D. 73, but the more pious Jews still looked to Jerusalem.
It is related that both Ptolemy VI and subsequently
Cleopatra III employed Jewish generals ; and a Jewish
mercenary, Abram, appears as a member of a Graeco-
Egyptian military association. In the civil war between
Cleopatra III and her son Ptolemy Lathyros the Jews
supported her, the beginning of tension in Alexandria
between Jew and Greek, for the Greeks favoured the
victorious Lathyros ; but the tension, which was primarily
political, only shewed itself in words ; anti-Semitism accompanied by violence was unknown in Egypt before the
Roman Empire. In the first century the Jews in Alex-

andria were the largest body outside Judaea; after A.D.
their number in Egypt is given as a million, and they largely
filled two of the five quarters of Alexandria within the
wall; but there was no Ghetto, and some lived scattered
throughout the other quarters.

The course of Jewish settlement in Asia is less easy to
trace. Certain religious phenomena (p. 179) make it
probable that much of the immigration into Asia Minor
came from Babylonia, and such was the tradition of the
Talmud, which alludes to the Jews of Asia Minor as the
Ten Tribes; if so, the immigration doubtless started
before the Seleucids lost Asia Minor in 188, for seemingly
at first they, like the Ptolemies, favoured the Jews as
good settlers, and there is no reason for rejecting the story
that Antiochus III settled 2,000 Jewish families in Lydia
and Phrygia, even if his letter has been doctored for propaganda purposes. We must suppose a parallel phenomenon
to the settlements in Egypt, though actual knowledge of
the great Jewish communities in many cities of Asia Minor
only dates from the first century; but by 140 the Sibylline
books could claim that every land was full of Jews. At
Sardes, and possibly in other cities, a special quarter of
the city was allotted to them. There was a community
of Jews on Delos before 100, and their handsome synagogue had been built before 88; the settlements known
later in Greece and Macedonia can hardly have been made
before Macedonia became a Roman province in 148. By
A.D. Jews had become very numerous in Damascus and
Syria generally, including Antioch; when the large settlement at Antioch began to form cannot be said. In this
sphere also, as in Egypt, it is generally supposed that there
was no active anti-Semitism before the Roman Empire.
Certainly the Jews of Delos once invoked curses on some
persons unknown who had shed the innocent blood of two
Jewish women; but this need not indicate an outbreak
against Jews as such.

As Jews filtered into a Greek city, their position was
at first merely that of metics; but as soon as they were

numerous enough, they set up a synagogue, and probably formed a private association for worship, as was the custom of other metics (p. 278). Such an association would have its officials—the ' ruler of the synagogue ' and others—to whom the Jews submitted their disputes according to Jewish law, in preference to going to the Greek courts ; this would be informal at first, but as all rulers were ready to favour the Jews, the privilege of judging themselves by their own law became in many places a right formally granted. In Rome the Jewish community had no organisation beyond these synagogue associations ; and when the Jewish prisoners whom Pompey took to Rome were freed and returned, they set up even in Jerusalem their own synagogue, built by one Theodotus, with a hostel, living-rooms, and baths. But in Greek cities this form of synagogue community, where it existed, ultimately passed from private law into public, and became the political form under which the Jewish body acted ; though this cannot be traced before A.D., it certainly antedates the destruction of Jerusalem.

In many cities, however, including the new Hellenistic foundations, the Jewish organisation went much beyond this ; the Jews, as they grew numerous, were allowed, or directed, to form a *politeuma* (p. 119), which made them quasi-autonomous ' settlers ' with rights greater than those of metics. Jewish *politeumata*, like others, managed their own internal and religious affairs, but in one respect they were privileged beyond any other : they ultimately acquired (at Alexandria not until after the third century) the right of being judged by their own magistrates according to their own law, which *probably* means that they were excepted from the jurisdiction of the Greek courts ; perhaps this, rather than religious exclusiveness, was the origin of the discontent Greeks began to feel later, seeing that Hellenistic Greeks held firmly to the principle that no man's religion was anyone else's business. The existence of these Jewish *politeumata* is explicitly attested for Alexandria and Berenice in the Cyrenaica, and seems certain in many cities, notably Hierapolis in Asia Minor. That in Alexandria was by Augustus' time governed by an ethnarch, who judged the people by Jewish law, but took into account Ptolemy's rescripts ; Augustus added a Council of Elders. At Berenice in 13 B.C. a board of nine archons governed the *politeuma*, and archons are referred to elsewhere ; probably after Augustus this became the usual form.

Josephus, however, claims that Jews as a body were full citizens in Alexandria, Antioch, and the cities of Ionia. Though many scholars have believed this, it was always impossible, for full citizenship, *i.e.* participation in government and legal administration, entailed worship of the city gods, which to a Jew meant apostasy ; and though individuals might bow down in the house of Rimmon, like that Nicetas of Jerusalem who at Iasos contributed to the Dionysia, or the two Jews who gave thanks in Pan's temple at Edfu, Jews as a rule, Hellenisers or otherwise, held fast to their religion. In fact, Jews in a city call themselves in inscriptions a racial unit only (*laos*), and never (I think) an enfranchised people (*demos*) ; and the recently discovered letter of the Emperor Claudius is (to me) conclusive that at Alexandria the Jews as a body never were citizens. Now Josephus is often untrustworthy over Hellenistic matters, and even uses falsified documents for propaganda purposes ; [1] but in this case he is guilty of nothing worse than a certain obscurity of terminology, pardonable enough in one dealing with new and partly fluid stateforms, and there is no ground for doubting either his statements that at Antioch and Alexandria the Jews called themselves Antiochenes and Alexandrians, or his account of the ' Ephesian process ', when the Greeks of Ephesus petitioned M. Agrippa not to let Jews participate in their citizenship. Moreover, Josephus apart, Paul's much-canvassed claim to be a citizen of Tarsus has to be considered. The expla-

----

[1] *E.g.* the decree of Sardes, *Antiq.* XIV, 10, 24, where οἱ κατοικοῦντες ἐν τῇ πόλει Ἰουδαῖοι πολῖται is a contradiction in terms ; the interpolation of πολῖται is self-evident.

nation is really very simple. Where the kings had power, as they had in new foundations like Alexandria or Antioch or in cities where, like Ephesus, the Seleucids restored democracy and could make terms, they gave the Jewish settlers isopolity, *potential* citizenship (p. 64) ; [1] that is, a Jew could become a citizen on demand, provided of course he apostatised by worshipping the city gods. This would explain, not only the Ephesian process, but also the ' Antiochenes ' and ' Alexandrians ' : when Aetolia, for example, gave Ceos isopolity the Ceans called themselves Aetolians. It would, literally, account for the insistence of Josephus and Jerome on the ' equal honour ' of the Jews. And there really seems no serious explanation of Paul's claim but potential citizenship, whether because the Jews of Antioch-Tarsus had isopolity or because he (or his father) had been given an honorary citizenship which of course had not been taken up ; the only alternative is that he worshipped the city gods, which need not be considered. A potential citizen might in an emergency appeal to his citizenship, and there is a parallel to Paul's case : when Alexander's treasurer Harpalus, who was an honorary citizen of Athens, revolted and was refused admission to Athens as a rebel, he sent away his army, appealed personally to his (potential) citizenship, and was received.

The great monument of the Hellenism of the Jewish Dispersion is the Septuagint or ' Book of the Seventy ', the translation of the Old Testament into Greek, the Bible

---

[1] The isopolity of the *Alexandrian* Jews is thrice mentioned : 3 Maccabees ii. 30 ; Josephus *Antiq.* XII, 8 ; and (the material passage) Claudius' edict *ib.* XIX, 281, ἴσης πολιτείας παρὰ τῶν βασιλέων τετευχότας. (This edict rightly calls the Jews συγκατοικισθέντας Ἀλεξανδρεῦσιν, *i.e.* a *politeuma* beside the Greek *politeuma*.) For Antioch, Josephus *Bell. Jud.* VII, 44, ἐξ ἴσου τῆς πόλεως μετέχειν. Except for some abbreviation, I have left my explanation as I wrote it, not knowing at the time (*mea culpa*) that Professor de Sanctis in *Riv. di filologia* 1924, p. 473, had already seen that isopolity is the key of the matter. He deals only with Alexandria ; but I hope he has ended the long controversy over Jewish ' citizenship '.

N

of Paul and of Philo; but it is a monument entirely of
form, not of substance. The Jewish tradition that Ptolemy
II called seventy Jewish elders together and requested
them to translate their Scriptures into Greek, the seventy
translations being found to agree exactly, is legend; but
it shews the Jewish belief that by the second generation
the Jews of Alexandria had adopted Greek speech and
lost their own, and also their belief that Ptolemy II was
sufficiently their friend for such action to be attributed
to him. The translation was really spread over a long
period; the *Pentateuch* was completed in the third century, *Isaiah* and *Jeremiah* between 170 and 132, the
prophets and *Psalms* generally by 132, the last book,
*Ecclesiastes*, not till about A.D. 100. The translation,
made from a much older Hebrew text than ours, has variations of considerable interest; for example, the witch of
Endor is a ventriloquist, and Greeks sometimes replace
Philistines as the oppressors.

Taken as a whole, the Jews of the Dispersion continued
to worship Yahweh, looked to Jerusalem as the Holy City,
and paid the half-shekel annual tribute for the Temple
service; the arrest of this tribute by a Roman governor
in 61 revealed the great number of Jews in the province
of Asia. But within these limits were many diversities,
for the Dispersion was spiritually, even if not racially,
the heir of the Northern Kingdom, and had some sympathy
with the religions of those around them and a tendency
to universalism; some were willing to believe that their
religion might save Gentiles as well as Jews, and *Jonah*
is an appeal to Jews to spread that religion throughout
the Hellenistic world. Doubtless there were orthodox
elements in the Dispersion, as there were Hellenisers in
Judaea; but on the whole the Dispersion was open to
Hellenistic influences. The fact that many Jews lost
Hebrew and spoke Aramaic rendered it easier to adopt
yet another language, and many Jews everywhere began
to speak Greek and take Greek names, preferably those
compounded with *Theos*, God, like Theodotus, Theophilus,

Dorothea ; even in the third century the Hebrew Scriptures were useless to many Alexandrian Jews. The services in many synagogues were conducted in Greek, and a long list of Greek words hebraised has been compiled, ranging from political terms to articles of domestic use. With Greek speech came Greek customs. Jewish settlers imitated their Greek neighbours ; they formed trade associations, like the purple-dippers and carpet-makers of Hierapolis, passed decrees in Greek form, set them up on steles before their synagogues, conferred the usual honours, like crowns, and instead of front seats at the games gave chief seats in the synagogue ; they gave titles and honours to women like Greeks, and copied Greek forms of manumission and Greek grave inscriptions. Some Jews in Asia Minor tolerated mixed marriages and dropped circumcision ; and, corresponding to this, beside the strict proselytes there were proselytes who were not compelled to be circumcised or to keep the whole Law, but who kept only the Sabbath and the food ordinances and worshipped Yahweh ; the Sabbatistai of Cilicia were probably a Gentile association who kept the Sabbath and worshipped Yahweh as Sabbatistes. These proselytes show that Jewish propaganda had some effect on Gentiles ; occasionally too Greeks adopted Jewish forms, like those Greek associations in Egypt and Chios whose head was called *archisynagogus*, ' ruler of the synagogue '.

But in Asia Minor and Syria some Jews went far beyond the imitation of Greek *forms* ; they adopted Graeco-Oriental cults. It may be evidence that they came from Babylonia (p. 174), for the eastern Jews had long been receptive in this respect ; women had learnt to wail for Tammuz and make cakes for the Queen of Heaven, Jews had taken Babylonian names, which " implied at all events an identification of Yahweh with Bel-Merodach and Nebo " (Charles), and a Persian demon figures in *Tobit*. In Asia Minor Yahweh himself took a Greek name as *Theos Hypsistos*, God the Highest, a name used later even by Philo ; the inscriptions from the synagogue at Delos are conclusive that Hypsistos often meant Yahweh. But when in Egypt the synagogue at Athribis was dedicated to Hypsistos by the local Jews, jointly with the prefect of police on behalf of Ptolemy V and his queen, possibly the Jews meant one thing and the prefect another ; for Hypsistos could mean other deities beside Yahweh, notably Zeus, and in Syria the term was applied to Zeus (Baal) of Heliopolis and other gods. But a Jewish synagogue in Mysia did actually worship Zeus Hypsistos ; and the ' synagogues of Satan ' at Smyrna and Philadelphia, " which say they are Jews but are not ", point to some worship of the kind, seeing that the altar of Zeus at Pergamum figures in *Revelations* as ' Satan's seat '. Sabazios too became a Jewish god, from a fancied identity of Lord Sabazios with Lord Sabaoth ; his mysteries, which purified men from ancestral sin, could be fitted to a religion which believed in the original sin of Adam. A society of Sabazios-worshippers is known who also worshipped Hypsistos, and in 139 some Jews were expelled from Rome for introducing the worship of Zeus Sabazios. Lastly, the name Sambathaios, Sabbath-born, common among Egyptian Jews, may really be derived, not from Sabbath, but from Sambethe, the Chaldean Sibyl who had a shrine, Sambatheion, at Thyateira ; probably her name was identified with Sabbath. Doubtless the Jewish devotees of these Judaeo-Pagan cults believed they were still worshipping the God of their fathers ; but they were influenced by Hellenistic syncretism, the belief that different peoples really worshipped the same god under different names, and that names and cults could therefore be united. These cults may conceivably have been sufficiently important to make Antiochus IV think that there would be no insuperable difficulty in introducing, even in Judaea, the worship of Zeus.

Apart from these cults, anything Jews took from Hellenism was only outward forms ; few learnt anything of its spirit. Whether a Jew adopted or rejected Greek forms he remained a Jew, a man whose ideals were not those of the Greek, even if expressed in the same words. Both

desired political freedom ; but, to the Greek, freedom was
an end, expressed in the free self-governing community,
making its own laws and worshipping what gods it pleased,
while to the Jew it was a means, preventing interference
with his devotion to a Law divinely given and unalterable
by man, and to a God beside Whom there could be no
other object of worship. Both praised Wisdom ; but, to
the Greek, wisdom was a thing which grew with the toil
of many brains, while to the Jew it was the fear of the
Lord, unchangeable for ever. Judaism by the first century
was offering the strange spectacle of a system which refused
to accept Greek thought while it opened its doors wide to
the infinitely lower influences of the east—astrology,
demonology, magic ; because of these it hoped to make
handmaids for its own spirit, while the Greek spirit could
be no handmaid. But if the ideals of the Jew and the
Greek conflicted, the world was to need both ; and it
was therefore to the good that, when Greek thought was
overrunning the east, the Jew should stand out against it.

But in one respect the Jew and the Greek had a parallel
experience. As the political decline of the self-governing
city state after Alexander made individualism inevitable
for the Greek, so the destruction of the old national State
and of the Temple had made it inevitable for the Jew ;
the idea of a blessed future for Israel was ultimately replaced by that of a blessed future for the Israelite. And
as the Greek had his problems of individualism and universalism, so, on other lines, had the Jew : would Yahweh
extend the hope of that blessed future to all mankind ?
Were men indeed to be brothers, not (as the Stoics hoped)
in this world, but nevertheless at the end ? In the second
century the idea of personal immortality, or rather of
resurrection from the dead, became firmly established in
certain Jewish circles. It is strange that some should
have believed that the Jew took his belief in immortality
from the Greek, seeing that the Hellenistic Greek had no
such belief : certain people might attain to immortality,
but certain people only. It seems clear that Jews evolved

this belief for themselves, though opinions have differed as to their reasons. It has been attributed to Antiochus' persecution (for unless the dead lived again, the upholder of the Law who suffered martyrdom was worse off than the ungodly who conformed), to the growing consciousness that the Messianic kingdom could not be realised in this world, and to the growing experience of personal communion with God. *All* these reasons may well have contributed to the new belief.

We must return to Judaea, where other things beside the belief in immortality developed amid the ferment of Antiochus' persecution and the rise of the Maccabees : a fresh outburst of literary activity, the formation of the Jewish sects, the growth and modification of the Messianic hope. The sects are too well known to require much notice here. Since Ezra there had been a strong body, the Chasidim or ' Pious Ones ', who stood for the whole Law ; naturally they opposed Hellenism, and from them in Maccabean times there developed the Pharisees, first actually mentioned in 120, who observed oral tradition as well as the written Law, and their allies the Scribes ; the name Pharisees is usually explained as ' Expounders ' of the Scriptures, but some take it to mean ' Those set apart '. The Sadducees, ' followers of Zadok ',—perhaps not David's priest, but some unknown founder,—developed out of the well-to-do governing class about the High Priest ; they were strict Jews, who rejected oral tradition and the new belief in immortality, unknown to the Old Testament, and had no connection with the Hellenisers ; they supported the Maccabee State, to which the Pharisees were sometimes in opposition after Jonathan became High Priest. There were smaller sects, like the ascetic Essenes, and the already noticed ' Covenanters ' of Damascus, who held themselves to be a remnant to whom God had revealed the hidden things in which all Israel, notably the Pharisees, erred, and who perhaps under the Maccabees returned to Judaea. Behind all the sects came the mass of the people ; they supported the Maccabees down to the reign of Jannaeus, and their prophets were the Apocalyptic writers.

It must now be asked whether any and what Greek influence can be traced in the Jewish literature of this period. There was no reverse influence; seemingly no Greek throughout these centuries so much as suspected that the Jews possessed a literature, still living and growing, which might rival his own. Except for the Babylonian revival (p. 109), other Oriental literatures were almost dead; the Egyptians, for instance, seemingly produced just one contribution, the queer jumble of prophecies called the *Demotic Chronicle*, a vague yearning for one of their own race who should come out of Ethiopia and deliver them from the Ptolemies. But from 200 onwards the Jews produced an enormous literature, in which three languages, Hebrew, Aramaic, and Greek, bore their part; among it were portions of the Old Testament Canon— *Ecclesiastes*, *Daniel* (a vivid monument of Antiochus' persecution), part of *Proverbs*, many *Psalms*—and most of the *Apocrypha*. This literature included psalms and wisdom-literature, some of the highest merit; the new religious orientation of the Apocalyptic writers; history, true and false; stories and proverbs, propaganda, magical books, and forgeries,—a literature of many complicated currents, testifying to the vitality of the people who produced it. Except for *Ecclesiasticus*, *II Maccabees*, and some of the propaganda writings, the names of the authors are in every case unknown; unlike the Greek, the Jew had no personal pride in authorship, probably because he so often felt himself the vehicle of something before which his own personality sank into insignificance.

Scholars have differed as to Hellenistic influences on this literature; some have traced such influence on a considerable scale, others have denied it altogether. Certain general considerations are of importance here. Both Jews and Greeks during the Hellenistic period were fond of attributing new works to great names of an older day, but as both peoples had begun the practice before they

came into contact we have here merely a naïve tendency
of the human mind ; but if in one undoubted case the
Greek and the Jewish mind ran parallel, the same phenomenon may occur elsewhere.  For instance, *I* and *II*
*Maccabees* quote state documents, true or forged, like
Greek historians ; but the model of the writers was the
books of *Kings*, and it does not follow that they borrowed
this obvious practice from Greeks, though the possibility
is not excluded.  Again, the mere resemblance of two
passages in two writers means nothing unless the matter
is such that two men would hardly think of it independently.
No one supposes that Ben Sira, when he wrote the famous
praise of his forefathers in *Ecclesiasticus*, was thinking of
the equally famous panegyric on the same theme in Aristophanes' *Wasps*, or that when Theocritus alludes to the
foxes in the vineyards he was copying from the *Song of
Songs*, which certainly he had never read ; for many people
might praise their fathers or observe the habits of foxes.
But when the author of *Daniel* says that Nebuchadnezzar
ate grass like an ox he is certainly drawing upon the lament
of Shubsi-meshrā-Nergal, the so-called ' Babylonian *Job* ' ;
for men do not eat grass, and this allegorical figure seemingly
never occurs elsewhere.  If these tests be applied, most
of the supposed Greek influence vanishes at once.  Perhaps
in the higher literature of the time, *Ecclesiastes* apart,
the one thing definite is that the learned Alexandrian Jew
who at the end of the first century wrote the beautiful
first part of *Wisdom* had *probably* read Plato ; God is to
him transcendent, without immediate contact with the
world, and immortality is a purely spiritual survival ; and
it has been suggested that Plato may have inspired the
passage beginning " The souls of the righteous are in the
hand of God ".  Nevertheless the author definitely writes
as a Jew, and holds to rewards and punishments after death,
though spiritual ones ; to read a thing is not necessarily
to be influenced by it.

*Ecclesiastes* is rather different.  The aristocratic author
of this fascinating book lived in Palestine *c.* 200 ; his

inclusion among 'the ungodly' in *Wisdom* shews that he
was considered a Helleniser, and his language is said to
be slightly affected by Greek ; one feels that in his time
he had somewhere breathed Greek air.  But all attempts
to prove direct Greek borrowings have broken down but
one : some who reject all else have believed, as Jerome
first suggested, that the passage IX, 7 *sqq.* was taken from
Epicurus.  But just as clear a parallel has been adduced
with a passage in the Babylonian Gilgamesh epic ; and,
while Greeks believed that the thought 'Let us eat and
drink, for tomorrow we die' was older than Epicurus and
first enunciated by an Assyrian king, *Daniel* shews that
some Jews of the time knew Babylonian literature.  That
*Ecclesiastes* borrowed from either source is possible.  But
it is quite unnecessary to suppose it ; for the thought
is as old as humanity, and must have been, as it still is,
acted on by many in many places who had never read
*Ecclesiastes* or Epicurus or Babylonian poetry.

I feel much diffidence in expressing opinions on Jewish
literature, but *Ecclesiastes* illustrates what seems to me
the true view.  Greeks and Jews were developing in the
same world, and some developed in the same way ; just
as today there was a body of thought in the air, call it
the spirit of the age or what you will, which unconsciously
affected men.  *Ecclesiastes* could not have been written
in Isaiah's time, but there is no need to seek definite
borrowing ; the Preacher lived in a world which was what
it was, and he felt it.  But, if a certain Hellenistic atmosphere may be traced in this or that Jewish writer, nowhere
is there any proof of a real penetration by Greek ideas.

Much the most important thing in the Jewish world of
the time was the Apocalyptic literature ; for the mass of
the people it replaced the prophets, whose roll was closed,
and its two greatest works,—the collection of writings
called *Enoch*, and the *Testaments of the Twelve Patriarchs*,
—considerably influenced the New Testament writers.  It
dealt with the future, which Yahweh was supposed to have
revealed to some sage of olden time, like Enoch or Moses ;

and its central thought was the Messiah, " the hope of those who are troubled at heart ", the Saviour who should come and who is sometimes called ' The Son of Man ' and ' The Christ '. The teaching concerning the Messiah varied greatly : sometimes he was divine and existent before the world, sometimes human and subject to death ; but thought steadily moved from a Messianic kingdom on earth, with resurrection of the body, to one eternal in heaven, with spiritual immortality. Usually immortality was for right- eous Jews only, but occasionally—the greatest thought of the time—it was extended to all men. This doctrine, and the parallel one of rewards and punishments after death, which seems first expressed in the earliest section of *Enoch* (*c.* 200–170), have influenced the world ever since. Both were connected with a problem which greatly exercised Greeks as well as Jews, the problem of the un- righteous flourishing ; its handling illustrates the two mentalities. The philosopher Carneades (p. 276) considered it, and argued that if there were gods who cared for the world they would never allow it ; therefore, even if there *were* gods, they did not care. The Jewish writers, certain that there was a God who cared, concluded that we could not be seeing the whole process ; there must be another life in which the balance would be redressed, the righteous rewarded and the wicked punished. It had nothing to do with the modern hope that some day we may reach true values ; for the writers were good Jews, to whom right- eousness meant the fulfilment of the Law. They themselves simply stated the reward of righteousness as a fact ; but the doctrine led, soon enough, to that abuse of it which has played such a part in the world : " Be virtuous in order that you may be rewarded ". Mankind was to travel far from the virile Stoic teaching : " Be virtuous because it is your duty ".

One book that stands apart must be noticed here : *Susannah*. About 95–80 the Pharisees were attempting to reform legal procedure, and *Susannah* is an extremely effective argument in favour of cross-examination as a means of eliciting the truth in legal processes. It is interesting to find a purely mundane matter in which Jews were in advance of Greeks ; for apparently this powerful instrument of justice was unknown to Hellenism.

Beside the great Jewish literature was a group of propaganda writers, who wrote in Greek ; these borrowed freely enough from Hellenism, but what they borrowed from was not philosophy or history, but that pseudo-history which always so attracts the half-educated. Manetho (c. 280) had early voiced a dislike of Jews, but he was an Egyptian priest ; however before 100 some Greek writers, of whom Apollonius, a rhetorician living at Rhodes, was the most notorious, were attacking the Jews, and even Poseidonius deigned to spread the story—whether the origin of or an outcome of the scandal that in the Holy of Holies was an ass's head—that Antiochus IV had found there a statue of a man (? Moses) riding on an ass. Naturally the Jews replied ; which side began cannot now be said, but the war of words was to culminate in the first century A.D. in Apion's attack and Josephus' answer. The accusations brought against the Jews were, that their culture was merely borrowed from others ; that they did not share any feeling of human brotherhood, but kept to themselves ; and that they were in fact atheists, because they said no god except Yahweh really existed at all, a charge they themselves did something to provoke by insisting that what other people worshipped was the actual image, and not (as the fact was) the god of whom the image was but a symbol.

Alexander Polyhistor has preserved the attempts of various hellenised Jews to show that Jewish culture was the oldest in the world and that Jews really taught other peoples. The first writer, Demetrius, gives Jewish history fairly correctly, but is interested in such trifles as proving that Jacob's 13 children could have been born within 7 years ; Leah becomes a mathematical scheme. To Eupolemus, history has no meaning at all : Abraham was of the giants who survived the Flood and built Babylon ;

he rediscovered astrology, originally discovered by Enoch who was Atlas, and taught the Egyptians, while Moses, the first philosopher, invented letters and taught the Greeks ; Hiram and Solomon correspond in the style of Hellenistic courts, and Solomon outdoes Alexander by spending 160,000 talents on the Temple in wages alone. Artapanus is not ashamed to quote *adespota*, the anonymous flotsam of Hellenistic writing : Joseph becomes the (Ptolemaic) *dioecetes* of Egypt and brings waste land into cultivation ; Moses invents almost everything—weapons, machines, ships, philosophy,—teaches the Egyptians to worship animals, and is deified after death in good Hellenistic phraseology. Cleodemus, less ambitious, merely made Abraham's sons outrival the Ptolemies by conquering, not only the Trogodytes, but the whole Spice-land of Arabia and Africa ; and Polyhistor himself was so confused by the nonsense he had collected that he made of Moses a woman, Moso. Probably allied to this literature was a group of Jewish poets ; Philo and Theodotus versified Jewish history in Greek hexameters, and Ezechiel wrote a tragedy on the Exodus, in which the catastrophe of the Red Sea was narrated by a messenger after the best Greek models.

Naturally Jews could write better propaganda than this. The letter attributed to Aristeas is a serious panegyric on Jewish law and Jewish sacred books put into the mouth of a heathen, who argues that all peoples worship Yahweh though they do not know it ; and the third book of the Sibylline oracles (the rest is post-Christian) makes a heathen prophetess witness, in Greek hexameters, to the superiority of the Jewish religion over all others. More important, if genuine, would be the work professedly written by the Jew Aristobulus under Ptolemy VI ; the author, a Peripatetic, knew Greek philosophy, and undertook to shew that the Jewish Law already contained all that was best in that philosophy, and that Pythagoras and Plato had learnt from Moses. But some hold that the work is a late forgery.

The distance between the highest and the lowest thought was thus as great among Jews as among Greeks ; and when in the later Hellenistic period the hand of the conquering Greek began to slacken and the east came flooding back on the west in one great stream of astrology and magic, the Jew played a conspicuous part ; Jewish magicians were reckoned second to none, and the Jewish exorcist was a familiar figure for centuries. The Jews had their own books of magic formulae, like those of which Paul's influence made a bonfire at Ephesus ; the most famous was the collection attributed to Solomon, of which, legend said, Hezekiah had once prohibited the use, since it seduced men from Yahweh's ordinances.

The fortunes of Hellenism in Judaea itself, after the country attained independence in 142 (p. 172), must now be followed. In 135 Simon was succeeded by his son John Hyrcanus, but his rule began unhappily, for in 134 the last strong Seleucid, Antiochus VII Sidetes, took Jerusalem and razed the walls. Sidetes could not carry out Epiphanes' policy, for he had no longer a party of hellenising Jews to support him ; Jonathan and Simon had almost wiped that party out. His Council advised him to exterminate the Jews and have done with trouble, but he followed the moderate course of leaving the High Priesthood to Hyrcanus and refusing to interfere with religious questions, merely making Hyrcanus a tributary vassal. But his death in 129 was the end of Seleucid power and authority, and Hyrcanus had a free hand. The rest of his reign was the golden age of the Maccabee dynasty. He set to work to restore the kingdom of David ; he refortified Jerusalem, conquered Edom and parts of Transjordania, secured Rome's alliance, took Shechem, and finally, after stubborn resistance, took and destroyed Samaria. The rise of the Maccabees, who were Levites, had had the consequence that the Apocalyptists now looked for a Messiah, not from Judah and the house of David, but from Levi and the house of Aaron ; and to the Galilean author of the chief monument of Hyrcanus' reign, the already mentioned *Testaments of the Twelve Patriarchs*, with its lofty anticipations of the Sermon on the Mount and its enunciation of the Golden Rule, Hyrcanus himself, prophet, priest, and king—king in fact though not in name—seemed the realisation of the Messianic hope ; to him the writer addresses two Messianic hymns.

But the glory soon faded. Hyrcanus' eldest son Aristobulus (105–104) murdered his mother, and his second son Alexander Jannaeus (104–76), who took the royal title, was about as bad as a man could be. A large section of the people, with the sympathy of the Pharisees, revolted against the brutal soldier ; after six years of civil war and much misery he mastered the revolt, and the final picture is of Jannaeus reclining at dinner among his harem and watching the crucifixion of the last 600 rebels. There was no more question of a Messianic kingdom on earth ; the Messiah was again to be of Judah, and the Messianic hope was transferred to a spiritual kingdom in heaven. One thing, however, the Maccabees, from Jonathan to Jannaeus, had achieved. As their forefathers had smitten the Canaanite and the Amalekite, so they had smitten the Helleniser and those neighbouring Syrian cities where Greek culture ruled ; a long list has been compiled of cities destroyed or ruined by them, largely by Jannaeus. The twenty years after Jannaeus' death were merely years of war between his sons Hyrcanus II, the High Priest, and Aristobulus II ; and it was well when in 63 Pompey appeared, took Jerusalem, abolished the monarchy, carried off Aristobulus, placed Hyrcanus under the Roman governor of Syria, and began to restore the towns the Maccabees had destroyed.

The attempt to hellenise Judaea had gone down in blood ; yet for a short time it was to be accomplished from the outside, when few remained in the country who desired it. The real power in Judaea under the weak Hyrcanus II was his minister, the Idumaean Antipater ; after Antipater's murder his son Herod persuaded the triumvirs to make him king of Judaea, and in 37 he took

Jerusalem and established the authority which, by grace of Rome, he was to wield for 43 years. Among the Roman client-kings of the transition period he is the outstanding personality ; able, cruel, and utterly unscrupulous,—the nature of the man is shewn in the recipe for success, as correct as abominable, which he gave to Antony : ' Kill Cleopatra '—he succeeded where the far greater Antiochus Epiphanes had failed, and forcibly made of Judaea a very passable imitation of a Hellenistic kingdom. He was not a Hellenistic king, but an Idumaean barbarian moderately well varnished ; but Hellenism was the only system he could apply to his mixed realm, stretching from the Lebanon to Egypt. His governors and officials reproduced the usual Seleucid forms ; but his numerous Greek cities were only subject towns, and petitioned Rome to transfer them to her province of Syria. As regards the Jews, it seems he never could make up his mind. He tried to conciliate the Pharisees, but butchered the Sadducees ; he forbore to build Caesar-temples in Judaea itself, but built a theatre, amphitheatre, and hippodrome in Jerusalem ; he tried to win the people by rebuilding the Temple with considerable magnificence, while he hankered after being a god himself and ultimately expressed his desire by putting on the Temple an eagle, the worst provocation Jews could receive. He built important cities—Sebaste to replace Samaria, Caesarea on the coast with a harbour larger than Piraeus—and helped to adorn Antioch and many other cities ; but the Jews disliked his Greek building, for the money was wrung from themselves. He needed masses of money ; he confiscated much land, and his private domains and their revenue must have been large ; his taxation was heavy, and was a perpetual source of discontent. He did give peace and prosperity, but he really ruled by fear and held Judaea down by fortresses ; he made and removed High Priests at his pleasure, and the Jews hated him principally for the danger they saw in him to their religion. They rose repeatedly till he became too strong ; his last years were a reign of terror, and they rose again the moment he was dead; and they took a belated revenge by ascribing to him a death too horrible to repeat (it was probably cancer of the bowels). His attempted Hellenisation of Judaea did not outlive him, for it was imposed by force from without on an unwilling people. On his death in A.D. 6 Judaea became a Roman province, and a new chapter of her history opened. It can only be said here that in the future, as in the past, the devotion of the Jew to his nationality and his religion was to prove a stronger force than any pressure from Graeco-Roman civilisation, and that what survived at the end was the full rigour of the Law.

# CHAPTER VII

## TRADE AND EXPLORATION

Alexander had opened to Greek influence a world which stretched from the Aegean to the Hindu Kush, from the Jaxartes to the Cataracts. Had he lived he would have enlarged it further, for at his death he had in hand the exploration of the Caspian and an attempt to complete the sea-route from India to Egypt (of which he had explored the section from India to Babylonia) by circumnavigating Arabia; his ships had already reached Bahrein and Ras Mussendam on one side, Yemen on the other. Though abandoned at his death, these plans were again taken up by his successors; but the only plan carried out in Hellenistic times other than his was the African exploration of the later Ptolemies. In particular, the wonderful voyage made up the coast of Britain to the Elbe and Jutland by Alexander's contemporary, Pytheas of Marseilles, the first Greek to hear of the Arctic Sea, remained fruitless; the empiric geographers even discredited its truth, though the mathematicians Eratosthenes and Hipparchus, with greater knowledge, wisely accepted it.

The Seleucids were too busy in other directions to give much thought to exploration. Seleucus, in accordance with Alexander's scheme to utilise the Persian Gulf, maintained a fleet there, colonised along the lower Tigris, and brought the Gerrhaeans of the Arabian coast into his sphere; but naturally he made no attempt to circumnavigate Arabia and divert the Indian trade from Seleuceia to the Red Sea for Ptolemy's benefit. In the north-east his general Demodamas again crossed the Jaxartes, and he or Antiochus I sent Patrocles, distinguished both as general

and geographer, to explore the Caspian. This sea and the
Aral were joined by one or more salt water connections,
and Alexander had at first taken the Aral for the Sea of
Azov ; subsequently, however, he had wondered whether an
old view, rejected by Aristotle, that the Caspian joined
Ocean might not after all be true. Patrocles started from
the Kizil Usen in Atropatene, and explored the south coast
and parts of the east and west coasts, but how he reached
his conclusion that the Caspian *was* a gulf of Ocean is
difficult to follow ; it may have been due to native stories
badly interpreted, and to the certain fact that he found
boats utilising some channel into the Caspian. Nothing
more was done in the north-east till the Graeco-Bactrian
kings, who seemingly colonised Ferghana, secured touch
with China through Chinese Turkestan, and before 120
were importing silk over the Silk Route ; they paved the
way for the ultimate extension eastward of Graeco-Persian
artistic influences.

From India Seleucus was debarred by the Mauryan
empire, and no Greek in arms again penetrated that country till that empire decayed, when Graeco-Bactrian kings
reached the sea through Sind, and Menander passed Alexander's bounds eastward and perhaps besieged Oude ; but
Megasthenes, whom Seleucus sent as envoy to Chandragupta
at his capital Pataliputra (Patna) on the Ganges, recently
excavated, enormously enlarged Greek *knowledge* of India.
He told some travellers' tales ; but he gave the west its
first knowledge of the Ganges and of the great empire of
Magadha, and his account of the organisation of the country
under Chandragupta's government, which can now be compared with the Artha-śastra, is first-rate. His book remained
for centuries the basis of all knowledge of Northern India.

Seleucid activity was connected with the question of the
Indian or eastern trade, a dominant factor throughout the
period. Our tradition assigns to this trade three main
routes, northern, central, and southern, this last bound up
with the history of the Ptolemies. Of the northern route
little need be said. It was supposed to run by Cabul,

Bactra (Balkh), down the Oxus, across the Caspian, and
along the Kur and Phasis to the Black Sea ; but the tradition is so unsatisfactory, and the problems connected
with the Oxus section so difficult, that it can only have
been of very minor importance. In Seleucus' time it was
still believed that Ocean washed the northern base of the
Himalaya and was near the Jaxartes, and undoubtedly
part of Patrocles' business was to ascertain if a northern
sea-route were possible ; later legends even made him partially explore that sea-route, and brought Indians by it to
the German coast. After Seleucus' death the Seleucids were
cut off from the Black Sea and had no further interest in
the northern route.

During the third century the important route was the
central. This came by sea from India to the Persian
Gulf and up the Tigris to Seleuceia, and was supplemented
by the overland caravan-trade which Seleuceia gathered
in ; one route came thither from India by Candahar–Persepolis–Susa, another, an old main road, ran Candahar–
Herat–Hecatompylos–Ecbatana–Seleuceia, and was joined
at Herat by the Taxila–Cabul–Bactra road. From Seleuceia
the accumulated trade passed westward, either by the new
Seleucid route up the Euphrates to Antioch, or by the old
road east of the Tigris which crossed the river at Jezireh,
swept northwards by Nisibis, where it collected the Armenian
trade, and so to Edessa, whence part took the traditional
road to Damascus and Tyre, while part went to Antioch,
crossing the Euphrates at Zeugma, which now superseded
Thapsacus. From Antioch a great through route ran by
Tarsus and Apamea in Phrygia to the sea at Ephesus (p.
122). The struggles between the Seleucids and the Ptolemies, which lasted from c. 280 to 198, though primarily
due to the dynastic ambition of the Ptolemies and their
desire for empire in the Aegean, were also partly connected
with this trade route ; its outlet at Ephesus changed hands
more than once, and the Ptolemies, by their possession of
Phoenicia and the Marsyas valley between Damascus and
Antioch, were probably able to exercise pressure on Seleu-

cid Damascus. In 198–7 the struggle ended with the expulsion of Egypt from Syria and Asia Minor; and the main lines of trade stood till the Seleucids lost Babylonia, and the central route, in Parthian hands, began to give ground to the southern. Various changes occurred after this; in the first century the route Edessa–Mazaca (Caesarea)–Apamea came into use, cutting out Antioch, and by 100 the short cut from Babylonia to Damascus across the desert by Palmyra was already becoming frequented; finally Rome, following in Pompey's steps, and reaching out from Pontus towards Armenia and the Caucasus for unexploited minerals, brought into some prominence the Caspian–Black Sea route along the Kur.

We turn to the southern route and the Ptolemaic exploration of Africa. This route came from India by sea to depôts in south or south-eastern Arabia, where the Indian shippers landed their goods, and they became part of the Arabian trade; the route was so entirely in Indian and Arabian hands that its very existence in the third century is only certain because Eratosthenes chanced to remark that cinnamon (which grew only in India) came from Arabia east of the Hadramaut. The Arabs guarded their monopoly so jealously that no Indian vessel was allowed inside Bab-el-Mandeb, and the early Ptolemies learnt hardly anything about Arabia; Eratosthenes knew nothing east of the Hadramaut, which Alexander's expedition had already heard of. The history of South Arabia is one of wars and combinations among its various peoples to control the Indian and incense trades; Solomon's Ophir was probably a name applied to whatever locality was at the time the Indian depôt. In the third and second centuries the dominant power was an alliance of the Habashat of Mahra and the Sabaeans of southern Yemen, the chief Indian emporium being the Sabaean Adana (Aden). The accumulated trade was brought north to Petra by the caravans of the Sabaeans and Minaeans, and from Petra it took three lines. Some went either to sea at Gaza, or to Arsinoe (Suez), and from either depôt to Alexandria;

the Gerrhaean caravans took goods between Petra and
Seleuceia across the desert ; and the rest went north.
Normally this last would go by Damascus to Antioch, as
it did after 198, when the importance of the Seleucid acqui-
sition of Syria is shewn by the display of gold, ivory, and
Indian spices made by Antiochus Epiphanes in the great
festival which he celebrated ; but while the Ptolemies held
Syria it also took a route they made by Philadelphia (Rabbath-Ammon) and Gerasa (Jerash) across Galilee to Ptolemais (Acre) and so to Phoenicia ; the importance of Ptolemais is shewn by the town retaining that name under the
Seleucids.  In the first century there was constant change
of power in South Arabia and no strong dominant state ;
but the movement which ultimately led to Egypt sharing
the southern route to India started in a side-issue, the
desire of Ptolemy II for elephants.

Ptolemy I had begun to explore the Red Sea, and his
admiral Philo had discovered the ' Topaz Island ', whence
some Ptolemy, anticipating St. Patrick's feat, expelled the
snakes.  Early in the reign of Ptolemy II his general
Satyrus founded Philotera on the Gulf of Suez ; Arsinoe
at its head must also belong to this reign.  Ptolemy II
then pushed steadily southward ; his generals in succession
founded Myos Hormos (Mussel Harbour) at Kosseir, Berenice of the Trogodytes on the ' Foul ' gulf (*i.e.* full of reefs),
whose ruins (latitude of Assouan) remain, and Ptolemais
of the Elephant-hunts near Suakim ; Ptolemy III founded
Berenice the Golden (perhaps Adulis) near Massowah, and
possibly Koloë (Kohaito) in Ethiopia, whose ruins are said
to be Ptolemaic ; later it was a depôt for ivory, which came
to sea at Adulis.  These settlements were fortified trading
posts and factories rather than towns, and the primary
business of this exploration was to collect ivory and capture elephants for war ; Ptolemy III organised the hunts
on a military basis under a general.  Expeditions fitted
out at the northern Berenice, whither the elephants were
shipped ; a well-equipped road ran thence to Coptos (Koft)
on the Nile, the main elephant park being at Memphis.

A fleet was maintained on the Red Sea for protection against piracy.

The loss of Syria and the Aegean under Ptolemy V induced a change in Egypt's attitude toward the Indian trade ; she now had to rely exclusively on the southern route. Under Ptolemy V, too, the elephant hunts began to die out, and the organisation created for them was presently diverted to the protection of trade and placed under the general of the Thebaid ; in 130 his duties included supervision of shipping and the collection of topazes, and protecting those who brought incense over the Coptos route. More attention was paid to sea-carriage up the Red Sea to Alexandria, as a rival to the Sabaean caravan trade. There was considerable activity in that sea in the second century ; in the north two new stations were founded, Berenice near Elath and Cleopatris near Suez, in the south the southern Arsinoe, not far from Bab-el-Mandeb. Philometor also pushed the boundary south up the Nile to Wady Halfa, and founded new settlements. Probably early in the century Egyptian generals had already reached the ' Horn of the South ', Cape Guardafui in Somaliland, afterwards called the Cape of Spices ; they founded no factories, but discovered many strange tribes of savages to add to the only savages so far known to the Greeks, the Fish-eaters of Gedrosia discovered by Nearchus ; the whole coast from the Gulf of Suez to Cape Guardafui was named Trogodyte (commonly misspelt Troglodyte), and the peoples distinguished as fish-eaters, root-eaters, turtle-eaters, ostrich-eaters, and locust-eaters.

By the end of the second century the growing demand in Italy for the products of Arabia and India made this trade more important than ever to Alexandria, and about 100 the Ptolemies had two strokes of fortune : the Sabaean power broke up, and Hippalus discovered the monsoons, probably long known to Indians, which made it comparatively easy to venture outside Bab-el-Mandeb and even sail to India direct. Full advantage was not taken of the discovery till Rome ruled Egypt, but the later Ptolemies did

a good deal ; their ships visited the South Arabian ports,
discovered Socotra, sometimes sailed direct to India, and
did something to break the monopoly of the Arab middle-
men.  They secured the straits of Bab-el-Mandeb by refounding Deire on the Straits as the southern Berenice,
while the nearer Myos Hormos began to replace the northern
Berenice as the port of Coptos ; and by 78 the general of
the Thebaid had become also general of the Red Sea and
the ' Indian Sea ', a new name which points to regular
connection with India.  Indian traders on their side began
to come direct to the Somali ports, and Indians appeared
in Egypt ; one, Sophon, travelled over the caravan route
to Coptos, and a gravestone with wheel and trisula attests
the presence of Buddhists in Alexandria.  These voyages
brought the first knowledge of southern India ; by 88
Malabar pepper, so much prized later, was known in Athens,
and with it must have come many other products.  Eastern
trade and exploration thus shew a steady evolution throughout the Ptolemaic period, whatever the merits or demerits
of the individual kings ; and when Cleopatra VII suggested abandoning the Mediterranean and ruling the Indian
seas instead she was not talking folly ; she might have
anticipated Albuquerque.

Whether any one at this time ever went south of Cape
Guardafui depends on a story told by Poseidonius.  Under
Ptolemy Euergetes II an Indian, sole survivor of his crew,
was picked up in the Gulf of Suez ; Eudoxus of Cyzicus,
in Ptolemy's service, sailed with the man to India and
back, and subsequently coasted along Africa ' beyond
Ethiopia ' and brought back the prow of a wrecked ship
identified as belonging to Gades in Spain ; he then went
to Gades and tried to sail round Africa to India in the
track of the Gades ship, but turned back just south of
Morocco owing to trouble with his crew.  The whole story
is quite possible ; but it is disfigured with absurd details,[1]
and Poseidonius was hardly the man to sift truth from

[1] For example, it displays ignorance of the Ptolemaic regulations
concerning imported spices, which Eudoxus would have known.

falsehood, nor does he say why he believed it when he disbelieved Herodotus' story of the Phoenician circumnavigation of Africa. The verdict must be 'not proven'.

The chief rival of the Ptolemies in this later period was the wonderful Nabataean city of Petra, "dwelling in the clefts of the rocks ". After the Parthians occupied Babylonia and controlled the central route from India, Petra became one of the greatest marts in Asia ; beside land caravans, her people were now getting sea-traffic through Aelana (Akaba), and they damaged Egypt's direct imports by founding Leuce Come on the Arabian coast, with which Egypt could not deal, and thence dominating the caravan route from Yemen. They extended north as well as south, and even for a time, from 85, ruled Damascus. The Nabataeans had a genius for trading, and Greeks remarked upon the strange fact that they never went to law with one another ; probably, like Chinese merchants, they always honoured their word.

When we come to the details of trade, we are met at the outset by the fact that among all the vast literature of Hellenism no work is recorded professedly dealing with its commerce, important as this was ; nor has modern scholarship yet filled the gap, except for selected portions of the field. Hellenistic trade is a palimpsest, buried under that of the Roman Empire as the Hellenistic road system beneath the Roman ; and one cannot merely argue backwards from the better-known Roman phenomena. Some of the material in later compilers is undoubtedly Hellenistic ; but the whole subject requires a thorough analysis.

The Persians had excluded Greek traders from inner Asia ; and the opening up of this continent by Alexander and his successors, the growing wealth and population of Asia and Egypt, the mass of new cities and settlements, an enhanced standard of living in the upper classes, all gave trade a tremendous impulse. The size of merchant ships increased till it culminated in Hiero's unmanageable Syracosia, with a load capacity of 4,200 tons, while the new habit of sailing direct from point to point instead of coasting increased the speed and scope of commercial operations. Many cities in the third century improved their ports, and the book of Timosthenes of Rhodes *On Harbours* filled the place now held by the *Mediterranean Pilot*. Many Greek cities signed conventions for the regulation of contractual disputes between their citizens, a movement fostered by Rhodes, and something was done towards filling the place now occupied by our banking and credit systems ; letters of credit were known, though not bills of exchange. Every Hellenistic king (unless the Antigonids) was a great merchant, and some Greek cities followed their example and instituted municipal trading ; mines of course had never been private property, but now Rhodes, Cnidus, and others made and stamped their own jars from their own claypits, Priene owned salt-works, Miletus had municipal sheep-runs and wool factories. Merchants too were free of one modern anxiety : demand normally outran supply, and if you could get a thing you could certainly sell it ; judging by Delos, retailers' profits were considerable, even 100 per cent being known, though 20 per cent to 30 per cent was more usual.

The amount of money actually in circulation increased enormously after Alexander instituted his international coinage, as was necessary for the increased trade ; and by the third century the world was divided into two main currency spheres. The Alexander-drachma was identical with the Attic, and this standard was used by Athens, Macedonia and her dependents, the Seleucid Empire and the far east, Pergamum, Bithynia, Cappadocia, the Black Sea (through Lysimachus' money), and Epirus ; it invaded Aetolia and Boeotia, while in 268 Rome, by adopting the denarius, at first equivalent to the Attic drachma, joined this standard. Ptolemy I at first adopted the Rhodian standard, owing to the close trade relations between Egypt and Rhodes ; but after acquiring Phoenicia he changed to the Phoenician standard, to which Rhodes also subsequently adhered ; this standard ruled in Egypt and her dependencies, Carthage and her empire, Rhodes, Syracuse, and Marseilles. The two international standards thus reflected the old opposition of Athens and Phoenicia. The Aeginetan standard was still used at Delphi and elsewhere, but had little importance ; Corinth too maintained her old standard, but her coinage would pass with the Attic. Carthage experimented with token money.

In the third century the trade preponderance definitely shifted from Greece to Egypt, Rhodes, and the coast of Asia ; but too much has been made of this, and the prosperity of Messene *c.* 100 (p. 95) shews the absurdity of talking about the poverty of Greece before Sulla's time. Athens' commerce certainly decayed, until the revival in the late second century ; but Corinth, with the transit trade between Asia and Italy, could in the second century perhaps vie with Ephesus ; in 205 Heracleides said Chalcis had the best equipped market in Hellas, while Boeotia was full of money ; Aetolia notoriously grew wealthy, Ambracia flourished as the port of entry from Italy till Rome diverted the traffic to Dyrrhacium, and the art of Pagasae attests a prosperous existence. What did happen was that much of the great *increase* went to the new countries ; in 170 the 2 per cent import and export duty produced at Rhodes a million drachmae, as against 200,000 at Athens in 401. But it is curious that most of the wealthiest cities of the world—Seleuceia, Antioch, Rhodes, Ephesus, Cyzicus, Corinth, Delos—were fed by *transit* trade ; Ephesus, a transit centre, gained steadily on her rival, manufacturing Miletus ; the fact suggests the dominant part played in international trade by oriental produce and manufactures. Beside Miletus, the chief exceptions were Alexandria and Pergamum, with their serf and slave factories, and Tyre ; but Alexandria and Tyre did great transit trades also. It is interesting to compare Alexandria, the greatest Hellenistic port, with Puteoli in Campania, when after 88 the latter became Italy's port of entry for the eastern trade. Alexandria imported all timber, all metals, wool, purple, marble, fine wines, spices, and horses, a formidable list ; nevertheless her exports—wheat, paper, glass, linen, woollen goods, ointments, perfumes, ivory, and luxury articles

generally—far exceeded her imports ; hence came part of
the Treasure of the Ptolemies. But at Puteoli imports far
exceeded exports ; and as Rome did not flood the Aegean
with coin, the balance represented a new thing in the world,
the plunder of the Roman tax-farmer.

We turn to objects of trade. As regards metals, the
general outline is clear : except for iron and copper, the
eastern Mediterranean was worked out. The gold of Pac-
tolus and Tmolus in Lydia, and of Asia Minor generally,
belonged to the past, as did the alluvial deposit of Scapte-
syle and the mines of Mount Bermion and Pieria in Macedonia ; some mines along the Strymon survived, but no
Antigonid king coined gold. There was some gold and
silver in Bactria and Carmania, but how far these provinces were exploited cannot be said ; the Bactrian kings
probably got gold from the Altai, as Cyzicus imported
electrum for her coinage from the Urals. The Ptolemies,
pushing southward, opened up valuable gold mines in Nubia
and in the mountains above Berenice the Golden, and had
a gold coinage from the start. But much of the gold used
must have come from Spain and India.—Silver is simple.
Mount Pangaeus in Macedonia kept producing throughout
the period ; Laurium failed steadily, and by Augustus'
time only the dumps were being worked over. There was
nothing else ; and the world was supplied from Spain, the
' Treasury of Empire ', where silver was nowise accounted
of ; it came from Gades through Carthage, and when
Jonah about 300 desired to fly to Tartessus (*i.e.* at that
date Gades) he at once found a ship going there. The
world required silver in masses for coinage, but the supply
was ample ; the Ptolemies could put Egypt on a silver
basis and amass a great treasure, and in 91 silver plate
was common at Messene, a little town in a backwater.—
The entire copper belt, from Cyprus to Sinai, was long
controlled by the Ptolemies, and Cyprus was probably too
rich in copper to fear even Spain's rivalry. Euboean
copper was worked out, but the Attalids had some local
mines.—Iron was still found everywhere ; and if certain

mines, like the Laconian, gave out, there were valuable
deposits in the islands never even touched.  The finest
quality, which came by sea to Cyzicus, was produced by
the Chalybes, now scattered about Pontus and Armenia ;
Chinese iron was also highly spoken of, but would hardly
come further west than Bactria.—Tin came from Cornwall
and Brittany, at first through Gades and Carthage, but
after 300 in increasing measure up the Loire and Garonne
and overland to Marseilles.  Possibly there was some in
Spain, but the Tin Islands are either a myth or a misunderstanding.—Quicksilver, in the form of cinnabar, chiefly
used to make vermilion, was obtained from three sources :
the Cappadocian mines which had once supplied Sinope
with her ' Sinopic earth ', the new Zizima mines near
Laodicea the Burnt, and a deposit near Ephesus ;  the
whole supply now came to Ephesus.

Speaking generally, mining was the gravest blot on
Hellenism.  There are shocking stories of the mortality
in the Laurium and the Cappadocian quicksilver mines ;
but it must suffice to quote Agatharcides' description of
the Nubian gold mines, which the Ptolemies worked, not
only with slaves and criminals (the usual practice), but
with prisoners of war, who might be free Greeks.  The
younger men, crawling with lamps on their foreheads,
tunnelled the quartz by hand, following the veins of gold.
The hewn quartz was dragged out by the children, and the
older men broke it small with hammers ;  the fragments
were then, preparatory to washing, ground to dust in spar-
mills, turned, not by oxen, but by the women, five to a
spar and naked.  They were guarded by armed Nubians ;
all were fettered and flogged, and were worked without
rest or care for their bodies ;  and all, says Agatharcides
drily, welcomed death when it came.

As to foodstuffs, corn was probably the greatest of all
trades, not excepting raw silver ;  Athens, Corinth, Delos,
many islands, Ionia, and perhaps other cities, were normally importers, while the great producers were Egypt (with
the Cyrenaica), and the Crimea.   Greece was supplied from

Egypt and the Crimea ; when in the second century the latter source began to fail, Numidia was ready to take its place, and in 180 Masinissa sent Delos corn at a cheap rate. Whether Babylonia competed with Egypt in supplying Ionia, or what happened to Babylonia's surplus, is unknown ; our ignorance of the whole Seleucid interior is colossal. It is now known that some Sicilian corn came to Greece ; but in any case Egypt's supremacy in the wheat market was unquestioned. The depôts of the international corn trade were Rhodes and Delos.—Wine was produced everywhere, but fine wines were a speciality of two countries : North Syria, whose wine was exported from Laodicea on the Sea, and Ionia with the coastal islands (except Samos) ; Lesbos, Chios, Cos, Cnidus, Ephesus, Smyrna, Tmolus, and the volcanic Katakekaumene were all famous. Alexandria insisted on Ionian wines, whatever the duty, as London insists on champagne, while Laodicean wine travelled even to South Arabia ; it was the vineyards which prevented Ionia growing enough corn, for vines gave roughly five times the profit of wheat off the same acreage. —Of other foodstuffs, Athens exported the finest oil, Athens and the Cyclades honey, Byzantium salt fish (partly Euxine re-exports), Bithynia cheese, Pontus fruit and nuts, Babylonia and Jericho dates ; the dried figs of Antioch on the Maeander, the raisins of Berytus, and the prunes of Damascus were celebrated. Indian sugar was known, but was used only as a medicine.

As to textiles. Alexandria supplied the world with linen, her only rival being the factories in bat-eating Borsippa ; the flax industries of Elis and Judaea were much later.— Aeolis and the Cyrenaica both produced wool, and Pergamum and Alexandria exported woollen goods, but the real centre of the wool industry was Miletus ; her home-grown wool was as yet the best in the world, though all Lydia and Phrygia wove wool ; the district about the salt Lake Tatta, where water was sold for money, and the Katakekaumene, whose wool was woven at Laodicea on the Lycus, carried great flocks. Doubtless too there was a large wool industry in Syria, for it cannot have started full-blown under Rome. Several places had specialities, like the curtains and gold-woven cloth of Pergamum, the carpets of Aeolis, and the rough cloaks of Cilicia ; while Alexandria also turned out cheap goods to trade to African natives.—Cotton, once cultivated in Assyria, was only known as a curiosity, though Indian muslins must have been imported, at least in the first century.—Silk probably came exclusively through India ; before 120 the Bactrians were getting Chinese silk overland, but there is nothing to shew it came west before the Roman empire ; heavy silks seem unknown, and Isidore knows nothing of the Silk Route or of any route through Bactria. Cos throughout the period imported Indian silk on bobbins and wove it into diaphanous stuffs for women's wear ; between wine, silk, and faith-healing, Cos prospered enormously, but the little island could hardly supply the world, and there must already have been a large silk industry in Phoenicia, for silk became so common that in 91 the women at Messene had to be prohibited from wearing transparent dresses during initiation. But Cleopatra's silks conceivably came from India direct.

A complete list of the known specialities of different places, produced or manufactured, would be a long one. Alexandria supplied the world with paper (papyrus), Alexandria and Sidon with glass. Parchment, from the second century, was Pergamum's monopoly, but the story that Eumenes II invented it is untrue ; it had long been known, and what he did was to utilise his wealth in cattle and leather, and his slave factories, to organise mass production. Macedonia and Mount Ida in the Troad competed in supplying the world with pitch ; the Antigonids had some system of export duties or licenses under which they lowered the price to their friends and raised it to their enemies. Egypt drew her bitumen for embalming from the Dead Sea fisheries, and it was plentiful in Babylonia ; bituminous earth, used for protecting vines from insects, was exported from Rhodes and Seleuceia in Pieria. Alexander's discovery of petroleum on the Oxus was never followed up. Parian marble held its own everywhere, and after 166 Athens was doing a large trade in Pentelic ; many others were used, sometimes only locally, but the taste for and trade in coloured marbles from Euboea and Thasos and serpentine from Egypt and Tenos must be largely Roman, for it was they who opened up the green marble of Taygetus and exploited the red-veined marble of Docimeum, only sparingly worked in Hellenistic times. Macedonia supplied Greece with timber, and treeless Egypt drew on the cedars of Lebanon (always a royal domain), the pines of Cyprus, and the oaks of Bashan, while through Arsinoe in Cilicia she tapped the Taurus forests ; by the time she lost her northern empire she was ready to import timber from the Trogodyte coast. Rare woods came from Pontus and Somaliland, and ebony, known at Delos, from India. The world's windows were made of Cappadocian talc. Egypt exported some granite, for about 130 it was used for the new docks at Delos. Purple mussels and sponges were fished for at many places in Greece, but the manufacture of purple was still the principal industry of Phoenicia, where Tyre and Aradus became exceedingly prosperous ; dyeing was also carried on at Teos in the third century, and in the first was a great industry in Asia Minor. Ivory from India was a Seleucid monopoly until between 269 and 250 Ptolemy II threw enough African ivory on the market to break the price ; with the decay of the Mauryas and the exploitation of Ethiopia African ivory must have gained steadily on its rival, and in the first century the Ptolemies made magnificent gifts of ivory to the temple of Didyma. Throughout the third and early second centuries there was a steady influx of slaves into the Greek cities from Thrace, Syria, and Asia Minor ; even before 200 there was *possibly* a slave market at Delos, though on a modest scale. Lastly, Pontus, whose great wealth was not really exploited till the first century, was the chief source of medical drugs. The importance to a city of some speciality, however modest, is illustrated by the prosperity which Tanagra derived from the manufacture of its little statuettes.

Of the luxury articles, gems came largely from India and Arabia, though Egypt produced amethysts and beryls, and obtained topazes from the Red Sea and emeralds from Talmis in Ethiopia ; India and the Persian Gulf sent pearls, highly valued by women as ornaments. But whether women used precious stones much seems doubtful ; diamonds were unknown, rubies extremely rare, and (except for pearls) Theophrastus deals only with the use of stones for gem engraving ; the sards of Sardes and Babylonia were noted, and gem engraving flourished at Alexandria. One trade, amber, was dead ; the Gallic migrations had destroyed the machinery of the old amber route from the Baltic to the Adriatic, and amber was a curiosity only till the route was re-established in Nero's reign. Tortoiseshell came from the Trogodyte coast, and Alexandria was a great centre of goldsmith's work ; but the real luxury trade was in spices. The demand was vast. India sent cinnamon and cassia, spikenard from the Himalaya, nard and bdellium (the two latter also came from Gedrosia) ; Arabia, beside frankincense, chiefly sent myrrh. Pisidia produced styrax and various gums, which probably made the prosperity of Selge ; Lake Gennesareth supplied scented rushes ; Jericho had a monopoly of balsam, the plant having been uprooted (as the Dutch once treated the clove) everywhere but in the famous balsam gardens, which Antony later presented to Cleopatra. Cinnamon was highly prized, but the trade was so entirely in Arab hands that Greeks believed it grew in Arabia and Somaliland. Alexandria was the centre of the spice trade ; spices were a royal monopoly, supervised by an official to whom all spices entering Egypt had to be delivered ; the working up of these imports into ointments and perfumes, and the export of the finished article, constituted a great industry. What an ointment now meant may be illustrated by that used at the coronation of the Parthian kings, which contained 27 separate ingredients, as against four in that used to anoint the High Priests at Jerusalem. What India took at this time in exchange for her exports seems unknown. But South Arabia was supposed to take only styrax, Laodicean wine, and Alexandrian glass and cloth ; hence arose the legend that South Arabia was bursting with accumulated money, a legend which played its part in Gallus' ill-fated expedition under Augustus.

One commodity, frankincense, stood apart from all others ; for it was as much a religion as a trade. No worship, Greek, Jewish, or barbarian, could be carried on without it, and it smoked on every altar of the ' inhabited world '. The quantities required were great ; Alexander captured 500 talents weight at Gaza, and the altar of Bel at Babylon alone consumed 1,000 talents annually. The frankincense country was the coastal district of South Arabia from the Yemen mountains eastward through the Hadramaut to beyond the plain of Dhofar, and the opposite Somali coast. The trees were sacred ; only men of certain families might tap them, and then only with religious rites, for they were drawing the life-blood of a divine creature ; the trees themselves were propitiated during tapping by burning styrax incense to them, as to gods. In the factories at Alexandria where frankincense was handled the workpeople on leaving work were stripped and searched like Kaffirs in the Kimberley diamond mines. Yet so little luxurious was Greek luxury that this most valued of all products, after all the expense and danger of its long caravan journey, fetched on reaching the Mediterranean just 5s. a lb. Whether Egypt ever succeeded in obtaining frankincense direct from Somaliland without Arab intermediaries does not appear.

The great trading races, beside the Greeks, were the southern Arabs and Nabataeans, already noticed, and the Phoenicians ; Phoenician merchants had even followed Alexander's terrible march through Gedrosia, and their later settlements on Delos shew that their keenness remained unimpaired. There is no evidence that the Jews played any particular part in commerce. Two cities, Rhodes and Cyzicus, kept out non-Greeks ; but this was

P

unusual. Foreign traders who settled in a city generally formed an association of their nationals, and probably brought their own gods ; the type may be seen in the Phoenician Poseidoniastae at Delos, whose establishment comprised a temple, porticoes for displaying merchandise, and ancillary buildings. Associations are found, however, whose basis was not nationalism but a particular trade, as the Italian oil-traders on Delos, or the associations at Athens and Alexandria of all export merchants. The later Hellenistic period saw a new phenomenon, the appearance in the Levant of the Roman trader, encouraged by the creation of the free port of Delos in 166 and the formation of the province of Asia in 130.

' Roman ' traders included all of Roman allegiance, some being Italian Greeks ; the first one known, Minatus, a Campanian, reached Delos in the third century, and by 230 there were some in Epirus. By 130 they were numerous in Greece, were much the largest body on Delos, and were pouring into Asia ; their way was made easy by the denarius (p. 201). By 74 they were plentiful in Bithynia, but did not penetrate further eastward in Asia Minor ; but after Pompey annexed Syria a strong body settled in Antioch, and under Augustus they reached Petra, which Greeks never did, but only when Petra was almost a Roman protectorate. In Alexandria they appear from 127 onwards, but were of small account ; Rome's chief contribution before Augustus to Egyptian business was the creation of a tourist traffic up the Nile. The Roman trader was not at first unpopular, either in Greece or Asia ; he often became a citizen, married a Greek wife, owned land, took part in the city life, perhaps held a magistracy, and sent his son to the gymnasium and through the ephebate ; some, as Zosimus at Priene, imitated the wealthy Greeks by spending money freely on municipal benefactions. They formed regular business houses with branches. But many were not free ; out of 231 Romans of known condition at Delos, 88 were free (27 being Italian Greeks), 95 freedmen, and 48 slaves, and this is said to be a high proportion of

free. They were expected, and sometimes even ordered
by the Roman Senate, to conform to the laws of the city
they settled in, but they had one enormous advantage over
their Greek and Oriental competitors : they could, and
often did, appeal from the city law to Roman law, and got
the benefit of edicts or allowances from complacent Roman
governors; the dice were, politically, weighted in their favour,
one reason why they clung to countries under Roman rule.
This ended, especially in Asia, by arousing a discontent
which commercial rivalry would not have done ; for the
Greek, given fair play, could hold his own in *that* field.

In 166 Rome broke Rhodes' power by making Delos
a free port, *i.e.* abolishing import, export, and harbour
duties ; and though Rhodes remained commercially prosperous, Delos soon took her place as the centre of international transit trade in the Aegean. The destruction of
Corinth in 146 gave Delos a further opportunity. Mommsen's view, that Rome destroyed Corinth for commercial
reasons, is at last being questioned ; for it is unlikely
that Corinth excluded Romans from participation in her
trade, and though her destruction was ultimately of advantage to the Romans on Delos, it is doubtful whether Mummius really looked so far ahead ; probably the act was
merely a warning to Greece. Something can be learnt
about the trade of Greece itself after 146 by noting where
Roman traders settled ; the strong body at Thespiae suggests that Thespiae secured some of Corinth's transit trade,
and they invaded Epirus because the desolated country
was now given over to breeding cattle and horses. It
seems that the modern ports of Salonica (Thessalonica)
and Patras (Patrae) now did little trade ; Thessalonica
fell with the Antigonids, and Macedonia's commercial
centre was again Amphipolis, while Italian traffic still
crossed from Brindisi to Ambracia, as in Pyrrhus' day ;
Patras only became important when Augustus made it a
colony. The one business the Romans perhaps created
was the supply of trade statuary to Italy (p. 260).

Delos in the third century had still been the holy island ;

but her trade had steadily increased with the increasing prosperity of her Asiatic background, as is shewn by the continued fall in agricultural rents after 250 and the enormous rise in house rents, and she was already a great corn-market, to which came the Antigonid officials from Thessalonica ; probably she owed part of her prosperity to Antigonid help. Many kings adorned her with buildings ; such were the house built by Ptolemy I for the ship he dedicated, and the porticoes of Antigonus Gonatas, Attalus I, and Philip V, this last certainly meant for the use of merchants. When Rome gave her back to Athens in 166 she was not badly equipped, in spite of her poor harbour, for an international commercial centre ; and under the rule of Athens and the Athenian cleruchs who expelled the Delians and settled on the island there was a vast influx of foreigners ; Romans flocked thither to meet the Orientals, as did the Orientals to meet the Romans. Her prosperity reacted on her mistress, and down to 88 Athens enjoyed an Indian summer ; shipping again sought the Piraeus, wealth increased, business men supplanted the old landowners, and larger families became not uncommon ; beside her exports of Pentelic marble and statuary, Athens manufactured articles of domestic use,—vases, lamps, beds. But this aftermath of prosperity originated in a great injustice to the Delians, and was partly due, not to Athenians, but to the Roman and the Phoenician who had worked in under Athens' skin.

In 130 the slaves on Delos rose ; the Athenian cleruchs were helpless, and the rising was suppressed by the whole business community. Thereon the rule of the cleruchs ended, and Delos became a unique kind of state-form : the foreign business associations became ' settlers ', and in their totality apparently constituted ' Delos ', seemingly without any city forms at all, but under an Athenian governor [1] ; that is, political precedents were subordinated to the requirements of trade. If gold can make a golden

[1] This was only the state-form composed of *politeumata* taken one step further.

age, Delos now enjoyed one ; she had part of Rhodes'
transit trade, most of Corinth's, and all that she created
for herself from the growing Italian demand for luxuries.
Building was taken up on an extensive scale by individuals
and corporations ; existing houses were divided into tene-
ments, and new warehouses erected along the sea-front,
with quays lined with Egyptian granite ; by 125 the artificial harbour, long in hand, was completed, and there rose a
mass of temples, magazines, meeting-places for the various
nationalities and their worships, culminating at the end
of the century in the market-place of the Italians ; cheap
building, much of it, adorned with uninspiring statues and
mosaics copied from an older art. Every Asiatic people
met there,—Egyptians, Phoenicians, Syrians, men from
Pontus and Bithynia ; Minaeans from South Arabia
brought their god Oadd ; by 100 there were Jews, who
built a synagogue. Between the third and first centuries
the Phoenician associations steadily became less religious
and more mercantile. Greeks were represented chiefly by
Athenians and cosmopolites like Simalos of Cyprus, who
acquired Tarentine citizenship and enrolled his son in an
Attic deme ; few came from Greece itself, Macedonia, the
Islands, or the old Greek cities of Asia. Far the strongest
element now was the Romans ; they were favoured by
the Athenian governors, Athens having consistently been
Rome's friend, and became the real power in the island.

Delos was purely a place of transit trade, and as such
received every kind of traffic, while the big motley population crowded on the little island made her of necessity
still an emporium of foodstuffs ; but much of her wealth
was due to a less reputable cause. The growing plantation
system of great estates in Italy and Sicily demanded masses
of slaves, while Rhodes, politically weakened, was no longer
an effective check upon piracy ; and Delos and the pirates,
in unholy alliance, undertook to supply what Italy required. Delos became the greatest slave-market yet known,
and as the eastern governments began to grow weaker
their subjects were drained away ; Bithynia is said to

have been half depopulated. Few Greeks were guiltless where slavery was concerned, but the decadence of Delos under Roman influence here stood confessed ; for while Apollo in Greek Delphi was doing what he could to free slaves, Apollo in cosmopolitan Delos looked down on such iniquity as no Greek soil had yet seen : the once holy island, within whose bounds none had made war on another, now boasted that she could easily handle over 10,000 slaves a day. The gold of the golden age was indeed tainted. The shame of Delos was reflected upon Athens ; but, except for Athenians, it does not appear that any Greeks had much part in this disgraceful traffic, which was mainly conducted by Romans and Orientals. Finally the power and audacity of the pirates, organised as a regular state in western Cilicia, compelled the Roman government to interfere, and the hospitality of Delos to the scourge ceased ; but it was only historical justice that the city, after being sacked in 88 by a general of Mithridates, the ally of the pirates, was in 69 finally destroyed as a trade centre by a pirate captain.

Of trade after the great catastrophe of 88 and the massacre of the Roman traders in Asia (p. 38) there seems little to say. Greece and Delos never recovered ; Puteoli, the ' lesser Delos ', took Delos' place as the emporium for eastern imports into Italy ; the Orientals followed the trade, and in Puteoli were settlements of Nabataeans, Phoenicians, and Syrians from Heliopolis and Palmyra. Roman traders flocked back to Asia after Sulla's settlement, and large bodies are known in many places, while Nabataeans settled in Miletus. Alexandria was not affected by the catastrophe ; but Phoenicia must have suffered from the disintegration of her Seleucid background, and the troubles of Asia generally at the hands of the contending generals in the Roman civil wars must have been reflected in trade depression ; and it seems probable that in this sphere, as in many others, the re-establishment of peace and decent government by Augustus came none too soon.

# CHAPTER VIII

## LITERATURE AND LEARNING

It was natural that, after the great upheaval of civilisation caused by Alexander's career, the number of those who tried in some fashion publicly to express themselves should increase enormously. Education, as the age progressed, became widely spread, but formed, as to-day, not one public but two: one of the highly educated, and a larger one which had education enough to read greedily but not to read seriously; both publics were catered for accordingly, one by the specialist, the other by popular literature. The systematisation in Greek hands of the production of papyrus, and subsequently of parchment, combined with the employment of educated slaves, enabled books to be produced on a scale heretofore unknown; and therewith presently appeared two new phenomena, the literary man, who wrote, not because he had something to say, but because to write books about other books was a pleasant thing to do, and the bibliophile, like Apellicon of Teos (c. 100) who made the romantic discovery of part of Aristotle's library hidden in a cellar. The great Hellenistic capitals enabled writers to concentrate in or for certain centres where there was a numerous public; while the improvement of communications, and the spread of a common civilisation and the 'common speech' over a large part of the 'inhabited world', meant that even the man from an outland city, like Borysthenes or Artemita, was secure of an audience; a considerable list has been made of writers from the Euphrates provinces. The rulers of the new kingdoms were generally helpful and

215

sometimes enthusiastic ; learning became a power, and was for a time rated above wealth. Poets or historians might be the friends of kings, philologists or architects their ambassadors ; an apt quotation once turned the fate of a treaty. Writers began to obtrude, instead of concealing, their personalities ; no one can guess what Thucydides was like, or the author of the story of Ahab and Elijah, but we all know Polybius and the Preacher.

Above all, the kings established libraries in their capitals. The idea of a library had probably come down from Assyria and Babylon, but before Alexander only an occasional tyrant had had the money to collect books ; and if Aristotle formed the first private library on any scale, Alexander supplied the means. State libraries now appeared at Antioch and Pergamum, and *possibly* at Rhodes ; but everything was eclipsed by the famous library in the Brucheion at Alexandria, founded by Ptolemy I and arranged under Ptolemy II, who founded the ' daughter ' library in the Serapeum, perhaps for duplicates. Beside the Library, Ptolemy I founded the Museum ; whether or no Demetrius of Phalerum gave him the idea, the foundation was in Aristotle's spirit. Henceforth, though Athens kept philosophy, Alexandria eclipsed her as the world's centre of science and literature, which sucked in workers from every quarter. Little is known of the Museum, an association of learned men, at their head a priest of the Muses, who lived and laboured in the building at Ptolemy's charges, freed by him from all worldly cares ; Timon the Sceptic called them ' fatted fowls in a coop '. It was broken up by Euergetes II, but seemingly re-formed again. The Library was in charge of an official Librarian, who was also the crown prince's tutor. Ships from every country dumped book rolls on the quays, and it was well on in Ptolemy II's reign before they were sorted out and arranged ; by the first century the Library had grown to perhaps 700,000 rolls, though the figure is uncertain. What Caesar burnt was not the Library but either some book-dump on the quay or books stacked there to be carried

off ; in compensation Antony gave to Cleopatra the 200,000
rolls of the library of Pergamum. The Alexandrian
Library was broken up and partly destroyed in A.D. 272,
when Aurelian burnt the Brucheion.

Of the six librarians who covered the great period [1]—
Zenodotus of Ephesus, Apollonius ' the Rhodian ', Eratosthenes (p. 246), Aristophanes of Byzantium, another
Apollonius, and Aristarchus of Samothrace—four at least
were philologists ; philology, already started by Theophrastus' pupil Praxiphanes of Mytilene, was at Alexandria to
find new scope and become the basis of her achievement.
Zenodotus invented textual criticism by comparison of
MSS, and the Alexandrian school established and handed
down the texts of the Greek classics and also introduced
accentuation. Zenodotus settled a text of Homer, ex-
punging many interpolated verses ; Aristophanes and
Aristarchus worked on his text, and our vulgate text is
largely Aristarchus' ; many other writers were similarly
treated. Zenodotus also began arranging the books ; he
took the epic and lyric poets, and his helpers, the poets
Lycophron and Alexander the Aetolian, the comedies and
tragedies respectively ; Callimachus (who was never
librarian) arranged the prose works and made and published
the catalogue, a stupendous work called *Pinakes* which
formed a guide to the authors, with biographies and other
information ; Aristophanes wrote a Supplement, while a
similar work was afterwards compiled for the library at
Pergamum, probably by Crates of Mallos. These men
made philology a science at which many worked down to
Roman times, producing commentaries, criticism, and a
whole literature of rare words, the foundation of lexico-
graphy, like the list of Macedonian words compiled by the
Macedonian Amerias. Part of the commentary on Demosthenes by Didymus of Alexandria (*c.* 40) has been recovered ;
it is really a substantive work on Demosthenes, full of
citations from historians and supplying useful historical

[1] The list *Oxyrynchos Papyri* X, 1241 omits Eratosthenes, who
is certain from Suidas.

material. Didymus wrote on most authors, and is said to have produced more books (3,500 rolls) than any man before or since ; he earned his nickname Chalcenteros (Brazen-Guts).

Including science and philosophy, over 1,100 Hellenistic writers are known, but most are little but names ; for the great bulk of Hellenistic literature has entirely perished. We possess only wreckage, though the sands of Egypt are steadily increasing the amount. How came so few Hellenistic writers to reach Constantinople ? The accepted explanation, that the Attic reaction of the second century A.D. made men contemptuous of Hellenistic work, seems inadequate ; for the worst of all Hellenistic styles, the Asianic, was still alive two centuries later. Third-hand compendiums, no doubt, ultimately killed off the original historians ; Hellenism was itself responsible for the modern fallacy of the short cut to knowledge. Many writers too perished because they were not read in schools ; one school about 2 B.C. was using Eudoxus' out-of-date astronomy. But, generally speaking, the causes of the great wreck, and the part played by Rome, are still obscure.

We may take the poets first. Poetry, by Alexander's day, had been almost crushed to death by the weight of the great masters ; none could approach them, and it was hardly worth trying. The one name of repute since Euripides was Antimachus of Colophon ; his *Lyde*, a collection of short poems on love themes addressed to his mistress, was imitated by Asclepiades of Samos (*c.* 300 ; lyrics rather than elegiacs), who invented the verse called ' Asclepiad ', by Hermesianax of Colophon (*c.* 290), who enumerated various people of importance who had been in love in their time—very poor stuff, and by Philetas of Cos (*c.* 300). Philetas' elegies to his wife Bittis were prized by the Augustans ; but the tutor of Ptolemy II and author of the first Greek lexicon really lived through the circle of scholars he formed, among them Zenodotus, Herondas, Callimachus, and Theocritus. This sort of love poetry did in form influence Propertius ; but in Greece its future was to be the epigram, of which Asclepiades was a master.

Tragedies continued to be manufactured in quantities, for quantities were required for the festivals, new and old ; seven writers of the early third century had enough temporary repute to be called the Pleiad, but the only one worth notice is Menedemus' young friend Lycophron, who went back to Phrynichus and wrote on contemporary subjects : a play on the sufferings of Cassandreia under its proletariat distatorship, and a satyr play on his master Menedemus, where doubtless, as with the carved Sileni in Plato, the grotesque shell was meant to reveal the divinity within ; we possess from this play a charming account of Menedemus' famous suppers, banquets of wit rather than of wine.   Comedy, on the other hand, flourished exceedingly till Philemon's death in 262 closed the roll of comedians.   Its form, the so-called New Comedy, or comedy of manners without a chorus, lineally descended from Aristophanes, was the most living style of art at Athens during the period—64 writers are known—but it was so typically Athenian that all attempts to transplant it to Alexandria or elsewhere failed ; Philemon's death dramatically coincided with the end of Athens' political importance.   The great name of the New Comedy is Menander (d. 292–1) ; enough has now been recovered from Egypt to enable us to study him directly, and not merely through Terence.   His importance to his age is undoubted ; also he was tremendously quotable, which helped him to live ;   three of his lines have become English proverbs.[1] Witty, elegant, more at home with men's mistresses than with their wives, he set a mark on literary history which lasted till Shakespeare and Molière ;   and it was not his fault that what he drew from life (of a sort) became for centuries a stereotyped convention.   It is proper to praise him without stint ;   certainly he would act well, while occasionally something better—Davus in the *Hero*, Glycera

---

[1] Whom the gods love die young.   Evil communications corrupt good manners.   Conscience makes cowards of the bravest.

in the *Perikeiromene*—does glimmer through his facile
tolerance. But to the writer he and his imitators seem
about the dreariest desert in literature. Life is not entirely
composed of seductions and unwanted children, coinci-
dences and recognitions of long-lost daughters, irate fathers
and impertinent slaves. Doubtless he had met these
things ; but, though his characters were types, the life was
not typical. The world, however, has decided that it *was*
typical, and on material drawn from the New Comedy is
chiefly based the traditional belief in Athens' decadence ;
it is perhaps too late to get the verdict reversed. But
anyone who wished could draw from the post-war London
stage a much more exciting picture of England's decadence.
We should rate the latter at its true value ; why accept
the former ?

Except for comedy, the revival of poetry largely centred
on Alexandria. Men's aim everywhere was rather to keep
poetry alive than to challenge the great masters, and for
this purpose to utilise the manifold interests of the enlarged
life of the time and bring poetry into touch with what men
were doing and thinking. This took many forms ; the
principal ones were the poetry of instruction, the idyll and
epigram (both of which included elegiacs), and the romantic
epic. It is curious that instructive poetry, allied to science,
was the one form not domiciled at Alexandria, the home
of science. Its chief name is Aratus of Soli, Antigonus
Gonatas' friend, who passed his time between Athens and
Pella, and wrote the hymns for Gonatas' marriage (276).
His *Phaenomena*, a versification in hexameters of Eudoxus'
old star-catalogue, was one of the most read and be-praised
poems of the age ; it helped to inspire Vergil's *Georgics*,
and its influence lasted into the Middle Ages. The popularity of this dry astronomical work is a puzzle. One
critic thinks it appealed to the public which desired knowledge conveyed in an easy form ; another, that men
welcomed its plain straightforwardness as a relief from poetic
conceits. Both may be true ; but I would rather attribute
its success mainly to its illustration of the Stoic doctrine

of Providence, drawn from the utility of the stars to sailor
and husbandman,—a note struck at once in the noble
prelude, akin to Cleanthes' great hymn ; and it was as an
appeal to Stoics that Paul quoted it.    Aratus set a fashion ;
Nicander of Colophon, *c.* 200, versified a scientific treatise
on poisons and antidotes, which was translated into Latin,
and also works on agriculture and bee-keeping, which
Vergil read, while Ovid used his collection of *Metamor-
phoses.*    Various poems by others on astronomy, geography,
and fishing are recorded ;   they probably had little to do
with poetry.    One historical poem remains, the *Alexandra*,
attributed to Lycophron but probably later ;  it belongs to
no class.    It survived because the utter obscurity of its
diction interested philologists ;   but it handled in small
compass a big theme, the struggle between Europe and
Asia from Troy to Rome.

The characteristic Alexandrian form was the Idyll, which
means a little picture complete in itself ;  it might take
many shapes, and was sometimes intended for recitation.
The master of the idyll, to his contemporaries, and the
most typical Alexandrian poet, was Callimachus of Cyrene
(*c.* 310–245), courtier and philologist.    He had been Philetas'
pupil, and he made the elegiac the fashionable vehicle it
was to remain.    We possess now some of his hymns, and
parts of the little epic *Hecale*, of a poem on Arsinoe's death,
and of his most important work, the *Aitia*—' causes ' of
various usages and cults.    But, were it not for his epigrams,
one might almost say he was not a poet but a learned man
writing verses.    All that care and polish could do, he did ;
and one gratefully admits that he avoided sentimentality
and rhetoric.    He was indeed scrupulous in avoidance ;   a
later critic called him " the faultless ", perhaps his sufficient
condemnation.    For he could not let himself go ;   and in
all his fastidious variations on a dead mythology—dead
even in his day to the educated—there is scarcely a line
with a human touch, and certainly not a line which ever
made anyone's pulse beat.    He is form without substance.
He set a standard, and influenced many ;   in form, he in-

fluenced Catullus ; but in spirit he had no spark of the fire which burst out in *Odi et amo*. But curiously enough his younger contemporary Euphorion had more effect later than he, though what of him has been recovered seems an inferior imitation of Callimachus. Euphorion lived at the court of Alexander of Corinth (*c.* 250), and afterwards became librarian at Antioch ; he played a part in the Augustan age and at one time affected Vergil.

Callimachus' epigrams, however, are on a different level ; there he can sometimes touch us. The beautiful lines on the death of his friend Heraclitus are familiar to many through Cary-Johnson's version in *Ionica* ; as good in another vein is the man deterred from marrying out of his station by hearing the children, at play with their tops, calling to one another ' Keep to your own line ' ; the little speech of the nautilus shell is unsurpassed for grace. But indeed a feature of the age was the widespread mastery of the epigram and the fact that in it writers were not ashamed to shew their feelings. It flourished from Leonidas and Asclepiades in the early period to the Syrian group— Antipater of Sidon, Meleager and Philodemus of Gadara— who lived in the political decay of the first century ; indeed it outlasted every other form of poetry and perished only with the Greek language. Meleager's love-poems in their grace and tenderness recall the flowers he so loved ; he compiled for one of his friends what was thought to be the first anthology or ' flower-garland ' of poetry until earlier examples were discovered in Egypt. Philodemus merely illustrates the luxurious sensuality of a Syrian city ; it is strange to recognise in him the laborious philosophic compiler of the Herculaneum papyri.

Callimachus was the arbiter of his day. But one man put the idyll to another use : Theocritus of Syracuse (born *c.* 315–312). Hints he may have got from earlier Sicilian poets ; something he owed to the peasant songs of the Mediterranean ; but the pastoral idyll of literature is his and his only,—so entirely his that from him derives the modern sense of ' idyllic '. He seemingly spent his boy-

hood in Sicily and his youth with Philetas at Cos (his Coan
friend Aratus, now known from inscriptions, was not Aratus
the poet); about 276–270 he was in Alexandria. How
long he remained there is unknown; one likes to think he
was homesick for the trees and flowers of Sicily, and that
it was he, not his Menalcas, who called on ' Etna, my
mother ', and thought wealth and power nothing if he
could sit with his beloved in the shade of a rock and watch
the blue home-sea. He indeed experimented with various
forms of the idyll, and in his hands even an official ode in
praise of Ptolemy, or the talk of the vulgar women at the
show in Alexandria, became poetry. But it is for the
pastorals that men have treasured him—the singing matches
of shepherd and goatherd, the forsaken girl trying to charm
back her lover, the two old fishermen in their reed cabin,
the Coan harvest festival with Lycidas' beautiful song,—
for these and for his love of plants and animals, the cicadas
chirping in the sun, the dog dreaming of a bear-hunt, the
little fox manœuvring round the boy's dinner. His men
and girls are living peasants. He perfected the pastoral,
and left nothing for others; his successors are far below
him, and Vergil's *Eclogues* seem artificial copies, an artifi-
ciality which grew until the end was Watteau and powdered
shepherdesses in hoops. Alone of the Alexandrians he has
become a classic, because, alone of the Alexandrians, he
could throw off all that Alexandria stood for and get back
to Nature. A great poet of Nature he was not, for he could
not see behind her; to him " the yellow bees in the ivy
bloom " would have been only bees, delightfully buzzing.
For her grandeur, too, he betrays no more feeling than
other Greeks; for that, in the Hellenistic age, we must
turn to the unknown Jew who wrote the *Song of the Three
Children*, and knew that the Lord was praised in the wind
and the storm, the flood and the snow. But for the sweet-
ness and mere beauty of natural things Theocritus had a
feeling such as no other Greek possessed; and he can never
die while every burn on the moor sings as he sang.[1]

[1] κατειβόμενον κελάρυσδε.

Epics continued to be written; and one at least was exciting, Rhianus' story (*c.* 250) of the Messenian war and the heroism of Aristomenes, a story which, through Pausanias' use of it, still had its place in the histories of our youth; we are the poorer without it, legendary though it be. Epic indeed had a certain future as a vehicle of local patriotism; for, as the city lost power before the monarchy, so pride grew in its past and its legends, and much poetry, often called epic, was written to glorify cities and peoples; any poet who came to a city and recited his poem on its history was liberally fêted and honoured. But there was one epic of a different type, the *Argonautica* of Apollonius of Alexandria, called the Rhodian. The reason and the details of the quarrel between Callimachus and Apollonius remain a mystery; but certainly the *Argonautica* expresses a revolt against Callimachus, who said of it that a big book was a big nuisance. He polemised against its author; but Apollonius, who as Librarian was Callimachus' superior, would hardly have quitted the empire for good on that account. But Callimachus and Apollonius' successor Eratosthenes were Cyrenaeans, and Ptolemy III married a princess of Cyrene; was the cause political, Cyrene against Alexandria? In any case Apollonius' epic stands alone. As a whole, it is a learned man's failure. He could draw a picture, but could not tell a story; the celestial machinery creaks badly, and the language is troublesome. But one part of it—Medea's love-story in book III—is quite extraordinarily good; for the first and the last time in Greece someone had dared to draw a girl honestly in love, and she was a particular Colchian girl, not a type. Apollonius had no successor till Vergil used him as a model; but the Medea of book III is far better done than Dido. Whatever Alexandria did to him, he has had his revenge; while none but scholars will ever read Callimachus, Apollonius (though the chain was broken) is the precursor of half modern literature.

But the idyll and epic were for the educated; the half-educated too required amusement, and were catered for by the Mime, both spoken and sung ; the former ultimately derived from Sicily, the latter from the loose ' Ionian songs ' of Asia Minor ; in the third century wandering companies of Mime actors were well established. The spoken Mime was a sketch of some incident of daily life, literary or otherwise ; Theocritus' famous ' Syracusan women ' is an example. We now have from Egypt a whole selection of the literary Mimes of Herondas (*c.* 240), apparently another member of Philetas' circle, written in scazons ; many are on unpleasant subjects, clever photographs of things not worth photographing, but valuable as illustrating how common people talked. Allied to this form, apparently, was cinaedology, compositions whose point lay in their indecency ; Sotades' verse on the marriage of Ptolemy II, for which Ptolemy's admiral Patroclus drowned him, is unprintable. The singing mime was divided into hilarody and magody, parodying tragedy and comedy respectively ; but if the now famous *Maiden's Lament*—the passionate appeal of a girl outside the door of a faithless lover—be really a mime, it was neither, but a piece for stage recitation. One example of hilarody has been recovered, the skeleton, to be filled out with gag, of a parody of the *Iphigenia in Tauris*, in which the barbarian king talks some Indian gibberish and the brother and sister escape by making him drunk.

Parody was of course employed in better literature than the Mime ; Timon the Sceptic wrote an entertaining skit called *Silloi* on other philosophers, living and dead, which naturally appealed only to a select few ; and Crates the Cynic produced a really good parody of Homer in the *Beggar's Wallet*, in which he glorified that symbol of Cynic poverty as the one refuge for an honest man, rising like an island from the wine-dark sea of universal humbug. But Crates' poem, though in form a parody, was serious enough, and possibly led to philosophy reviving the long-dead fashion of using serious verse as a vehicle. The best example is the fine *Hymn to Zeus* of the Stoic Cleanthes, the high-water mark of Greek religious poetry, very different from

Q

the orthodox hymns and paeans written to order, of which a number are now known ; but almost as notable in its way is the poem in which Cercidas of Megalopolis, a politician with ' Cynic ' leanings—everyone dissatisfied with the existing order was called a Cynic—exhorted his friends to meet the threat of social revolution by healing the sick and giving to the poor ; it stands out from the commonplace moralising poetry of the time,—*e.g.* Phoenix of Colophon, *c.* 286,—which has no depth. Lastly, we possess one popular (political) song, sung in the streets of Athens in 290 ; very catching it is.

The influence of Alexandrian poetry on Roman was great. Some well-known points have been noticed, and new ones continually come to light ; a recent discovery has revealed, in a treatise preserved in Philodemus' work *On Poems*, the Hellenistic original of the doctrine and much of the detail of Horace's *Ars Poetica*. But Hellenism only gave the Romans form, and subjects to treat ; it did not give them the vital matter of poetry itself, the essential difference between the poet and the painstaking literary man ; for that, the great poets—Lucretius, Catullus, Vergil —looked into their own souls.

Before turning to prose proper, the spoken word must be noticed. The judicial commissions killed forensic oratory—no great loss—but political oratory flourished for a century after Alexander. Deinarchus and Demosthenes' nephew Demochares were indeed only relics of Demosthenes' age, though Demetrius of Phalerum (317– 307) perhaps took his own line ; but Aratus of Sicyon (271– 213) was obviously a great orator, for during a long career he consistently swayed the Achaean Assembly as Demosthenes never did the Athenian. As no speech of his remains, it is not known how he did it ; but Plutarch says he disdained the forms of art, *i.e.* rhetoric, and possibly he spoke extemporary and said just what he thought ; the effect on men soaked in rhetorical artifices might be startling. The most important speech of which Polybius gives a précis, Agelaus' appeal for Greek unity at the conference of Naupactus (217), with its two unforgettable images, must have been really good ; Pyrrhus' minister Cineas was ranked by contemporaries with Demosthenes.

But political oratory ultimately died also ; and from the second century everything was swamped by the growth of rhetoric. It is not worth enumerating the professors of this art, increasingly numerous down to Roman times. Hegesias of Magnesia-under-Sipylos (*c.* 250) helped to popularise the flowery Asianic style, whose laboured rhythms can be cut up into lengths resembling modern *vers libre* (it is uncertain whether he or Timaeus invented it) ; Hermagoras of Temnos (*c.* 150), whose *Handbook* became authoritative, marks a stage on the road back to Atticism. Rhetoric was capable of some good, by teaching men to arrange their thoughts clearly ; but it became one of the curses of Hellenism. Men concluded that style was everything and substance nothing ; what you said was immaterial provided you said it according to rule and avoided hiatus. For some reason rhetoric intoxicated Greeks ; it took the place filled to-day by cheap journalism and the cinema ; men flocked to rhetorical displays as to a theatre. It debased everything it touched. Petronius said it taught people much about pirates and so forth but little about life ; and Martial summed it up in his bitter jibe at an advocate who could make fine speeches about Hannibal but was useless in a petty larceny case.

In prose, history took first place. Under the stimulus of the opening up of Asia, the two generations after Alexander witnessed a large output ; but all these historians have perished, and are now known only through their use by later writers. The vice of writing for effect, introduced by Isocrates and his pupils, was not dead or going to die ; but there was a sense of reality in the new world which led some, especially in military circles which had known Alexander, to react against rhetoric. When Ptolemy I (after 301) wrote his history of Alexander from the official *Journal* and other official documents, supplemented by his own notes and recollections, he was doing a new thing,—

he was the man of action writing down what he knew and
had seen ; it is well for us that he did.  Similarly Nearchus,
in the account of his voyage (before 312), produced perhaps
the most trustworthy chronicle in Greek ; both these men
had been Alexander's friends from boyhood and had felt
his directness.  Halfway between them and the vulgate
stands Aristobulus of Cassandreia ;  he knew a certain
amount about Alexander, and was good on geography, but
his accounts of events are not always trustworthy.  These
three are represented for us by Arrian.  Aristotle's nephew,
Callisthenes of Olynthus, wrote very differently ;  his influential history (c. 330) was written to advertise Alexander,
and was full of extravagances which caught the world's
ear a generation before more sober accounts were available.
But he at least was able, while the books about Alexander
produced in the outer circle, by Onesicritus the pilot, Chares
the chamberlain, Ephippus the gossip-monger, were full of
worthless trivialities or inventions ;  a man can only see
what he is big enough to see.  Subsequently Cleitarchus of
Alexandria, a writer of ability, not devoid of imagination
and hero-worship, using Callisthenes and the smaller writers
freely, the better tradition sparingly, and a floating mass
of stories drawn from many lost sources—propaganda,
mercenaries, and what not—produced (not before 280–270)
a rhetorical history of Alexander which fixed the vulgate
tradition and held the field for $4\frac{1}{2}$ centuries ; it was read as
eagerly as a novel, and perhaps rather resembled one.  It
is known only through its use by Diodorus and Curtius.

Soon after 264 Timaeus of Tauromenium completed at
Athens his big history of the Western Greeks to that year,
which for two centuries exercised much influence.  He was
learned and industrious, well travelled, and diligent in
collecting epigraphic evidence, but his mind had no depth,
and he did not really understand Dionysius and Agathocles ;
he wrote as a rhetorician in the Asianic style, and related
wonders and legends, though he introduced the clumsy
dating by Olympiads, which gained some vogue and was
employed by Cleitarchus, Polybius, and Castor.  Diodorus'

Agathocles goes back to him. An innovation was attempted by Duris, sometime tyrant of Samos, who wrote a history of the period from Leuctra to 280 ; he aimed at making history interesting by dramatising characters and motives and using the accessories of the theatre ; what can be traced of his work is tolerably remote from fact. A better man, Nymphis of Heraclea Pontica (active 280), wrote a history of Alexander's Successors which has perished without trace ; but his history of Heraclea, represented by Memnon, seems to have been good and vivid. Diyllus at Athens wrote a history of Greece from the Sacred War to Cassander's death in 297, favourable to Cassander, which has left traces in Diodorus ; Demetrius of Phalerum left a history of his rule in Athens, besides much other work ; Demochares wrote a rhetorical history of his own times from the Nationalist standpoint ; Demetrius of Byzantium narrated in minute detail the Gallic invasion of Asia ; Proxenus wrote on Pyrrhus' Epirus ; and Pyrrhus himself left a volume of *Memoirs* dealing with his wars, if indeed the work was not merely an edition of his official *Journal*.

But the great history of the half-century after Alexander, probably one of the greatest histories Greece produced, was written by Hieronymus of Cardia, the friend, possibly the relative, of Eumenes, who after Eumenes' death served Antigonus I, Demetrius, and Gonatas as general and administrator ; it ran from the death of Alexander to (probably) that of Pyrrhus. It stands behind Diodorus and Arrian's *Diadochi*, was partly used by Plutarch in his *Lives* of Eumenes and Demetrius, and exercised a steadying force on the whole of our broken tradition of the period ; the more that period is studied, the stronger the conviction grows of the presence of a great lost writer behind it. He dated by campaign years, like Thucydides, and his figures seem to have been trustworthy, a rare phenomenon. He neglected style, and consequently perished ; but he was careful to tell the truth as he saw it—and he had played an active part in the history he related,—and there are in-

dications enough that he could draw both pictures and
characters ; indeed the astonishing fact that, even now, we
can trace some *development* in the character of Demetrius,
if due to him (as it must be), would set him in this respect
above any previous historian ; for to Greeks generally
character was static.  He illustrated what Polybius emphasised, that in Greece only men of action could write
good history.  The Antigonid dynasty were fortunate in
his services, and he makes it possible for a time to understand Macedonia a little.  Neither Seleucid Asia nor
Ptolemaic Egypt ever produced a competent historian ;
the early Seleucids, at least, deserved a better fate.

The interval between Hieronymus and Polybius was, as
regards Greece, covered by Phylarchus, who wrote in
Athens and continued Duris' history to Cleomenes' death
(219) ; he is represented by Plutarch's *Lives* of Agis and
Cleomenes, and colours a good deal else.  It is usual to
treat him merely as another Duris, partly for his dramatic
introductions of female characters ; but though he was a
convinced partisan of Cleomenes, he grows in importance
the more his period is analysed, and where he clashes with
Polybius it is not always Polybius who is right.  Aratus
of Sicyon covered much of the latter half of the century
in his *Memoirs*, really his autobiography ; strongly partisan,
and unfair to opponents, he yet enables us to know the
Achaean League, and he was frank about his own failings ;
he is represented by Plutarch's *Life*, and was Polybius'
primary source for this period.  Sosylos' history of Hannibal
is a real loss, as the one fragment shews ; for he was with
Hannibal in Italy.

The second century belongs to Polybius of Megalopolis
(*c.* 198–117), a man who played his part in the politics and
warfare of the Achaean League, was carried off to Rome
after Pydna, became the friend of Panaetius and Scipio
Aemilianus, and returned to Greece in 146.  His great
history told the story of the ' inhabited world ' from 221
to 146.  Only the first five books remain, with long extracts
from others ; but Livy represents him, though mixed with

inferior material. He treated Ephorus and Timaeus as his
predecessors, and gave a preliminary account of Greece and
Rome to bridge the gap between Timaeus and 221; he was
attracted by the wide field they covered, though he properly
hated rhetoric and, as became Panaetius' friend, discarded
all wonders. Hieronymus, unhappily, he ignored, as he
disliked Macedonia; and the development in Aratus'
character probably comes from Aratus. Polybius is not
pleasant reading; his style is that of rescripts and des-
patches, and desperately long-winded; like Timaeus, he
interrupts his narrative with polemical discussions which
to-day would form appendices. In military matters he
compares badly with Hieronymus; and Livy knew more
about ships than the Arcadian could teach him. He used
official archives where he could, and utilised many sources
of evidence, but he was deficient in scientific training; his
mind was a politician's, and for politicians he wrote; he
believed the present could learn from the past, and on
politics he is solid, if dull, though he has queer gaps, like
his omission to describe the Achaean constitution. He is
not impartial; his own party among the Achaeans
resembles 'God's Whigs' in certain English writers, and
his attitude to Aetolia and Macedonia calls for constant
mental adjustment on the reader's part; but though a
partisan of Rome, he makes some effort to be fair to Hannibal, though not to Carthage. But if one emphasises his
defects, it is because he is almost big enough to carry them
off. He had a great subject and gave it full scope; his
hero is Rome, and his theme Rome's expansion over the
Mediterranean world; all his rivulets run into that river.
His history is the epic of Rome's heroic age. He understood the time, and the men it produced; he knew both
Greece and Rome from the inside. He could draw fine
pictures when he chose; he did try, though not deeply
enough, to understand the causes of events; and he was
not afraid of ethical judgments. Above all, he emphasised
that history's sole concern is truth. Mommsen's way of
regarding the second among Greek historians remains the

right one : contrast the darkness before and after him with the period when his sun scatters the clouds.

Polybius' history was continued by Poseidonius (p. 288). He was picturesque and full of detail, but as an historian quite superficial. He related many marvels, and his much praised picture of the Celts reveals little insight into Celtic character ; if Caesar really went to him for their psychology, no wonder Caesar had trouble. His standpoint was the narrow one of the Roman optimates, and comparative darkness falls on Rome between the Gracchi and Sulla; nowhere do we feel a great writer behind the extant tradition. His quality is shewn by his long surviving account of Athens joining Mithridates ; instead of explaining the nature and reason of the hatred Rome evoked, he relates that a little people, secure and peaceful, who had waged no war for a century, suddenly rose and fought to the death against her as they had against Xerxes, because—a plausible sophist told them to. A better historian may have been Nicolaus of Damascus, philosopher and historian at the court of Herod I, with some practical knowledge of affairs. He wrote a universal history ; the section on Herod survives in substance in Josephus, and is the reason so much is known about Herod, while greater men are forgotten. Of the general history of the world by Agatharcides of Cnidus (c. 120) nothing is known ; and it is quite uncertain whether the book of Timagenes of Alexandria (c. 20) called *Of the kings* was really a history of the Macedonian monarchies. Apollodorus of Artemita wrote a Parthian history, from which a few fragments on the Graeco-Bactrians survive. Lastly, a tribute of thanks must be paid to Diodorus of Sicily, who wrote his *Historical Library* about 27 B.C. He is not an historian, but a conduit-pipe ; his work, always pleasant to read, is good or bad according to the writer he is summarising at the time. But he has thus preserved much that would otherwise have perished, Iambulus for instance ; and it is primarily to him that we owe our knowledge of Hieronymus.

There were other forms of historical writing beside the

formal histories. Early in the third century two priests, Berossus of Babylon and Manetho of Egypt, attempted to make their countries' history available to Greeks ; but few cared to study barbarian history seriously, though Theophrastus knew of the Avesta and Berossus' astrology was welcomed ; the Calendar of Sais, a calendar of the Egyptian year and festivals written in Greek about 300, is however notable. Under Ptolemy I Hecataeus of Abdera wrote on Egypt as a Greek saw it ; later one Menander worked up some Phoenician chronicles. Alexander Polyhistor of Miletus (c. 50), who collected the literature about many countries, Greek and barbarian, has preserved some Jewish propaganda (p. 187). The local patriotism which influenced poetry also influenced history, and a long list of local or town chronicles is known ; such chronicles might also embody the labours of the antiquarian and epigraphist, like the *Attis* or Athenian Chronicle of the learned Philochorus (c. 261), which gave much information on the constitution, festivals, and ceremonies of Athens ; doubtless there were works which rendered similar service for other cities. Craterus, whom tradition identifies with Gonatas' half-brother (this is doubtful), compiled a corpus of Athenian decrees with a sound historical commentary ; but the outstanding name in the antiquarian field is Polemon of Ilium (second century). He spent half his life studying inscriptions in many countries ; having acquired his knowledge, he then wrote voluminously on the foundation, antiquities, and customs of many cities, and on epigraphy itself, together with critical *adversaria* of every kind. He was regarded as very trustworthy ; but nothing of his remains, and he is probably our worst loss after Hieronymus. Many imitated his travels (*periegesis*) and writings, though not his great knowledge ; Pausanias probably used him more than he admits. Eratosthenes (p. 246), who beside his other activities was a genuine historical critic, founded the study of chronology ; Apollodorus of Athens in 144 worked his chronology into a rhyming chronicle, whose fragments are for that reason of value, and Castor of Rhodes (d. 42) used

Apollodorus in compiling a set of synchronised chronological tables which were in turn used by Varro and by Eusebius' predecessor, Julius Africanus ; there is thus a chain linking Eratosthenes with Eusebius' ambitious chronological scheme.

The Peripatetic school, with their love of collecting facts, naturally handled historical work from the start. Theophrastus wrote a history of scientific studies, others wrote histories of medicine and mathematics ; two of Theophrastus' pupils, Duris the historian and Chamaeleon of Heraclea Pontica, produced the first histories of art and poetry respectively, and were to have many followers. Dicaearchus (c. 300) wrote an important work called *The Life of Hellas*, probably a history of culture. All these works are lost, as is Dicaearchus' important *Constitution of Sparta* ; Theophrastus' little sketches of human types, called *Characters*, of some interest for social history, alone survive. But the Peripatetic influence on history proper was to become thoroughly bad ; they created, or fixed, that doctrine of Fortune which gained such vogue (p. 280), and from their diligence in collecting every scrap of everything sprang the so prevalent habit of mixing up truth and legend without discrimination, a habit which quickly enough became nothing but a passion for scandal. There is no more unpleasant feature of the time than the propaganda they carried on against Alexander and his house ; they had not even the wit to avoid mutually exclusive allegations, and this the first known propaganda campaign was typically unwholesome. They specialised in biography, which the individualism of the third century inevitably brought into prominence ; but their habit of mixing up true and false, which already appears full-blown in a very early work, Clearchus of Soli's *Lives*, was to be its curse. Biographers of influence at Alexandria were Satyrus (c. 220), whose recovered *Life* of Euripides, written in dialogue form, is better than one expected, and Callimachus' pupil Hermippus of Smyrna ; and in their footsteps Alexandria piled up masses of biographical material, but so uncritically that when later Plutarch took the material and from it produced

great works of art, truth and falsehood had become hope-
lessly fused ; for instance, no one yet has even attempted
to analyse Plutarch's *Life* of Alexander. Hellenism, however, produced one serious and competent biographer to
whom we owe much, the sculptor Antigonus of Carystus
(d. after 225), who wrote the lives of the third century
philosophers ; he partly survives, together with much
inferior material, in Diogenes Laertius.

Hellenistic geography begins in science (Chap. IX) and
ends in literature. Eratosthenes' great *Geography* gave a
description of the world he knew, good for the Mediterranean
and for what Alexander, Patrocles, Megasthenes and
Pytheas (whose voyage he wisely recognised as true) had
made known (Chap. VII) ; the fringes were conjectural,
for he naturally knew nothing of the African and Indian
peninsulas, the world east of the Ganges, or northern
Europe and Asia ; but he first mentioned the Seres, the
people through whom silk came westward, and his account
of Asia beyond Euphrates for long held the field. But it
was Polybius' utilitarianism which chiefly turned men's
thoughts to descriptive geography. His younger contemporary Agatharcides of Cnidus has left an excellent
account of the Red Sea coast and its strange peoples, based
on Egypt's penetration southward (Chap. VII) ; Apollodorus of Artemita wrote on Bactria and Chinese Turkestan ;
the much-travelled Artemidorus of Ephesus (*c.* 100) produced
an important general work, utilising his predecessors and
rich in detail, known only from Strabo's use of it. Poseidonius' works were full of descriptive geography, brilliant
and picturesque ; it is now thought that from him come
Strabo's accounts of the peoples of Western Europe and of
the mineral wealth of Spain, of the volcanic districts of
Asia Minor and elsewhere (which Strabo might well have
known himself), and of the strange Cran d'Arles at the
Rhône mouth, and also Diodorus' flaming description of
the wonders of Arabia.

Though Strabo of Amasa wrote his *Geography* under
Tiberius he must be mentioned here, for there are few

writers to whom we owe more. His book is the swan-song
of Hellenism ; through his eyes we survey that world as
a whole as it passed away. He is no original geographer ;
he embodies his predecessors, but he writes well and is a
tolerably sane critic ; to suggest that we should value him
less had we Artemidorus and Poseidonius is true but un-
grateful. One might wish that the world around him,
which he knew so intimately, had been the Hellenistic
kingdoms in their bloom ; that we had more of the Bactrians and less of Roman client-kings. But the mass of
information he has collected on the serious matters—
geographical theory, Greek cities, economics—is great ;
while he had learnt more about the interior of further Asia
(not the coast) than anyone was to know again till Marco
Polo. His book is shot through with pictures. Here we
have the glory of Alexandria and Rhodes and the social
system of Bengal ; Cappadocian priest-kings, Indian fakirs,
German priestesses, Gallic Druids pass before us ; he tells
of the strange festivals of Thrace and Persia, the couvade
of the Iberians, the head-hunters of Carmania ; in his
company we can discover Britain with Pytheas or explore
the Caspian with Patrocles, watch the mongoose killing the
crocodile, or gather crocuses in the Corycian grotto ; we
can fish for fresh water in the Phoenician sea, spear sword-
fishes off Sicily, stalk ostriches in Nubia, or ferret rabbits
in Spain. No more picturesque book remains since
Herodotus.

The underside of geography was the ' traveller's tale ' ;
its type was settled by Antiphanes of Berge, author of the
story about the country where it was so cold that in autumn
a man's words froze in the air and you did not hear what
he was saying till they thawed in the spring ; ' Bergean '
became Greek for ' fish story '. Hecataeus on the Hyper-
boreans and Amometus on the Uttara Kurus (Attacori) of
the Himalaya were books of this type, and a surviving
specimen is Lucian's amusing *True Story*, lineal ancestor
of *Sindbad the Sailor*. The underside of history, which was
occupied with mythical and romantic tales, was even more

prolific ; among other things the Aeneas legend and the story of the founding of Rome were worked up in Hellenistic circles, where Geoffrey of Monmouth would have been welcomed as a brother craftsman.  But the principal achievement was the Alexander-romance, a fusion of ideas taken from Egypt, Babylon, and the last debased form of the Cleitarchean tradition, originating in Egypt and subsequently attributed to Callisthenes ; for though the Greek text of Pseudo-Callisthenes did not take final shape till *c*. A.D. 300, the roots may go back to the second century B.C.  The story, with endless variations, ultimately spread over Asia to Malaya and Siam, and came westward to France and Britain.  History itself tended to become more and more a thing of textbooks and compendiums, boiled down from the greater writers and repeated from one to another, gradually growing worse ;  Justin and Orosius, though later, will illustrate the type.

Indeed the forms and content of prose writing were endless ; for there was no branch of human thought or activity which was not a subject for literature.  The Utopias have already been mentioned (p. 104).  The letter became a serious vehicle, used by philosophers ; but letters, forged or doctored, also played a part both in the spread of literary history and in the war of pamphlets and propaganda which accompanied the military struggles after Alexander's death ; of the published correspondence of Alexander, Olympias, Antigonus Gonatus, and others, only part at best was genuine.  Imaginary conversations between historical personages were written (two have recently been found) ;  and the satires of Menippus of Gadara (*c.* 280), much used by Lucian, written in prose and verse mixed, were also sometimes cast in dialogue form, as were Satyrus' *Lives*.  A large class desired short and easy reading, and there grew up a whole literature of snippets on every subject,[1]—history, war, banquets, theatres, moral philosophy, miscellaneous gossip ; they ranged from genuine

[1] Such collections were called ὑπομνήματα, which also means (*a*) a king's official Journal, and (*b*) what we call Memoirs.

historical extracts to the most untrustworthy anecdotes.
Polyaenus and Aelian exhibit the type, and Athenaeus'
vast hodge-podge, invaluable for all the otherwise unknown
writers it has preserved, is only a glorified example. Alexander's supposed *Memoirs* were a second-century compilation
of the kind; combining truth and falsehood ; Ptolemy
Euergetes II seemingly published his own commonplace
book. Greeks had no feeling about plagiarism, and to copy
out a predecessor was a compliment ; the end can be seen
in Augustus' protégé, Juba II of Mauretania, who would
buy any forgery and compiled large uncritical works on
many subjects by the simple use of paste and scissors ;
Pliny's *Natural History* is only a better example of the same
type. Of course such writers preserved many true things
as well as false, but the two became so fused that it is now
often impossible to distinguish them.

Others compiled lists ; the ten Attic orators, the seven
wonders of the world, the list of ' inventors ' used by Pliny,
are all Hellenistic ; Phlegon knew a list of centenarians,
and somebody made one of teetotallers. There was a
whole literature of wonders and marvels, often attributed
to great names of the past, as indeed were many sorts of
books. The romantic love-tale (not serious attempts at
portraying love, like Apollonius') appears in many places
and contexts—Hero and Leander; Sappho and Phaon,
Pyramus and Thisbe, Antiochus I and Stratonice—and
paved the way for the so-called Greek novel of Roman
times ; Parthenius of Nicaea in 73 brought a book of such
love-stories to Rome. There was much literature on special
subjects, some good, like the book of Timosthenes of Rhodes
*On Harbours* ; Poseidonius' pupil Asclepiodotus has left a
pedantic book on drill and tactics ; we hear of works on
agriculture, bee-keeping, fruit-trees, gardens, horse-breeding,
fishing, precious stones, the interpretation of dreams ;
there were descriptions of special festivals, or of the great
ships of Ptolemy IV and Hiero ; a whole literature on
gastronomy and the demi-monde. A work on cosmetics
was naturally attributed to Cleopatra.

One work must be named for the evil it did : the late third-century book *On the wantonness of past times*. The object of the writer, who pretended to be Socrates' pupil Aristippus, was to attach to every honoured name as much scandalous matter as he could invent ; there is plenty of him, now universally discredited, in Diogenes Laertius' *Lives* of the philosophers. It was scarcely the only book of the kind ; and anyone who wants to understand Hellenism must be prepared to treat as it deserves the scandal-mongering he will meet with in some extant literary sources. Philip II, no model character, might have shamed many a writer when after Chaeronea he gazed on the Sacred Band of Thebes lying dead in their ranks and cursed those who had spoken evil of such men.

# CHAPTER IX

# SCIENCE AND ART

It was after Alexander that Greek science came into its own. A good beginning had been made long before his time in mathematics and medicine ; the Pythagoreans and Plato and his school had brought geometry to an advanced stage—the inscription over Plato's Academy, ' Let none enter who knows not geometry ', is famous— and Hippocrates, whose oath the modern doctor still takes, had laid solid foundations of the science of medicine ; while Aristotle, for whose work Alexander had liberally provided, had not only systematised the whole province of learning, but had settled the principle governing research, the collection of a mass of data from which deductions could be drawn. Everything was ready for an outburst of activity, which came as soon as Alexander had in effect quadrupled the size of the known world. He himself provided the material for an increase of knowledge on many lines, botany, zoology, geography, ethnography, hydrography ; but it was probably of greater importance that he brought Babylon into the Greek sphere. The result was that for a few generations after his death there was such a growth of true science as the world was not to see again for very many centuries ; the supremacy of this period, till quite modern times, is unquestionable. But it contained also one of those queer contradictions of which Hellenism was full ; we regard science as essentially European, but Hellenistic astronomy was partly due to Babylonians.

We may take astronomy first. Babylon had for long collected empirical observations of the heavens, and the Greek picture of the sky with its planets and constellations

was, like our own, Babylonian ; but in the Persian period
—it is dated to 523—scientific astronomy, in the sense of
the *use* of recorded observations, started in Babylonia,
where there were three schools, those of Uruk, Sippar,
and Babylon with Borsippa. The great name after Alexander's time is Kidinnu of Sippar (Kidenas), though whether
he was late fourth or third century seems uncertain. Professor Schnabel has recently attributed to him the exciting
discovery of the precession of the equinoxes, though this
is at present in dispute [1] ; and he makes his calculation of
the year 365 days 5 hours 41 minutes 4·16", only 7 minutes
16" too short on modern calculations for the year 300.

Among Greeks the accepted view of the universe since
Eudoxus (fourth century) had been that sun, moon and
planets revolved round a fixed earth in concentric spheres ;
but Aristotle's younger contemporary, Heracleides of Heraclea Pontica, had discovered that the earth turned on its
axis and that Mercury and Venus revolved round the sun.
These views were accepted by Aristarchus of Samos (*c.*
310–230), a pupil of Strato the Peripatetic, who followed
them up with the discovery that the sun was far larger
than the earth,—some 300 times its mass, he thought. It
was probably this which to him made the geocentric
theory impossible ; and he propounded the view that the
earth and all the planets revolved round the sun in circles,
while the sun and fixed stars were stationary, the latter
being an enormous distance away. In the realm of thought
the suggestion, though he could not prove it, should have
been epoch-making ; but the great geometricians who followed him—Archimedes, Apollonius, Hipparchus—naturally
could not make observed phenomena agree with the sun
as centre of a circle, and therefore rejected his system ;

---

[1] P. Schnabel, *Berossos und die babylonisch-hellenistische Literatur*,
Leipzig, 1923. *Contra :* F. X. Kugler, *Sternkunde und Sterndienst
in Babel*, Vol. II, Part II, 2, pp. 582–630 (Münster i. W., 1924).
Schnabel's reply, *Zeits. f. Assyriologie*, 1926, p. 1. The arguments
are extremely technical ; but several writers have accepted
Schnabel's discovery.

Hipparchus was right enough, from the geometrical standpoint, in saying one must ' save the phenomena ', *i.e.* stick
to observations.  Unfortunately this did not lead to the
discovery of elliptical orbits, but to the further evolution
of Heracleides' idea of epicycles ;  and someone in the
third century, very likely Apollonius, produced Tycho
Brahe's system—the planets went round the sun and the
sun round the earth ;  this also was not fated to endure.
Among other third-century astronomers Archimedes' friend
Conon of Alexandria must be mentioned, for he named
the constellation *Coma Berenicis* after the lock of hair
Berenice dedicated for the safety of her husband Ptolemy
III, one of the few constellations in our sky which do not
go back to Babylon.  Meanwhile a group of Babylonians
—Sudines is notable among them—were translating into
Greek, and by the second century rendered available to
Greeks, much Babylonian material, including Kidenas.

The great name of the second century was Hipparchus
of Nicea (*c.* 146–126).  His contemporary the Chaldean
Seleucus, an intriguing figure, was defending Aristarchus'
heliocentric theory and striving to find proofs for it ;  Hipparchus took up epicycles and eccentric circles, handled
them better than Apollonius, and produced that geocentric
system which, copied later by Claudius Ptolemy, was to
rule the world till Copernicus ;  Seleucus lost his battle,
Apollonius' system expired, and the world settled down to
the sun, moon and planets revolving round the earth.
Hipparchus got the sun's apparent movement right, but
could never quite manage the moon.  The pity of it was
that, could heliocentricism have been established, it would
have killed astrology and saved the world infinite trouble.
Hipparchus used to be supposed to have discovered the
precession of the equinoxes ;  his calculation made the
equinoctial point go forward 36″ a year (really 50·3757″).
Whether he was the real discoverer or not depends on
Kidenas' alleged priority (p. 241).  Hipparchus certainly
used Babylonian eclipses and a good deal of other information—it is doubtful where his debt to Babylon is going to

stop—and he knew Kidenas' work, for an express statement is said to have come to light shewing that he took from Kidenas the equation 251 lunations = 269 anomalistic months. His calculation of the year, however, differed from that attributed to Kidenas, being 6 minutes 14·3″ longer than the mean tropic year ; but the fact which they established, that the year was not 365¼ days, was neglected in practice till the Gregorian calendar. Hipparchus' calculation of the length of the mean lunar month was less than 1″ out, and his figures for the moon's distance and diameter approximated closely to reality ; he made the sun's mass 1,880 times that of the earth, and began to recognise its enormous distance, making it 1,245 earth-diameters away against Aristarchus' 180 ; unfortunately Ptolemy went back to 605. In his observations he used parallax, already known to Archimedes. His greatest work was his catalogue of over 805 fixed stars, placed by latitude and longitude and divided into three classes of brightness, a catalogue somewhat enlarged by Ptolemy. He was the last of the scientific astronomers, unless Ptolemy be included ; he already faced a new world, that of astrology (p. 288).

One first-century name, however, must be given here, because of two brilliant guesses. Poseidonius (p. 288) made the sun's diameter 39¼ earth-diameters against Hipparchus' 12⅓ and Aristarchus' 6¾, and its distance from the earth 6,545 earth-diameters against Hipparchus' 1,245 ; that is, respectively three-eighths and five-eighths of the true figures. But he got the distance by taking from Archimedes the diameter of the sun's apparent orbit as *equal to* 10,000 earth-diameters, whereas Archimedes had been shewing, for another purpose, that it must be *less than* 10,000—a good example of Poseidonius' methods. Ptolemy unhappily took for the sun's size and mass much smaller figures even than Aristarchus ; and Ptolemy was to be authoritative for very many centuries.

Mathematics were closely allied to astronomy, and the same men were often active in both fields. Probably the third-century achievement in mathematics was actually far greater than that in any other science. Geometry had to be the foundation of everything, figures for numerals being unknown ; probably it was the very perfection of their geometry which prevented Greeks inventing a numeral notation. Euclid (c. 300) was not an original mathematician, though he wrote on many subjects, and his famous geometry, though he tightened up some proofs, was really a textbook of existing learning ; but he was a wise man, who like Plato and Archimedes believed in knowledge for its own sake, and he once told Ptolemy I that there was no 'royal road' to geometry. His book was the world's textbook of geometry through Greek, Roman, Arabian, mediaeval, and modern times, down to a generation still living. Greek geometry had always included much that would now be treated as algebra, but it is thought that quadratic equations were already applied to finding numerical values in Euclid's time ; the first step toward an algebraic notation was, however, not to be taken till Diophantus in the third century A.D. Eratosthenes handled mathematics among his other activities ; Archimedes dedicated to him his book *On Method*, and when the gods demanded, as a condition of staying a plague at Delos, that an altar there, cubic in form, should be doubled, it was Eratosthenes who discovered how to duplicate a cube. Apollonius of Perge, of Euclid's school, somewhat younger than Archimedes, is probably the second name in pure mathematics ; his great work on Conic Sections, of which the latter part was dedicated to Attalus I, marked such an advance in knowledge that seemingly it left little for others to do, and it was possibly he who made a beginning with trigonometry, though the first systematic use of trigonometry was due later to Hipparchus, who (among other things) employed triangulation in his criticism of Eratosthenes' map.

The greatest name of all is Archimedes of Syracuse (d. 212). He wrote monographs on very many subjects, and the mere list of his technical achievements is a long one ; among other things, he calculated limits for the value of $\pi$ (the ratio between the circumference of a circle and its

diameter), though Apollonius subsequently got a little
closer ; invented a terminology for expressing numbers up
to any magnitude ; laid the foundations of the calculus of
the infinite ; and founded the whole science of hydrostatics.
On his tomb, which was lost and rediscovered by Cicero,
there was engraved at his wish the figure of a sphere within
a cylinder, indicating that he considered his proof of the
relation of the volume of a sphere to a circumscribing right
cylinder his finest achievement. He was also the greatest
theoretical mechanician of the ancient world ; and though
he held with Plato that a philosopher should not put his
knowledge to practical use, it was in fact the practical use
he made of his knowledge which caught the world's imagination. He made a planetarium, worked by water, to
represent the motions of the heavenly bodies (the planets
must have been moved by hand) ; he invented the compound pulley, and the endless screw, used to pump out
ships and drain the fields after the Nile flood, which survives in our Archimedean drills. Everyone knows the
stories about him : how he was too absent-minded to
remember to eat ; how one day he discovered specific
gravity by noticing the water he displaced in his bath,
and jumped out and ran home naked, shouting *Eureka*,
' I have found it ' ; how when difficulties arose over the
launching of Hiero's great Syracosia he launched the ship
by himself, and told the king " Give me where to stand
and I will move the earth " ; and how during the siege of
Syracuse the solitary geometrician kept the whole strength
of Rome at bay for three years with his grapnels and
burning-glasses and improved catapults. He is the only
mathematician who ever became a legend.

Archimedes apart, practical mechanics (as distinct from
engineering) came to very little, and chiefly meant siege-
engines and catapults, on which various treatises remain,
and mechanical toys ; labour was too cheap for much
thought to be given to machinery, though Ctesibius invented a catapult worked by compressed air, someone else
invented a water-mill, and the younger Ctesibius a water-

organ, used in the early Church. Heron had some idea of the expansive power of steam ; but some place him after A.D. 200. The most useful invention was the *dioptra* or portable water level, which took the theodolite's place in land surveying ; Hipparchus constructed a more elaborate form for astronomical use, it is thought on Babylonian models. Aristarchus made an improved sun-dial, and by 200 the *baroulcos*, a windlass for moving heavy weights, was in use. Mathematics remained vigorous, but the first-century attitude is shown by the Epicurean Zeno of Sidon attacking the very foundations of geometry ; Poseidonius refuted him, and the period closes with a vast history of mathematics written by Poseidonius' pupil Geminus, a summary of the results obtained.

In scientific, as distinct from descriptive, geography, there was great activity, which revived again under the Antonines. The beginning was the series of measurements made by Alexander's surveying section (bematists), which for long formed the basis of the geography of Asia ; and about 300 the Peripatetic Dicaearchus, with pecuniary help from Cassander or Lysimachus, made a map of the world, calculated the heights of various Greek mountains, and (probably) calculated the earth's circumference ; using Syene-Lysimacheia as base line, he made it 300,000 stades, considerably too large, but meritorious for the first attempt. But the great geographer of the third century, and one of the greatest men it produced, was Eratosthenes of Cyrene (275–200), a pupil of Ariston the Stoic at Athens, who worked at Alexandria. He almost rivalled Aristotle in the number of fields of learning he covered ; beside his studies in historical criticism and chronology, he published works on mathematics and philosophy and a history of comedy which superseded Lycophron's, and wrote poetry ; his nickname was *Beta* (Number Two), meaning that on a poll of learned men he would have gained the ' vote of Themistocles ' in every branch of study. He measured the circumference of the earth by calculating what fraction of an arc of meridian equalled the known distance from Alexandria to Syene, and made it 252,000 stades ; the length of the stade he used is disputed, but the most probable calculation makes his measurement 24,662 miles, the true mean circumference being 24,857 miles. His actual error, whatever it was, arose from his not possessing the means of determining whether Alexandria and Syene had precisely the same longitude (they have not) ; but it was an amazing feat, and never improved upon till modern times. The ' inhabited earth ' he made some 8,910 by 4,340 miles, divided latitudinally by the parallel of Rhodes (36°), which he treated as equivalent to the Taurus-Hindu Kush line ; this latter division he took from the gazetteer of Alexander's empire made shortly before Alexander's death. He also drew certain parallels of latitude and longitude.

The question of whether India and Africa joined or not, which had so perplexed Aristotle, had been settled by Alexander, and Eratosthenes' strongly critical mind never doubted that all the oceans were one and that the inhabited world, Europe-Asia-Africa, was an island ; he pointed to the similarity of the tides in the Indian and Atlantic oceans, and rightly deduced that one could sail from Spain round Africa to India, a voyage which was not actually made before Vasco da Gama, though the philologist Crates of Mallos (c. 168), in his controversy with the philologist Aristarchus over Homer's geography, made Menelaus take it,[1] and Poseidonius utilised the idea in the Eudoxus story (p. 199). In some ways Eratosthenes had juster views than any of his successors ; but his weakness was his difficulty over longitudes, and Hipparchus, with improved knowledge, was able to subject his map to serious criticism in this respect. Hipparchus himself had the fine idea of getting the latitude and longitude of a large number of places astronomically fixed by the co-operation of different observers all over the world ; the political position made it impossible, but that it ultimately bore fruit is suggested by the number of places fixed by latitude and longitude

[1] Not to India across the Atlantic ; Strabo 1, 38 says περιπλοῦς, not πλοῦς.

in the later geography of Claudius Ptolemy, which was to dominate the world till Columbus.

Polybius did much to render Greek geography after him descriptive, as being the only sort useful to the historian ; and the only advance in scientific geography between Hipparchus and the Roman period came from Poseidonius (p. 288), whose curiosity about the things of the earth was boundless, and who wrote on meteorology and volcanic phenomena beside his famous work *On the Ocean*, a title taken from Pytheas. Neither scientific nor critical, he nevertheless rendered services to science. His huge collection of phenomena, volcanic and aqueous, to illustrate changes in the earth's surface shewed what his idea of evidence was ; myth or history, the destruction of Atlantis or the destruction of Helice, was all one to him, but out of it all there did emerge the European-Anatolian earthquake belt as a whole. He employed some strange assumptions in calculating the earth's circumference, which he made 180,000 stades [1] ; what stade he used is unknown, but in any case he thought the earth too small. He is the author of our five zones, for Polybius had made six, and Eratosthenes seven by dividing the tropic zone into two burning belts and a habitable equatorial belt between them, a wonderfully good guess at the actual desert belts ; Poseidonius took the midday shadow as the criterion, whether during the year it fell one way, both ways, or all round. Luckily he followed Eratosthenes' conviction that all the oceans were one, a belief which was to be lost again to the world owing to its rejection by the astronomers Hipparchus and Seleucus ; and he made a famous journey to Gades (Cadiz), where he studied the Atlantic tides. Aristotle and Dicaearchus had thought the sun made the tides by raising a wind, and it was that very great traveller Pytheas who first shewed it was the moon. Seleucus,

---

[1] That 240,000, also assigned to him, is only a later adjustment may be shewn by his taking 140,000 as the circumference of the parallel of Rhodes. But conceivably he was merely employing different hypotheses as arguments against Eratosthenes.

observing the Persian Gulf, discovered the inequality of the tides (spring and neap tides) and attributed this to the moon's position in the zodiac ; Poseidonius took the observation of inequalities further, and attributed them to the moon's phases. But for agent he went back to Aristotle's wind, whereas Seleucus thought that the interaction of moon and earth set up some form of pressure or current ; he may have been groping in a direction which, if followed up, might have led to the discovery of gravitation.

However, Poseidonius' journey threw light on more than the tides ; it ultimately led to the discovery of America. Someone, probably Eratosthenes, had suggested that the Atlantic might be divided longitudinally by land (*i.e.* America), a suggestion which inspired Seneca's famous prophecy of the discovery of a New World. Poseidonius, however, not only rejected this idea, but, having got the size of the earth too small, believed that, on the parallel of Rhodes (36°), the 'inhabited world ', which he made 70,000 stades across, was half the circumference ; so, looking at the Atlantic, he very naturally remarked that a man sailing west for 70,000 stades would come to India. This remark was the ultimate foundation of Columbus' confidence ; and it was only historical justice that he should set sail for India from Poseidonius' Cadiz.

In medicine, the two great names of the early third century were Herophilus of Chalcedon and Erasistratus of Iulis in Ceos, who founded rival schools ; Herophilus worked in, and his school became identified with, Alexandria, though it invaded Asia ; of Erasistratus' life and place of work nothing is known, for the stories about him, especially that which makes him Seleucus' physician, have no value. Both made important advances in anatomy and physiology. Herophilus discovered the nerves, previously unknown, which he understood ran from the brain and the spinal cord, and distinguished the cerebrum and cerebellum ; he also found out that the arteries carried blood, not air (as had been believed), and pulsed, not of themselves, but from the heart ; therewith he practically discovered the circulation of the blood, lost again till Harvey. Some of his names for parts of the body, as the duodenum and the torcular Herophili, are still in use. Erasistratus improved on the anatomy of the heart, but his chief discovery was the distinction between the motor and the sensory nerves ; unfortunately he went back to the belief that the arteries carried air. Both men performed serious operations, and dissected corpses. Vivisection of animals was already known to Aristotle ; but Celsus, a sober and competent writer, has a horrible story that Herophilus vivisected criminals given him by Ptolemy I (anaesthetics were unknown), and the same is implied of Erasistratus.

Their schools made no great advance on the two masters, and were ultimately eclipsed by a third, the empiric, founded by Herophilus' pupil Philinus of Cos, which, influenced perhaps by the scepticism of the Academy, is supposed to have neglected anatomy and to have held that disease was curable without a knowledge of physiology ; but its best known member, Heracleides of Tarentum, did practise dissection, and its concentration upon medicines did much for the study of drugs. One interesting personality, Asclepiades of Prusa, appeared in the first century, when science everywhere was dying ; he was not a trained physician, but he undertook to cure disease without drugs by dieting, walking, massage, and cold baths, and achieved such success that a legend grew up that he (like Empedocles) had raised a man from the dead ; the origin of this legend can, for once, be traced, for Celsus says that he once recognised that a man being carried out to burial was still alive. Under Augustus, Celsus closes the age with a medical encyclopaedia, a summary of the advances made in knowledge since Hippocrates, parallel to Geminus' history of mathematics. Naturally all through the period scientific medicine had its half-world, the cures in the temples of Asclepius and Serapis, where the patient slept in the precinct and was healed in a dream by the god ; some of the recorded cures are amusing stories, but doubtless some patients really were healed by suggestion.

By the first century the wandering magician was a serious rival to both doctor and priest.

Zoology and botany did little more than make a start. Theophrastus and his successor Strato wrote on zoology, but essentially the science remained where Aristotle had left it, and all that was done was to familiarise the Greek world with various new animals ; Seleucus sent an Indian tiger to Athens, and Ptolemy II had a zoological garden containing leopards, panthers, lynxes, Indian and African buffaloes, wild asses from Moab, a giraffe, a rhinoceros, and a polar bear (whose journey south must have been exciting), together with parrots, peacocks, guinea-fowl, pheasants, and many African birds. Botany fared rather better ; Theophrastus' great *History of Plants*, which incorporated the results of Alexander's expedition, was for long the high-water mark of that science ; all that was added to it was more precise knowledge of plants like the Arabian frankincense tree, and of drugs. The empiric school of medicine did much for the knowledge of drugs, and there was a whole literature of poisons and antidotes, in which Attalus III and Mithridates Eupator were specially interested ; Attalus had a garden of strange plants for his study of the subject. But botany never attained to a classification and nomenclature, though Mithridates' physician Crateuas did something to diminish the uncertainty of verbal description by introducing the method of representing plants pictorially.

Too much must not be made of Hellenistic science, exciting as it is, since of the two sciences which to-day bulk so large, physics and chemistry, chemistry never got started and physics died with Strato, who made a limited use of Democritus' atomic (really molecular) theory ; for the adoption of that theory by Epicurus had nothing to do with science (p. 269), though in Lucretius' account of evolution, based on Empedocles' idea that many ill-adapted animal forms had perished, there was the germ of a true evolutionary hypothesis, had science taken it up. The Greek got no further than he did because he had no scientific instruments, and, except in surgery, rarely experimented; he had, perhaps for his happiness, no gift for instruments and machines, and probably he went about as far as was possible without the telescope, the microscope, and the test-tube. Mr. Cornford has said that if some Archimedes had overcome the Greek prejudice against mechanical crafts and invented optical glass the whole course of history would have been changed.[1] But the (rather later) legend of the glass on the Pharos which enabled ships to be detected beyond the range of vision shews that the properties of the concave lens were at least suspected; but this was not followed up, for the bent of the Greek mind was to try and think the thing out by itself; philosophy rather than science was the goddess to be served, and of the sciences mathematics, for this reason, far surpassed the others.

The transition from science to art was formed by architecture and town-planning; for in some respects Hellenistic architecture was an alliance of the older Greek architecture with engineering, which perhaps first came definitely to birth with Philo's arsenal and dockhouses at Athens in Alexander's reign. If mass of construction counts for anything, the century or so after Alexander was one of the great blossoming times of architecture, with its multitudes of new cities, each of which, so far as it was Greek, would now contain a theatre, market-place, town hall, gymnasium, and at least one temple; the theatre at Ephesus held 25,000 people. Some description of Alexandria and Pergamum has already been given, and Antioch and Seleuceia on the Tigris were ultimately not much less populous than Alexandria. Antioch was four distinct walled towns or ' quarters ' enclosed in a general ring wall; Demetrias was a double city, one ring wall enclosing Demetrias and Pagasae. The great advance in siege machinery due to Alexander's engineer Diades and still more to Demetrius had led to corresponding improvements in the city wall; the magnificent fortifications of Heraclea-Latmos, a city

[1] *Cambridge Ancient History*, Vol. IV, pp. 577 *sq.*

of the second class, can still be traced, going straight across mountain and ravine with towers at intervals ; the little Melitoea in Oeta had walls no ladder could scale. Normally the wall followed the city contour on the flat and took in part of the hill behind ; it left no room for expansion, which explains why Antioch, for example, as it grew, became a cluster of towns with separate walls. No Hellenistic city ever challenged the 17-mile circuit of the wall of Syracuse. Alexandria's huge wall was possibly 10 miles round, Ephesus' $7\frac{1}{2}$, Miletus' 7, that of Seleuceia on the Tigris only $4\frac{1}{8}$ (p. 126) ; but the extraordinary wall-circuits of some Acarnanian towns, meant to shelter the country population, might rival Ephesus. Of course at Alexandria and Seleuceia there was a great native population outside the wall.

The characteristic of the Hellenistic city was its rectangular streets, which cut it up into blocks like a chessboard ; Hippodamus of Miletus had introduced the system at Piraeus in Pericles' time, but it now became usual. Polybius compares the Hellenistic city to the camp of a Roman legion, with two main streets crossing at right angles, dividing the town into four quarters, with four gates at each end of the main streets ; but, though cities of this type must therefore have existed, none have been excavated, and the only one whose extant description corresponds to this formation is Antigoneia-Nicea in Bithynia. A city was naturally conditioned by the lie of the ground : Priene may be typical of the usual form on the slope of a hill, and there, though the chess-board pattern is maintained, the two main streets both run parallel to the long axis ; at Miletus, on the flat, the plan seems to consist in distributing the public buildings to the best advantage. Smyrna was a horseshoe round a hill, built in three separate blocks, each with rectangular streets but differently orientated, which may explain the number of kings who are said to have ' built ' it ; Seleuceia in Pieria rose in terraces up a cliff ; Delos just grew anyhow. In fact there was no stereotyped planning ; the architects achieved beauty by

adapting things to their ends ; for example, the main
street usually formed one side of the market-place, but
the street was planned to lead to the market, the market
did not grow out of the street. There is, however, some
evidence that orientation was so arranged as to secure the
greatest amount of sun for the houses in winter.

Alexandria apart, where the main street is called 100
feet broad, the streets were not yet as wide as the Roman.
At Pergamum the main streets had by law to be 33 feet
wide ; the broadest street at Priene is about 24 feet, at
Magnesia 26½. Cross streets run about 14 to 15 feet wide,
though 10½ is known ; the cheapness of labour is illustrated
by little Assos cutting streets through the living rock.
Smyrna boasted that she was the first city to pave her
streets ; but Hellenistic paving, though known, is rare, and
Miletus, Antioch, and Alexandria were not paved at all.
The first covered colonnade alongside a main street, common in Roman times, was built by Herod I at Antioch.
Great attention was paid to the water supply ; where
possible, the water was merely led downhill by gravitation
into a reservoir and thence distributed ; but, judging by
Priene, the distribution of water to single houses was only
very occasionally done. The underground cisterns at Alexandria were a thing apart, and the statement that every
house in Antioch had water laid on belongs to a far later
period ; but the extremely severe penalties imposed by
the Pergamene Public Health law for fouling the town
water illustrate a new regard for health. Where a gravitation supply was impossible, pressure was well understood ;
the supply for the hill at Pergamum was forced up the last
two miles through metal pipes under a pressure of 18
atmospheres. Baths became common, and were in every
well-equipped gymnasium ; there were apparently public
lavatories at Pergamum, but open drains from the houses
remained the rule till the Romans built sewers.

Architectural technique altered little. The arch and
the vault, long known in Babylonia, and the cupola came
in during this period to reinforce the older forms of con-

struction derived from wood, but are only occasionally met
with ; arches occur at Pergamum and Didyma, but the
buttressing necessitated by the outward thrust of the arch
seems to have been foreign to Greek instincts ; the vault-
ing of the Alexandrian cisterns is said to be Arab. The
Corinthian capital gained steadily in popularity at the expense of the older orders ; in the first century the temple of
Zeus Aizani in Phrygia exhibited a mixed Ionic-Corinthian
style. Otherwise architectural innovations related to the
forms of buildings. Private houses were still of the type
which opened on a central court, but were greatly improved and more luxurious ; in the second century the
peristyle—a colonnade round the court—begins to occur at
Delos. Building had to vary with the available material ;
it was said Alexandria could never be burnt because there
was no wood anywhere, while the absence of marble in
Egypt led to the invention of ' incrustation ', the panelling
of inner walls with thin slabs of that material ; walls too
were painted to look like marble, while on the other hand
there were cities like Mylasa where the abundant local
marble was used even to build private houses. Sometimes,
too, the wall-panels of a room were painted with gardens
or colonnades, so that you seemed to be in a hall open
on all sides. At Tyre and Aradus, whose island sites
afforded no lateral space, houses ran up many stories high ;
and this was perhaps so at Alexandria within the wall by
c. 100, for the city began with houses only half the distance apart that was compulsory at Athens, and seemingly
the intervening space could be built over upon payment.

One would like to illustrate Hellenistic architecture by
describing the palace quarter at Alexandria ; but nothing
is known about it, except that the palaces stood in gardens. Ptolemy's abode must be figured, not as an oriental
palace, but as strictly Greek, a cluster of juxtaposed halls
and living rooms ; Philopator's houseboat, a magnificent
villa of halls and shrines surrounded by a colonnade and
mounted on a barge, may illustrate the type, and imported
marble must have been freely used. The palace at Per-

gamum was only a large private house, but one cannot
argue from this to other dynasties, for it was part of the
Attalid pose (p. 131). It was an age of pillared colonnades, especially for the use of merchants ; king's gifts
often took this shape, like the porticoes of Antigonus
Gonatas, Attalus I, and Philip V at Delos, and of Antiochus I at Miletus. The normal type of market-place had
colonnades round three sides, the fourth abutting on the
road, and the great cities began to separate its mercantile
and political functions, as they separated the mercantile
and military functions of the harbour ; the double harbour of Alexandria was copied where the lie of the land
permitted, and an important city would be able to close
one of its harbours with chains, though perhaps no other
city, unless Cyzicus, ever rivalled the advantage Athens
had had in being able to close *all* her harbours. But
Sostratus' lighthouse on the Pharos at Alexandria, built
as a tower of three diminishing stories, nearly 400 feet
high, was unique ; the third story was the ' lantern ',
eight columns supporting a cupola, under which burnt a
fire of resinous wood, the light possibly being thrown out
by convex mirrors ; a lift ran up to it. It perhaps gave
Arab architects the idea of the minaret. The amphitheatre, though not common, certainly goes back to Hellenism, which had some fancy for circular buildings, several
being known ; a temple at Samothrace has a rounded apse
like a Christian basilica.

The number of temples built was very great, as, beside
the new cities, many settlements and associations required
one ; but the Serapeum at Delos shews that these last
must, inevitably, have often been poor cheap work ; clubs
of 50 members could not afford much of a chapel. An
unexplained phenomenon is the building with raised tiers
of seats like a theatre annexed to the temple of Artemis
Nanaia at Doura ; it is thought that in it some sacred
dance was performed. Among the great temples of the
time the most notable were Parmeniscus' Serapeum at
Alexandria, where a Roman pillar still marks the site of

the Serapis column, and the temples of Zeus Olympius at
Athens, completed under Hadrian, and of Apollo at Didyma
near Miletus, never really finished at all; most beautiful
was said to be that of Artemis Leukophryene at Magnesia
on the Maeander, planned by Hermogenes and completed
in 129. The Artemision at Ephesus, the wonder of the
world, can hardly be included here, as it is essentially
fourth century; but a short description of Didyma may
be given. Strabo calls Didyma the greatest of Greek
temples, but in fact Sicily has the honour, the dimensions
in feet of the five largest being : Zeus at Acragas, 363 by
182 ; G at Selinus, 360 by 163 ; Didyma, 354 by 160 ;
Artemis at Ephesus, 342 by 164 ; Zeus at Athens, 354 by
135.

The old temple at Didyma had been burnt in the Ionian
revolt, and Miletus began the new one about 300. Didyma
could only be reached by sea, and the Sacred Way from
the landing-place to the temple was still bordered by the
original archaic figures of worshippers ; this idea, which
came from the sphinx-bordered temple avenues of Egypt,
now returned again to Egypt from Didyma, the approach
to the Serapeum at Memphis being bordered by statues
of distinguished Greeks. The precinct of the temple was
shaped like a stadium, and some believe races were run
round it, Greek athletic sports being always part of a
festival primarily religious. The temple was dipteral and
decastyle, that is, it was surrounded by two rows of columns
and was ten columns in breadth along the front, no other
temple being more than eight. Instead of the usual two
columns *in antis*, *i.e.* in the recess between the cella walls,
there were twelve, in three rows of four each ; the impression made on the approaching visitor was of a forest of slender
Ionic columns, which suggested some Egyptian or Persian
hall, and was intended to divert his mind from the fact
that he could see no *naos*, the roofed room which held
the temple statue. For when he entered the *prodromos*
(vestibule), before him rose a six-foot screen of stone,
blocking all further view. At either side were staircases

s

with arched roofs ; passing down one, he entered what
replaced the *naos*, a court fourteen feet below the floor
level and open to the sky. Beyond it was the shrine of
Canachus' Apollo, carried off by Darius I and sent back
in 295 by Seleucus ; but the visitor, turning his back on
Apollo, saw before him the grand stairway of 22 steps,
leading back the way he had come and up to the chamber
between the court and the *prodromos*, the ' oracle bureau ' ;
at the head of the stairway were three doors, two leading to upper rooms, possibly treasuries, while the central
one was the great door of the ' oracle bureau ', which
Ptolemy XIV covered with ivory. Didyma thus differed
absolutely from the well-known form of every other Greek
temple.   But the sculptured bases of its columns, and still
more the twelve columns *in antis*, went back to the sixth
century Artemision at Ephesus, just as the Sacred Way
belonged to an older world ; while one of the architects
of Didyma, Paeonius, had worked on the new Artemision
and probably desired to avoid repeating himself. Didyma
thus became a unique combination of audacious novelty
and conscious archaising.

With Hellenism, art changes its character. Classical
restraint goes ; there are no longer limitations, for it is a
time that tries all things and explores many new paths.
All the tendencies of the time are in its sculpture : lack
of repose, for indeed the age knew little ; self-conscious-
ness, expressed in the theatricalism which has left its mark
at Pergamum ; romanticism, and realism even to ugliness.
Individualism breaks through in the outburst of portrait
statuary, the brotherhood of human beings in the representation of old working people, like the rather wonderful
old shepherdess and fisherman of the Conservatori palace
at Rome.   The Fortune of Antioch reminds us that Fortune was the typical worship of the third century, just as
the Isis of Delos introduces the new world of the first ;
Struggle is personified in the Pergamene frieze, and Triumph
is glorified, as never before or since, in the Victory of
Samothrace.   Happily every attempt to express something

otherwise than had been done by Phidias or Praxiteles is
no longer condemned offhand, and no one need feel a sense
of guilt in admiring some Hellenistic work. Decadence
ultimately shewed, of course ; things like the Alexandrian
grotesques, the degradation of Eros into a cupid, the transition from Theocritus to the artificial ' nature ' of the
pastoral reliefs, statues like the once-admired Laocoon, all
illustrate tendencies at work. Idealism gradually declined,
and inspiration began to be drawn, not from the artist's
soul, but from the past. But even so, technical skill never
failed till sculpture at the end became a trade ; and the
continuing love of beauty may be illustrated by the fact
that the Aphrodite of Melos (Venus of Milo) and the Aphrodite Anadyomene of Cyrene are both now assigned to the
late second century.

Much work has been done on the tendencies of these
three centuries ; local schools have been traced, or the
time has been divided into periods without regard to
locality, sometimes labelled with terms of an alien art,
baroque or rococo ; perhaps one who is not an art-critic
may be pardoned a certain distrust in face of a science of
criticism which during the last few years has succeeded
in placing the Victory of Samothrace everywhere from 322
to 31, including dates which, to the historian, are frankly
absurd. That sculpture was a living force is shewn by
the enormous output and the occasional prices paid ;
though about £120 was a usual price for a good statue,
Attalus II is said once to have paid £25,000 for one ;
Philip V found 2,000 statues at Thermum and the Romans
took 1,000 from Ambracia, both places which were certainly not art-centres. The considerable mass of Hellenistic work still known, in originals, fragments, and copies,
bears no relation at all to what once existed ; for this
was the age of the honorary and votive statue, and every
Greek city set up considerable numbers, some doubtless
good ; but the hereditary families of sculptors known illustrate the gradual transition from art to craft in this matter.
The final step came after the Roman conquests, when the

plunder of a Mummius or a Verres induced at Rome a taste
for Greek statuary in bulk, as a self-made man furnishes
a library. Athens' commercial resurrection after 146 was
partly due to her supplying Rome's need, both by original
work based on older statues and by good copies, and other
cities imitated her ; the better things of the sort can be
seen in the over-muscled Farnese Hercules and the over-
graceful Apollo Belvedere. Ultimately a Roman firm, the
Cossutii, set up branches throughout Greece wherever there
was marble and engaged Greeks to turn out statues wholesale for the Roman market ; and sculpture, which began
as a religion, ended as a trade.

There was seemingly a school at Alexandria, though she
was primarily a collecting centre ; but the work so far
found in Egypt is chiefly second-rate, and the Alexandrian
grave-reliefs are hardly even that, unless for the one generation when Athenian artists, quitting Athens because Demetrius of Phalerum's prohibition of grave-reliefs had spoilt
their livelihood, settled in Alexandria ; it was in Egypt
that the practice arose of putting on statues' hair in
stucco. Praxiteles' influence remained great, and not
only at Alexandria, but the smoothness of his skin-texture
became exaggerated ; the beautiful Cyrene Aphrodite illustrates the style, which sometimes merely covered slack work.
Alexandria's real strength was in the smaller arts ; probably she invented mosaic and cameo-cutting, while Pyrgoteles' gem-engraving was far superior to anything previously
seen. Curiously, though idealism fared badly in Alexandrian art, the city contained one strongly idealist work, the
cult-statue of Serapis. The original statue, possibly of the
Asclepius type, may really have been the work of Scopas'
pupil Bryaxis, wherever Ptolemy I brought it from ; but
the statue whose description and copies survive was possibly a replacement of it somewhere about 200. This
statue was coloured dark blue, and the eyes were jewelled,
to gleam through the darkened temple from the richly
decorated and lighted cella ; the face is described as mild,
majestic, and mysterious, as befitted the god of the under-

world, and on the head was a *modius* or corn-measure,
significant of that great granary, Egypt.

Lysippus' influence lived on at Rhodes, where his pupil
Chares of Lindus, to commemorate Rhodes' resistance to
Demetrius in 304, carved that colossal statue of the Sun
which was one of the wonders of the world ; it was destroyed
by the earthquake of 225, and nothing remains to suggest
what it was like.   The Rhodian was a virile school, a school
of athletic men and carefully draped women ;  the well-
known Praying Boy of Berlin and the so-called Hellenistic
Ruler at Naples may illustrate its best period, and even in
the first century, when it had declined to the tortured
forms of the Laocoon and the Farnese Bull groups, its
technical mastery remained astonishing.   But the most
influential work of Lysippus' school was the famous Fortune of Antioch, made for Antioch by his pupil Eutychides,
a gracious and charming woman with a pensive face, seated
on her mountain with the river god Orontes at her feet ;
she was fully draped and wore a turreted crown, thenceforth the universal mark of the city-goddess, and held a
palm-leaf in her hand.   To say that she has not the dignity
or austerity of an older goddess is otiose, for she was not a
goddess (though she became one) ; she was the personifica-
tion, the individuality, of the group of men and women
who were Antioch (p. 281).   The type, with many variations to suit local circumstances, was copied by innumerable
cities throughout Asia.

The earlier history of the school of Pergamum is only
of technical interest, and Pergamene great art, in which
Scopas' influence lived again, dated from the two victories
of Attalus I over the Gauls (before 230).   Some marble
copies, probably contemporary, remain of Gallic figures
from his monument of victory, the best known being the
Dying Gaul of the Capitol, immortalised by Byron as the
Dying Gladiator, and the group of the Gaul who has killed
his wife and is stabbing himself.   They are rated highly ;
the artists of the monument have found a new kind of
realism in rendering the strange type and rough-hewn

features of the barbarians, fearless of death though impatient of defeat ; they have caught more of the Celtic spirit than the literary men ever did. The second phase of this art is shewn in the titanic frieze of the altar of Zeus at Pergamum, more than 400 feet long, which exhibits, with vast learning, the battle of the gods against the Titans. The strange shapes of the Earth-born, some ending in serpents, the multiplied attitudes and incidents of every form of contest, some impressive, some theatrical, the wild turmoil and motion of the whole, are like nothing else in Greek art ; whatever else the frieze was, it must have been enormously effective, and Christian literature was not far wrong in calling the altar ' Satan's seat ', for it expressed Hellenism as nothing else ever did ; the whole tumult of the age, the meeting of civilisation and barbarism, the conflict of good and evil, the striving with unfamiliar ways of expression, knowing no rest—all is there. It inevitably calls to mind another altar, the beautiful restful figure of Earth with her fruits on Augustus' *Ara Pacis*, when the struggle that was Hellenism had worn itself out, and the world asked of the Roman victor one boon only, peace.

The artistic affinities of the masterpiece of the age, the Victory of Samothrace, are, like her date, disputed ; but *some* connection with the Victory of Demetrius' coin, set up to commemorate his naval victory over Ptolemy I at Salamis in 306, seems assured, and the most satisfying view to the historian is Professor Studniczka's, which sees in her a monument set up in filial piety by Demetrius' son Antigonus Gonatas to commemorate *his* naval victory over Ptolemy II at Cos (*c.* 258). Viewed from the side as she stands in the Louvre, her mighty wings seem almost too large, which leaves little question that she was slightly tilted forward to balance them ; she was not standing, but alighting, on the galley's prow, and if Cos were really her battle her upraised right arm bore the Isthmian victor's crown. In this attitude her drapery is correct ; it shews the sweep of the sea-wind through it as she stays her flight.

Little imaginative work came from the Greek mainland,

where inartistic peoples, Achaeans and Aetolians, were supreme ; but Damophon's attempt (second century), in his colossal group of Despoina and Kora at Lycosura in Arcadia, to recapture the detached serenity of the older gods is interesting. Lysippus' portraits of Alexander, however, gave a tremendous impulse to portraiture, which spread outward from the mainland ; Polyeuctus' well-known Demosthenes (c. 280) is good, and conjecture to-day has a fair field among the great number of extant portrait-heads, some striking enough. But to realise what could be done we must go to the coins, where among much conventional work is found some of the very best, like the beautiful idealised Alexander-heads on Lysimachus' pieces, or that artistic mystery, high-water mark of Greek portraiture, the heads of the Graeco-Bactrian kings. Much relief work exists beside coins, but Schreiber's long series of Hellenistic reliefs belongs only in part to Hellenism ; a very beautiful set of early high reliefs, painted, are those on the Sidon sarcophagus depicting a battle and lion-hunt of Alexander. With relief, sculpture and painting join hands and mutually influence each other ; beside grave-reliefs painted over there stand other gravestones only painted.

These gravestones—those from Pagasae, though second-rate, are the best—are the only Hellenistic paintings extant in the original ; for vase-painting was over. The repute of the great masters shews that Greeks thought their painting as valuable as their sculpture ; what it was at its best can barely be guessed, for easel pictures have perished, and nothing remains of the historical painting of Apelles and his time except literary notices and one copy, the mosaic of Alexander's battle. All we have is wall decoration, an art essentially Hellenistic ; except for one or two tombs, it means Pompeii, where the first period derives from Alexandria. But Pompeii rarely even furnishes copies ; much of it is trade work, itself adapted from cheap trade copies—mythological subjects, grotesques, vapid cupids ; there are graceful little pieces of flowers and landscape, but they tell no more of great art than the Greek Anthology of great poetry. It seems possible to trace how the painted figure gradually shook itself free of its fourth-century affinity to sculpture,—perhaps the real work done by Hellenistic painting,—and how a knowledge both of perspective and of landscape emerged ; but though the Greek loved sun and air, his poetry shews little feeling for landscape ; the Pompeii landscapes are conventional and devoid of atmosphere, and probably landscape in painting was never much more than a setting for figures.

Two sets of figures, however, at Pompeii stand right out from the mass, and can be looked at for their own sakes and not as antiquarian curiosities. One is the beautiful group of women on the extreme right of the long scene of Dionysiac ritual in the Villa Item, which Pfuhl holds must go back to some great fresco ; the other, even more important, is the frescoes of the Villa Boscoreale, which give us portraiture, otherwise known only from the dreadful Fayum mummy-cases. These are supposed to be true copies (first century) of fine early third-century work representing the family group of Demetrius I ; their affinities are with the school of Lysippus. The rugged figure of the philosopher, with grand head and streaming white beard,—a figure of painting, not of sculpture,—might be some mediaeval John the Baptist grown old ; the sad thoughtfulness in the eyes of the woman called Eurydice is not easily forgotten. Above all, even the copy conveys the suggestion that these were in truth great men and women.

Except perhaps for certain influences on the temple at Didyma, the art here considered is purely a Greek development. Some interaction took place between Greek and Oriental art in this period ; but this difficult question is essentially one for experts, and most of the material, such as the architecture of Syria, the paintings from Doura, the important Gandhara school of sculpture in India, the necropolis of Kom-el-Chougafa in Egypt, belongs to the Roman Imperial age, whether its roots in any case go back to Hellenism or not. The sculptures of the monument of Antiochus I of Commagene (p. 136) shew local stone-cutters imitating late Greek work. The massive remains of the Tobiad stronghold at Arâk il-Emîr near Heshbon (second century), whether a temple or a fortress, reveal a Greek building with certain Persian and Phoenician borrowings. The Nabatean tomb of Hamrath at Suwêdā in the Haurân (c. 85–60) is also Greek, but the great Nabatean temple of Balsamem (Ba'al Shamin) at Sî in the Haurân (c. 33) shews little that is Greek beyond some inscriptions and the influence of the Corinthian column, an influence also traced in the arrangement of the palm-leaves on the capitals of the Egyptian (Ptolemaic) temples at Edfu and Esneh. Some Alexandrian grave-steles exhibit Egyptian influence ; and in the first century a revived native Egyptian sculpture began to turn out portraits under Greek influence. But most striking is the tomb (c. 300) near el Amarna of the Egyptian official Petosiris, discovered in 1920.[1] It resembles some Greek Heroön, though the architecture is Egyptian ; the motives of the reliefs are purely Egyptian, but Greek influence in execution is strong, notably in the sacrifice for the hero and the mourning women : also the women and peasants wear Greek costume, and the artist, who knows something of perspective, has tried to introduce Greek realism into the attitudes. Except for this tomb, it seems at present, to the layman, as if Greek influence on Oriental art did not amount to much before the Roman period.

This chapter must remain incomplete ; for nothing can be said here of Hellenistic music except that it played as great a part as to-day, and its appeal was not confined to the educated. Two hymns, written in five time, have been recovered from Delphi ; but music is a lost world, not merely because it has perished, but because, if we had it, few would now understand it, since Greek music was based on the employment of finer intervals than the semitone.

[1] A recent attempt has been made to date this monument in the Persian period.

# CHAPTER X

# PHILOSOPHY AND RELIGION

The philosophy of the Hellenistic world was the Stoa ; all else was secondary. What we see, broadly speaking, as we look down the three centuries, is that Aristotle's school loses all importance, and Plato's, for a century and a half, becomes a parasite upon the Stoa in the sense that its life as a school of scepticism consists wholly in combating Stoic doctrine ; Epicurus' school continues unchanged, but only attracts small minorities ; but the Stoa, which meanwhile has taken under its shield both popular and astral religion and many forms of superstition, finally masters Scepticism, in fact though not in argument, and takes to itself enough of a revived Platonism to form that modified Stoicism or Eclecticism which was the distinguishing philosophy of the earlier Roman empire.

Athens was the centre of philosophy throughout the entire period, though later on two great Stoics did work in Rhodes. Soon after 317 Demetrius of Phalerum procured for Aristotle's successor, the alien Theophrastus, the right to hold land and form Aristotle's school (the Peripatetics) into a legally organised association, like Plato's Academy ; in 306 the Athenian Epicurus came from Lampsacus and set up his school in his garden ; Zeno came to Athens after 317 and began to teach in the Painted Porch, the Stoa, in 302 ; and the early third century saw the four schools, like great colleges, working side by side. Aristotle's school had its brief day of power from 317 onwards ; Cassander favoured it, Theophrastus inspired the laws of Demetrius of Phalerum, and Demetrius himself after his fall helped Ptolemy I to found the Museum. Theophrastus was a many-sided man of great learning; but after the death of his successor Strato the school abandoned its founder's search for theoretic knowledge, and by the middle of the third century its work was over; it had rendered much service to science and much disservice to history, but it did nothing more for the world except to contribute a few elements later to eclecticism. Like Aristotle himself, it was alien to Athens and usually antipathetic to the Antigonids; it might have had a better chance had it moved to Alexandria with Demetrius. Plato's school could not die, for it was Athenian of Athens; but it also abandoned the search for knowledge, and when Arcesilaus revivified it, it was to be on lines which, though they might go back to Socrates, had little to do with Plato.

The small local schools died out or merged in the Middle Academy of Arcesilaus, though Menedemus of Eretria, the teacher and friend of Antigonus Gonatas, was a notable and attractive figure, a man of strong sense and character and the centre of a brilliant literary circle; his friends compared him to Socrates, but he left neither writings nor successor, and his influence, which depended on his personality, died with him. The Cynics, however, remained an active body. They had no established centre, as became their profession of poverty; but their appeal was largely to the poor, and their roughness and studied neglect of ordinary decorums and courtesies rather discounted the manliness of their attitude toward life, though they did affect the early Stoa. But Zeno's teacher the Cynic Crates, the 'physician of souls', seems to have been a man; he had much wit and more earnestness, stripped himself of a large fortune to lead the life of a beggar and a preacher, and, though ugly, so won the devotion of his pupil Hipparchia that she too gave up everything to marry him and share his way of life; a man who in that age attacked sexual immorality as scathingly as he did was something of a portent. But the weakness of the Cynics was precisely that 'beggar's wallet' which Crates glorified: they saved their souls by living on common people who had no time to save their own. That strange creature Bion of Borysthenes, another friend of Antigonus Gonatas, was also three parts Cynic. He had risen from a lowly origin, and was vain of his wit and with something of the vulgar mountebank about him ; but beneath the outer husk lay humanity and a sort of simple manliness, and his influence was great, for he was the first of a long line of wandering teachers who popularised philosophy and whom Origen afterwards compared to the wandering Christian preachers ; they gave the age a sort of spiritual background. Though no original thinker, he had force enough to make men listen ; and even at the Rhodian docks he drew the sailors in crowds with his usual message—do your duty, be content with little if so it be, and face your fortune like a man. To understand what that feat meant, translate it to the London docks to-day.

The two new philosophies, those of Epicurus and Zeno, were both products of the new world which Alexander had made, and primarily of the feeling that a man was no longer merely a part of his city ; he was an individual, and as such needed new guidance. The two philosophies both aimed, not at the discovery of truth, but at the satisfaction of practical needs ; and they accordingly had certain things in common. The aim of philosophy was the happiness of the individual ; and what mattered was conduct. Both therefore went back behind Plato and Aristotle to Socrates. Both were content to take sense-impressions as true, Epicurus saying that all were true, while Zeno made the criterion of truth the impression which so grips you that disbelief is impossible ; both treated the universe, including man's soul, as composed of something material (though to the Stoics, who were really intensely spiritual, this was a mere matter of words) and adopted existing physical explanations, Epicurus that of Democritus, Zeno that of Heraclitus. Both desired the avoidance of passions and emotions, which bring the unhappiness of unsatisfied desire. Both laid their full stress on ethics, morality, which they absolutely divorced from politics ; neither cared for science or learning. But there the resemblance ends ; in essentials they were as far asunder as the poles. The new world was affecting men in two ways. The majority felt that they belonged to it, but were sailing an uncharted sea ; this the Stoa set out to chart. But a minority felt oppressed and fearful, and desired escape ; and for them Epicurus pointed a way.

The world they dreaded, he said, was only a machine. No gods, good or evil, affected it ; it was not made or guided by design ; it came into being through certain mechanical principles. He revived Democritus' atomic theory : atoms (he meant molecules) fell in a ceaseless rain through the void, and their clashing formed the world. But at once he met two difficulties. Atoms falling in a straight line through the void could not, as he understood it, clash. Also he cared nothing for atoms, and very much for ethics ; and there could be no morality without free-will. He solved his two problems together : the atoms had the power of deliberately swerving a little, in order to meet ; that is, he gave them free-will. His mechanical world, then, had something more than mechanics in it from the start ; the materialist could only make a world at all by denying his own principles. The rest was easy, and Empedocles' idea that many less adapted animal forms had been tried and had died out helped him ; the result can be seen in the wonderful description of the evolution of life on the earth in the supreme monument of this school, Lucretius' poem *On the Nature of Things*. Epicurus' aim was, by constructing a world on scientific principles, to free men from fear of the gods and the evils of superstition ; man's soul at death dissolved again into the atoms which made it. His school did render good service by refusing to touch divination and astrology. But he conceded this much to popular belief, that gods existed ; only they *did* nothing, except exhibit an ideal happiness. They were a little company of Epicurean philosophers, of extreme tenuity, living in intra-mundane space, and conversing perpetually, probably in Greek ; one slides insensibly into Cicero's parody that their sole occupation was to say to each other ' How happy I am '.

But his ethics were serious enough. Happiness was the aim ; and happiness meant pleasure ; pleasure was the one true good. But not the physical or sensual pleasures of his predecessors the Cyrenaics ; intellectual pleasure primarily, for the mind matters most. And passive pleasure rather than active,—repose, freedom from passions, desires, needs, above all absence of pain ; the keyword of man's effort was to be *ataraxia*, escape from worry. Virtue was vital, but not, as the Stoics taught, for its own sake,—that had no meaning ; it was vital because without it happiness could not be. This constituted a doctrine of renunciation, a renunciation of active effort and positive happiness, and his followers formed little isles of quietude apart, bound together by the friendship he so stressed ; except that they lived among their fellows and enjoyed family life, one might call them, spiritually, the first monks. They never influenced the great world ; they had no wish to. They never altered or added to what their founder taught. But they met a perpetual human need, and they never died out ; in the second century A.D. an unknown Diogenes at Oenoanda in Lycia set up their teaching in a long inscription on a stone because it had brought him a happiness and peace which he wanted his fellow-men to share. Epicurus himself, who died in 270, was a gentle frugal man, who bore his last painful illness with quiet fortitude ; his personal success in Athens was considerable, and the lives of his own circle, which included women, were not only exemplary but a fragrant oasis in a stormy age ; and if his doctrine of pleasure was sometimes abused, this was not done by those who really followed his teaching. The real reproach against his philosophy was that it taught men to shirk living ; it was a running away.

Very different was the gaunt ascetic Phoenician who founded the Stoa, Zeno of Citium in Cyprus, the noblest man of his age. Shy and silent, a foreigner who spoke and

wrote indifferent Greek, he made headway but slowly ;
he had no centre for his followers like Epicurus' Garden,
and talked to those who came in a public colonnade, a
forecast of the fact that the Stoic teachers were never to
be tied to a centre at Athens, but were to spread throughout
the world. But early in his career he attracted Antigonus
Gonatas, who became his pupil and his life-long friend,
doubtless a help to him in the worldly sense, and long
before his death his personality had conquered Athens,
especially the young men, over whom his influence is said
to have been great ; though Antigonus' friend, he kept
clear of politics, and when he died after the war between
Antigonus and Athens, which must to him have been acute
torture, Athens gave him a public funeral and one of the
most beautiful testimonials any man ever received ; for
the striking decree which accompanied the honours voted
to him after death ended with the words " He made his life
a pattern to all, for he followed his own teaching." He
left a notable circle of pupils, among them Ariston, who
taught Eratosthenes ; Persaeus, who went to Antigonus
as spiritual adviser ; and Sphaerus, who inspired Cleomenes'
revolution at Sparta. Zeno's successor, Cleanthes of Assos,
author of the greatest religious hymn in Greek, was to
bring out the religious side of his doctrine ; Cleanthes'
successor Chrysippus of Soli, a voluminous writer, got the
tenets of the school elaborately laid down in many books ;
Panaetius and Poseidonius we shall meet later. Unhappily
the writings of Zeno and Chrysippus are lost, except for
fragments, and no Stoic writings survive in completeness
till we come to the Eclectics of the Roman Empire—
Seneca, Marcus Aurelius, Epictetus ; though Cicero's *De
Officiis* represents Panaetius' treatise *On Duties*. Zeno at
the start owed something to Heraclitus, possibly something
to Babylon (p. 287), and much to the Cynics ; but the great
system of ethics developed by himself and his successors
was very different from anything the Cynics ever envisaged.

The Stoic idea of brotherhood and a World State has
already been noticed (p. 69). Their Universe was in fact

one great city ;  and it was ruled by one Supreme Power
whom the Stoics envisaged under many aspects and names
—Destiny, Zeus, Providence, the Universal Law, Nature.
From this Power, conceived of in their material terminology as a fifth element or divine Fire, came all that exists,
heaven and earth and all that is therein, including the
soul of man ;  everything was a derivative of God, and in
a derivative sense *was* God ;  the spark in man's nature
was akin to the divine.   The universe, at the end of every
world-period—a recurring cycle of enormous length,—was
reabsorbed into the divine Fire, and then started afresh
to run an exact repetition of its course ;  ages hence another
Socrates would teach in another Athens, and there was
nothing new under the sun ;  all had happened before,
and history merely repeated itself, a strange idea but
familiar to us from the superb lyric at the close of Shelley's
*Hellas*.   Hence the Power that ruled the universe was
Destiny ;  but it differed from the terrible Babylonian
Fate, for it was all-wise, and that which it decreed for men
was best for them.   Indeed it was God, for the universe
was the product of design, and He had made the laws which
ruled it, summed up in that Universal Law which was
really Himself ;  He too obeyed the law He had created.
He was not a God devoid of moral attributes, for His
design was all-wise and all-good ;  the stars did not turn
blindly in their courses, but illustrated His Providence
for sailor and husbandman.   In the hands of the religious
Cleanthes He is even a merciful God ;  He makes all the
odds even, and that which is dear to none other is dear
unto Him.   Still, everything was determined ;  and in
Determinism the Stoics encountered the usual difficulty,
for first and foremost their system was a moral one, and
without free-will there could be no morality ;  the logical
outcome of Determinism is antinomianism—I may do what
evil I will, for that too is fated.

Another difficulty they met was in the practical bearing
of the idea of a World State.   As all men were citizens
of one City, all ought to be equal.   But in fact men differed

in character, ability, circumstances ; in Chrysippus' metaphor, nothing could prevent some seats in the theatre being better than others ; all men therefore were not and could not be alike, and equality was only a theory. Also their World State was in practice unrealisable ; for the world was composed of ordinary men, ruled by people who were not philosophers and had no knowledge of the Universal Law. Fortunately the Stoics were content to do what they could ; they stood behind the king's throne and advised ; they wrote treatises on how States should be governed ; they were ready to fight against bad governments, notably tyranny, or, like Sphaerus at Sparta and Blossius at Pergamum, to work for any reform which promised greater equality to the people, any step towards their own form of Communism, which meant Concord and the abolition of class-war.

Consistently with their principles, then, they seemingly could not admit either free-will or inequality, and yet they had to accept both. Their solution of both dilemmas was to go back to the root principle of Wisdom or Mind. Human minds were sparks of the divine Fire, but the human body was clay ; therefore the body mattered nothing. Zeno said that all that had to do with the body—strength and weakness, sickness and health, wealth and poverty— was matter of indifference ; and this, in theory, remained their attitude throughout. The Stoic sage, the Wise Man, would neglect such things, and turn only to the things of the soul. But these were, or could be, the same for all men ; the slave in the silver mines, brutalised in body, might still in his soul follow after Wisdom and be the peer of the philosopher or the saint. Men then *were* equal after all, for all, if they wished, could be equal in their souls ; in that realm the beggar might be king.

Through Wisdom they also solved Determinism. Certainly their Wise Man was a monster, passionless, pitiless, perfect ; he would do good, but without feeling for others, for his calm must remain unruffled ; in Paul's words, he would give his body to be burnt, but he had not love, and

T

it is strange that Zeno, who had based his Ideal State upon Love, gave no place to love of others in the Wise Man's composition. But man reads what he will into his ideal, and that the Wise Man acted as an ideal is unquestionable; he was something to aim at, but never (fortunately) to reach. But Wisdom was of the Divine Power; true wisdom therefore on earth must be coincident with the Divine, and the wise man would desire that which God or Destiny in its wisdom had ordained for him. Therewith, for Stoics, the contradiction of determinism and free-will was transcended by a new philosophic concept, duty; man *had* free-will, but it was his imperative duty so to employ it as to approximate to the Divine Will. Whether he submitted to Destiny, or kicked against the pricks, made no difference in the material sphere; he had to go the way marked out for him. But in proportion as he attained to wisdom, so would he recognise that that way was the right way, and find peace of mind, and the truly wise would need neither driving nor leading; he would see, and gladly anticipate, that which Destiny intended; the free exercise of his own will would simply bring him into unison with the will of God. The ideal man, when he came, would say ' Thy will be done.'

Therewith too, for himself, the Stoic solved the ancient problem of happiness. Unhappiness usually arose from wanting something you had not got or could not get; the way to be happy, then, was to want what you got, that is, to go in accord with the Divine will. This is what they meant by ' living according to Nature ', and not the rather material sense in which the Cynics employed that phrase; for Nature too was God. Certainly they used this conception to discard from consideration luxury and pleasure, wealth and success, the complexities of civilisation, which were no part of the Divine plan. But accordance with the Divine will meant far more than neglecting these material things : the Stoic will not grieve for his son's death, for the decree is all-wise, and nothing better could have happened. For the Supreme Power is not only all-wise but all-virtuous ; what it does is best. To reach harmony with that Power, therefore, the thing most necessary is Virtue ; and virtue, and nothing else, is therefore happiness ; virtue *is* its own sufficient reward. For centuries many men believed this, and some practised it.

Virtue was the central point of Stoic ethics. On this Zeno was uncompromising ; the intention to do evil, he said, was equivalent to doing it. At first he said that all that was not absolute virtue was vice ; but this rule was so unworkable that he had to modify it himself before he died by granting a middle sphere of things indifferent, which subsequently became divided into things to be preferred and things to be rejected, the Stoic being bound to choose the former ; on these lines the main Stoic conception of duty was strongly reinforced. That you *ought* to follow the moral course was to them not an assumption, for Stoicism's first postulate was that it was itself a moral system, and it could claim that the contrary course must be wrong because it introduced discord into the cosmic order, which was a bigger thing than mankind. Now man's means of getting into harmony with God were wisdom and virtue, and in both these matters progress was possible ; the Stoic was thus led to examine the progress he was making, and the idea arose of conscious moral growth. Moreover the Supreme Power had had forethought for men, and they had an aid on the path ; there now first appeared in philosophy the conception of conscience. Conscience and Duty were the corner-stones of Stoic ethics.

The influence of those ethics on the world and on Christianity was to be great. Critics might carry the outworks of the system, or wits riddle the Wise Man with their arrows, but the central fortress, the philosophy of conduct, was to stand firm. Stoicism in fact was as much a religion as a philosophy, and a virile one, as it was to show. Strength was needed to despise the things of the body, and on strong natures it acted as a tonic ; the true Stoic, whatever else he was, was captain of his soul, or, in their phrase, *autarkes*, sufficient to himself. And he was master of his fate ; fate could not hurt him, for what it brought him was what he would have chosen. But to all, strong and weak, it had a message, its insistence on the things of the soul. Whatever the world did to you, in one sphere the world had no power ; you could withdraw into your own soul, and there find peace ; for none could harm you *there* but yourself.

The Sceptic school started with Pyrrhon of Elis, who in youth accompanied Alexander to India ; but he wrote nothing, and is known only through his disciple Timon the ' sillographer ' (p. 225). Timon's doctrine was simple. The source of trouble is contradictory knowledge, but nothing can be known, therefore suspend your judgment and never dogmatise ; remember too that nothing matters, not even whether you live or die ; thus you will attain the goal, imperturbability. He attained to a good deal of money by preaching this throughout the world, but did not attain to imperturbability, for much of his life was spent in attacking Arcesilaus for poaching on his preserve ; and he left no successor, for with Arcesilaus (c. 264–242) Scepticism passed over to the Academy. Arcesilaus was a patriotic Athenian of fine character, but as a philosopher he was a negative force ; he too believed that knowledge was impossible, and thought that he had demonstrated this merely by overthrowing the Stoic theory of knowledge, the ' irresistible impression ', a tribute to the position the Stoa had attained. His greater successor Carneades (213– 129) was so occupied in fighting the Stoa that he said of himself that he would never have been anybody but for Chrysippus. He did good service by attacking the Stoa's shadow side, divination and astrology, and forcing Panaetius to modify his position in this regard ; and it was not difficult to destroy the ' irresistible impression '. But Carneades produced no real effect ; he could not touch the essentials of Stoicism, and the world simply passed him by. For the world had somehow to live and act, and here Carneades had nothing to offer. Knowledge being impossible, Arcesilaus had said the guide of action must be Reasonableness, which meant nothing ; Carneades substituted Probability, but could only interpret it to mean ' Do as your neighbours do.' He also laid himself open to much misconstruction by his habit of arguing for or against any thesis indiscriminately, as an intellectual exercise ; he tried this at Rome in 156, and plain Romans were shocked at such immoral levity ; even his pupil, the Carthaginian Hasdrubal-Clitomachus, who composed 400 rolls in an attempt to reduce Carneades' oral teaching to writing, confessed that he sometimes did not know which was Carneades' real view. But Carneades, though he had a sort of passion for destruction, was a man of good personal repute, and one of the acutest minds Greece ever produced ; and some of the difficulties he raised have never been answered. Scepticism died with him, but revived again with Cicero's contemporary Aenesidemus, and again under the Antonines ; it did supply a want, for it was useful that someone should criticise and prune dogmatic philosophy.

It has been truly said that in the religious sphere the only vital things in Hellenism were philosophy and the Oriental religions. Twilight was indeed falling on the Olympians, in spite of external show—new epiphanies, new festivals, the attempted religious revival in Greece after 146 (p. 36). The great temples that were built and completed were generally to some alien deity, like Serapis of Alexandria or the Fair-browed goddess of Magnesia ; the chief exception was that of Athene Polias at Pergamum, built by the Attalid kings for political reasons, for their real god, ancestor of their line, was Dionysus. What was happening can be seen in the one great temple a Greek city planned to a Greek god : Apollo's temple at Didyma was still unfinished four centuries later, not for lack of money at Miletus, but for lack of that living faith which had formerly enabled cities to complete their temples in a generation. Once Zeus at Dodona had himself spoken to his devotees as a god might, in the wind in the oak tree, the bubbles on the spring ; at Didyma oracle-giving was a business, conducted from a bureau. Many things conspired to decide the fate of the Olympians. They belonged

to, and fell with, the city state ; philosophy killed them
for the educated, individualism for the common man ;
he was no longer part of the city, content with whatever
its corporate worship might be, but wanted something
that spoke to himself. But perhaps what settled the
matter was the conquest of Asia and Egypt ; for it was a
conquest by the sword alone, not the spirit. Greece was
ready to adopt the gods of the foreigner, but the foreigner
rarely reciprocated ;  Greek Doura freely admitted the
gods of Babylon, but no Greek god entered Babylonian
Uruk. Foreign gods might take Greek names ; they took
little else. They were the stronger, and the conquest of
Asia was bound to fail as soon as the East, in the religious
sphere, had gauged its own strength and Greek weakness ;
for what Greece could give to Asia, science and philosophy,
only a chosen few could take ; these things were never for
the mass. Had Ptolemy I enthroned Zeus in Alexandria
and persecuted Osiris, Egypt would have fought but would
have understood ; that the Ptolemies instead built temples
to Egyptian deities meant to Egyptians not toleration but
weakness—the invader had no faith in his own gods. From
the second century Hellenism was between the hammer
and the anvil, the sword of Rome and the spirit of Egypt
and Babylon. One man saw it—Antiochus Epiphanes—
and has been called a madman ever since. But his attempt
to unify his realm on a basis of Greek religion and culture
failed ; and Greek religion got no second chance.

Individualism shewed itself in the enormous outburst
of private associations after 300 (p. 81). They were the
regular channel by which foreign worships entered a Greek
city ; a few foreigners settled there would club together
to worship their own god, and Greeks might join them.
These associations probably made for diversity in cult-
practice ; for example, many a Dionysus club in Egypt
had its own *hieros logos* or ritual book. A foreign club
might worship the god of the city in which it settled, as
the Haliastai at Rhodes worshipped Helios ; but a Greek
club, though it often worshipped some Olympian, never

worshipped its own city-god. The Muses came into prominence as the official deities of the great corporations of
learning, the four philosophic schools at Athens and the
Museum at Alexandria ; the worship of a whole class of
helping or protecting demons—Amynos and Hypodectes
at Athens, Pasios at Cos, Anthister at Thera—helped to
prepare the way for Oriental demonology ; family clubs
would worship their ancestor as a hero. But one thing,
in the third century, the clubs never did : they never worshipped the deified king, a strong indication that king-
worship in its inception was a purely political phenomenon.
The first case of such king-worship was when the Asiatic
branch of the Dionysiac artists, under the lead of Craton
of Teos, worshipped Eumenes II, and Craton founded the
club of Attalistai ; for the Egyptian Basilistai always
worshipped some god.

Far the most important Greek god of the age outside
Greece was Dionysus, whom the Dionysiac artists carried
all over the world ; art and literature gave him a trium-
phal progress across Asia on the model of Alexander's.
His name Sabazios was equated with Sabaoth, and he thus
affected the Jewish Diaspora (p. 180) ; the Orphics identified him with very many deities, and in Egypt he was
identified with Serapis through the Osiris element in the
latter. He became ancestor of the Ptolemies, as well as
of the Attalids, and possibly his enthusiastic devotee
Ptolemy IV dreamt of making him the chief god of his
composite empire (p. 168). Certainly if any Greek god
was to conquer the world, Dionysus was the only one
possible. But great as the influence of the Orphics subsequently became, it was not on these lines that things were
to shape themselves.

A dominant factor of the time was the striving after
one god. Alexander had transcended national states,
which implied transcending national cults ; and though
there was no longer one empire, there was one ' inhabited
world ' and one culture, which imported (it seemed) one
god, an idea to which philosophy had accustomed the

educated. This might take the form of the national god claiming to be god of the whole earth, as Yahweh in Judaea ; but another movement, very typically Hellenistic, was a great expansion of syncretism, the equation or fusion of one god with another as being alike forms of the one divinity behind them. Men would worship any god impartially ; when Stratonice, wife of Antiochus I, enriched Apollo of Delos, rebuilt the temple of the Syrian Atargatis at Hiera-polis, and joined a club at Smyrna which worshipped the Egyptian Anubis, she doubtless saw in them merely forms of one deity. The process was assisted by Stoicism. The Stoics did not reject the gods of the people ; they made them *daimones*, and brought them into their pantheistic system by allegorising all the myths, however barbarous ; they sought to explain, not destroy, for the gods too were part of the beneficent world-order, veils mercifully granted to the common man to spare his eyes the too dazzling nakedness of truth.

One deity, however, stood apart ; even the Stoics could not assimilate Fortune. Fortune was a thoroughly Hellen-istic conception. The first Peripatetics, Demetrius of Phalerum and Theophrastus, moulded her form ; Men-ander suggested she might be Providence ; an unknown poet compared her to Iris, the messenger of the gods. She dominated the third century, and even Polybius and Poseidonius later did not disdain the concession to popular belief implied in the use of her name. She was not blind chance, but some order of affairs which men could not comprehend. But all could see her. Fortune had brought this general of Alexander's to a throne, that to a grave ; Fortune had decreed that Macedonia should strike down Persia and would herself (so Demetrius prophesied) fall in turn ; after Cynoscephalae the Greeks sympathised with Philip V because Fortune had reversed her wheel. She was not altogether an unkindly goddess, for she did not deprive men of hope : to-day to thee, but to-morrow to me. Each man had his own Fortune, his *daimon*,— Romans called it his *Genius* ; it was almost his individuality. Cities swore by the king's *daimon*, men had an implicit belief in the ' Fortune ' of Alexander or Antigonus Doson, and the great influence of Eutychides' statue of the Fortune of Antioch ultimately made of a city's Fortune the city goddess.

For the educated, the place of religion was being taken by philosophy and science. But these hardly affected the common man ; he must worship something, and, as the Olympians faded, a more real religious feeling began to develop, and the appeal of the intimate and confident oriental worships became irresistible. In this sphere the East led its conqueror captive ; and though the movement did not perhaps culminate till after the Christian era, it was gathering strength all through the Hellenistic period. One must, however, distinguish between the countries.[1] Of Persia, ultimately so great a force, nothing can be said here ; what Zoroastrianism was doing is most obscure, and the day of Mithras the Unconquerable was not yet, though the Cilician pirates worshipped him in the first century ; the Mithraion mentioned in Egypt was only a local chapel of some Persian mercenaries. The two world-influences came from Babylon and Egypt ; the cults of Syria and Anatolia exercised much local influence, but (except perhaps for the Anatolian mysteries) only sporadically affected other centres.

In Syria the old religions grew in power, though partly under Graecised forms ; the coins, especially of the Roman period, reveal a very medley of cults and syncretisms. But though several old priest-states of the Anatolian type are known, there was no really dominant deity, doubtless because Syria had always been politically divided into several kingdoms or spheres of influence. The most powerful god was Hadad of Damascus (Rimmon of the Old Testament), who absorbed many local Baals ; he became Zeus of Damascus and Zeus of Heliopolis (Baalbek), but his chief temple was at Hierapolis-Bambyce (Mabbog), where he was Zeus before 150. His consort at Damascus and

[1] For Judaism, see Chap. VI.

Hierapolis, Atargatis, Lucian's 'Syrian goddess', was originally a pointed stone (betyl), but had long since become a woman under the influence of the invading Persian goddess Anahita (Anaïtis) ; subsequently she often became a Greek city-goddess. Her most famous temples were those at Hierapolis, whither at the biennial festival men came from all over Asia to be purified in her sacred pool and where tame lions and bears lived in the precinct, and at Ascalon, where she was a mermaid, with the local name of Derceto ; wherever she went she brought her sacred pool and sacred fish, the fishes of the Euphrates who had assisted at her birth and been rewarded with a place in the Zodiac ; her fish-pond, eunuchs, and lions relate her to Artemis of Ephesus and the Anatolian goddess, the 'Lady of the Wild'. Her temples were the home of clouds of pigeons, as some mosques to-day. Hadad had reached Delos before 100, but Atargatis went further ; she was one element of that 'Syrian Aphrodite'—the other being the Phoenician Astarte—who travelled all over Greece and even reached Macedonia, and whose club at Athens shared the precinct of her kinswoman the Anatolian Mother.

Atargatis was not the only betyl in Syria ; the black stone at Emesa, Elagabal, was to play a great part at Rome later, and another stone throws some light on a Seleucid city, Seleuceia in Pieria. For the two gods of Seleuceia's worship were a thunder-god, Zeus Keraunios (probably Balsamem, the 'Lord of Heaven'), and Zeus Kasios, a conical stone enshrined on the neighbouring Mount Kasios ; Seleuceia therefore had officially adopted the local native worships, as Doura officially adopted Adad and Nanaia from Babylon. Zeus Kasios travelled to Egypt, and thence to Delos ; but at Seleuceia he remained a stone, and did not achieve human form till Hadrian's time. Similarly the Ammonite Milcom (Moloch) survived throughout as a god of the hellenised Rabbath-Ammon (Philadelphia). But the most interesting god of all was the local deity of the little town of Doliche in Commagene, who lived

' where the iron grew ' [1] ; for he was really Teïsbas (the Hittite Teschub), god of that strange broken people the Chaldi or Chalybes, the greatest iron-smiths of the world west of China, who had once ruled a kingdom in Armenia, but were now scattered in groups wherever there was iron to enable them to set up their forges and practise their inherited technique ; later, as Jupiter Dolichenus, their little iron-god with his hammer was to spread throughout the Roman Empire in the track of the Roman sword.

The temple states of Asia Minor have already been described (Chap. IV). How old the worship of the Anatolian nature-goddess and her son and consort was cannot be said ; but Greeks, from Herodotus to Hippolytus, had a persistent tradition that the ' Phrygians ' were the oldest race on earth and their religion older than the Egyptian. The true Anatolian worship was probably far older than Phrygians or Hittites, but it cannot be said to what lost people it goes back, or what were the original names of the goddess and her son, which may always have varied locally ; perhaps Ma looks as old as anything. The original worship had been overlaid and syncretised by layer after layer of invaders ; the Hittites apparently contributed a peasant deity, who reinforced the god ; the Indo-European Phrygians brought their sky-god, who in the sanctuaries he invaded elevated the god at the expense of the goddess and took the respectable name of Zeus ; the Persians brought Anaïtis, who reinforced the goddess. The temple prostitutes also occur in Babylonia, but it cannot be said which borrowed from which, or if both go back to some earlier world. Certainly, though the Greeks brought their own gods to the cities, many of the Greek names in Anatolia are modern appellations of native gods. The connection of the Anatolian goddess with Greece may be extremely old ; but as regards Hellenism, though Meter—the Anatolian Mother—had her associations for worship in Athens

---

[1] Iron was supposed also to ' grow ' afresh in the Elba mines, and Hippolytus records that the Naassenes believed that minerals had life ' because they grew '.

from the fourth century onwards and as Cybele ultimately reached Rome, and though Attis and Adonis penetrated the Hellenistic clubs, the Anatolian religion on the whole remained rooted to the soil of Anatolia. But in its own land it was enormously strong ; even at Ephesus Artemis maintained herself as a State within the State till Lysimachus' time. Valuable statistics have been collected for the most hellenised province, Lydia, outside the Greek cities ; 117 inscriptions refer to Greek cults and 237 to Asiatic, of which 112 relate to the Anatolian goddess and her son ; the figures shew how completely the Greek spirit failed to master Anatolia, and, as they comprise the whole Roman period, statistics for Hellenism alone would be even more unfavourable.

The history of Mēn Askaenos, who was the Anatolian god probably syncretised with the Babylonian moon-god Sin, is notable in this respect. When the Seleucids built Pisidian Antioch it was found necessary, for the sake of the native settlers, to establish on Mount Karakuyu near the city a new sanctuary of Mēn ; the Sacred Way and Hall of Initiation have now been excavated, and the inscriptions show that Greek Antioch also was worshipping Mēn in the first century. Augustus replaced the priest by his own procurator, and thus became himself the god of the god's peasants ; but Mēn, though he lived beside a large Hellenistic city, resisted every attempt to displace him, and in the fourth century A.D. his worship was still so vigorous that, as god of the association called the Tekmoreian Guestfriends, he became the centre of the last fight of Paganism against Christianity in Asia Minor, and the temple on Karakuyu was destroyed by the victors like the Serapeum at Alexandria. The symbol of his initiates, the moon-god's crescent, is in its horseshoe form identical with the oldest form of horseshoe found in Scotland ; those who hang up horseshoes for luck may be the last practitioners of a pagan cult which was hoary when Greece was born.

Babylonia's great contribution was star-worship, which

we call astrology.   Its roots go very far back ;  and though
in the Seleucid age many Babylonian astronomers refused
to touch it, it had developed in Babylonia into a full-grown
system.   The stars, and above all the planets, obviously
moved in the vault of heaven according to fixed laws ;
and a doctrine of ' correspondence ' had arisen—this was
the vital matter—according to which the heavens above
and the earth beneath were the counterpart of each other,
and what happened in the sidereal world was reproduced
on earth.   But the movements of the sidereal world were
fixed ;  if then there was correspondence, what happened
on earth was also fixed ;  and men's actions too were fixed,
for man was a microcosm, a little world, the counterpart of
the great world or universe, and his soul was a spark of
that celestial fire which glowed in the stars.   From this
sprang one of the most terrible doctrines which ever oppressed humanity, the Babylonian *Heimarmene* or Fate,
which ruled alike stars, earth, and men ;  all their motions
were fixed by an immutable Power, non-moral, which
neither loved nor hated, but held on its course as inexorably
as the planets across the firmament.

Greeks had heard of astrology by 400 ;  Plato shews
some acquaintance with it in his later period, and Eudoxus
and Theophrastus knew that Chaldeans cast horoscopes.
Effective knowledge of Babylonian star-worship was brought
to Greeks by Berossus, *c.* 280, but its time really came in
the second century, when science was beginning to fail,
and the irresistible advance of Rome might well seem
Fate's counterpart upon earth.   It ultimately penetrated
and coloured many religions.   Astronomy might have
killed it ;  instead, by the end of the second century, it
had killed astronomy (Chap. IX), and thenceforth it had
a free field till Copernicus.   It had reached Egypt also by
the second century, when those writings appeared (before
150) which attributed the discovery of astrology to a
mythical Egyptian king Nechepso and his priest Petosiris ;
and it was from the accessible Alexandria as a secondary
centre that it spread over the Mediterranean world.   The

details of star-worship were probably further elaborated all through the Roman period. There was more than one system ; in one the planets were most prominent, in another the twelve signs of the Zodiac, developed in Egypt into the 36 decans, corresponding to the 36 decades of the Egyptian year, and ruled by 36 demons with extraordinary names,—Chnumen and Chnachnumen, Smat, Srat, and Sikat,—who also governed the 36 parts of the body. But planetary astrology had the greater power ; the seven planets—Sun, Moon, Mercury, Venus, Mars, Jupiter, Saturn—were the interpreters of Fate, the seats of the awful Cosmocrators or ' rulers of this world ', who subsequently became definitely evil and hostile to man's soul. To the seven planets were assigned their own colours, corresponding to the seven stages of a Babylonian temple, their own minerals, plants and animals ; the seven vowels of the Greek alphabet became their signs ; and from them came that persistent use of ' seven ' [1] which survives in our (Hellenistic) week, and appeared in the seven sleepers, the seven wonders of the world, the seven ages of man (which Shakespeare took from astrology), the seven stoles of Isis, the seven-stepped ladder of Mithras, the seven joys of the righteous in the Salathiel apocalypse, the seven angels and vials of *Revelations*, the seven gates of hell, and the seventh heaven.

The Zodiacal signs governed the destinies of various cities ; coins testify that Antioch and Nisibis were under Aries, Edessa under Aquarius, Singara and Rhesaena under Sagittarius. But what mattered to men was that *their* destinies were fixed at birth by their stars, and a competent practitioner could foretell them by casting horoscopes. The English language is full of the terminology of this outworn creed ; men are still jovial, mercurial, or saturnine, talk of fortunate conjunctions of events, believe in unlucky numbers, and thank their stars. By the first century Fate was in a fair way to oust the more kindly Fortune as the arbiter of men's lives. Later, prob-

[1] Some believe this antedates astrology.

ably under Stoic influence, some were to welcome Fate
as an escape from the caprices of Fortune and the decep-
tions of Hope ; but to the majority Fate was the negation
of freedom, an impossible tyranny, and the pressure on
men's minds would have become unbearable but for certain
ways of escape which will presently be indicated.

It was unfortunate, but perhaps inevitable, that the
Stoa, many of whose chief exponents came from Asia,
should take up astrology ; the weakness of Stoicism was
its detachment from the scientific spirit, and astrology
was to be its shadow side. Some now believe that Zeno
was influenced by astrology from the start ; certainly
Chrysippus regarded the Chaldeans as allies, and the
resemblances of the two systems were patent. To each
the universe was an organic whole, ruled by one almighty
Power and bound together by something which the Stoic
called sympathy [1] and the Babylonian correspondence ; to
each, man was a microcosm and his soul a spark of the
ethereal fire ; the destruction and identical renovation of
the world at the end of each world-period was, in some
form, common to both. But there was one crucial difference : the Babylonian Fate was a non-moral Force,
the Stoic Destiny a moral Providence, which at the start
had taken forethought for men. Stoicism struggled hard
to mould Fate into the semblance of Providence. It was
illogical, but men's need was great ; possibly the continuing repute of Aratus' *Phaenomena* (p. 220) was partly
due to its argument that Providence had created the stars.
Epicurus' school, to its honour, rejected astrology. Carneades attacked it as he attacked the Stoa, and propounded
the crux : " Why do men fated to die at different times die
in the same shipwreck ? " But astrology was to escape
from worse difficulties than that, and slipped away on a
theory of general influences which overrode the special
ones. But he forced the great Stoic Panaetius of Rhodes,
the friend of Polybius and Scipio, to discard astrology

[1] The roots of this idea seemingly go back behind its chief ex-
ponent, Poseidonius, to Chrysippus anyhow.

and the popular gods from his system ; and it was important that it was Panaetius' Stoicism, rationalist and strongly moral, which through Scipio's circle found its way to Rome ; what Rome first took from the Stoa was the philosophy of conduct alone. The man who might have done more than Carneades was the astronomer Hipparchus (p. 242) ; had he used his enormous mathematical ability to amend instead of to destroy Aristarchus' heliocentricism, he might have saved the world many centuries of astrology ; for to astrology heliocentricism meant death. As it was, he merely reversed the traditional rôles of Europe and Asia ; while Seleucus the Chaldean was defending heliocentricism, the Greek astronomer was championing the connection of the soul and the stars. But whatever Hipparchus' responsibility, the man who did most to establish astrology and its kin firmly in Europe was Panaetius' successor Poseidonius.

Poseidonius of Apamea in Syria (135–51), who worked in Rhodes and there held high civic office, was the last great intellectual force which Hellenism, untouched by Rome, produced ; his learning ranged over many fields, Cicero was his pupil, and he dominated the first half of the first century as Eratosthenes had dominated the end of the third. His work as historian, geographer, and descriptive writer has been noticed ; it reveals his strength and weakness, a mind of great scope and boundless desire for knowledge, but quite uncritical and without the scientific spirit. As a philosopher, he blended some Platonism with the Stoa ; but he blended much more than that. In his religious-philosophic activity he is a most difficult figure to grasp ; nothing of his remains, and but little of the mass of material in later writers is definitely attributed to him. It has been usual to call everything which exhibits certain tendencies Poseidonius, and to represent him as a double mind, standing between east and west and drawing from both, a philosopher and man of science, an astrologer and oriental mystic and what not, author of a great system which combined all the floating tendencies

of the time, science and superstition, star-worship and
popular worship, heaven and earth, men, gods, and demons ;
one in whom all things met and from whom they passed
out to influence the future.  Is this Poseidonius, or only a
label for the spirit of the first century ?  He is perhaps
too shadowy to dogmatise overmuch about ; the compound
of influences often called Poseidonius can perhaps hardly
be disentangled.  It is certain that he set Zeus above
Destiny instead of identifying them ; that is, his world
was a religious world, ruled by Reason and Will.  It seems
likely that he was working on a scheme ; he wanted to
prove the close inter-relation of earth and heaven.  So
far, science and philosophy had run separate courses ; he
would blend them, but science was to serve his philosophy.
For it is not true to say that, in science, he wanted to find
out the reasons of things ; he wanted to find there *his*
reason for things, the connection of earth and heaven ;
he took trouble to shew that the moon governed the tides,
that climate affected races, that the sun painted the pea-
cock of India or ripened the beryl in the Arabian mine,
because all these things were useful for his thesis, his doctrine
of vital force by which heaven acted on earth and which
pulsated through the universe.  His vast collection of
data to illustrate the changes in the earth's surface was
meant to prove the parallelism of earth and man, the fire
and water which ran through the veins of the earth as
blood and air through the veins of a man ; block the vein,
and both suffer alike,—the volcano explodes, the man's
vein bursts.

But what else came into his cosmic system beside heaven
and earth, Zeus and man ?  The gods we know did ; astrology is fairly certain.  He would have repudiated the
accusation of superstition ; his pantheistic deity, immanent
in every portion of the Universe, *was* Nature ; everything
that exists is equally in Nature.  The trouble is the number
of things he accepted as existent.  He believed in, and
wrote on, divination ; it was in Nature.  He wrote on
daimons ; and there is just enough to shew that he did

U

believe the soul became a daimon and inhabited the upper air. And supernatural beings spoke to men in dreams. His own system, then, lofty in some respects as were his ideas of the correlation of the universe under the rule of a divine Providence, was not so very far from what we have called the spirit of the time ; his Universe admitted too much, for he did not distinguish between what existed and what men believed to exist. He opened the door to demonology and much else. That he did not enter the open door with the crowd matters little ; what the crowd saw was that his presence made their proceedings respectable ; for if a daimon appeared in dreams, why not in a crystal, and if in a crystal . . . there is no halting on *that* slope. Every forsaken lover or speculative trader who hired some wandering Egyptian to call down a demon for him with an ibis' egg and a bit of garlic might claim that he was only carrying out to its logical conclusion the teaching of the great Poseidonius.

We come to the ways by which man could escape from Fate. One was provided by the heavens themselves ; certain phenomena, such as comets, could not be brought under any fixed order, so there was something at work beside the fixed revolutions of the spheres. Correspondingly, astrology itself admitted many quite illogical elements ; it managed to incorporate Fortune, and it presently provided a doctrine of ' opportunities ', fortunate planetary conjunctions which might be seized on by one bold enough. But, speaking generally, there were three main lines on which man sought to escape from his stars, all depending on a belief that some god was really more powerful than that Fate which ruled the gods ; it was the human mind reacting for itself, as it always has done, against the dead weight of Determinism, and declaring that there should be no such thing ; its weapon was the ineradicable belief of men in some helping deity, could they but find him. These three lines were Gnosis, magic, and the eastern mystery-religions. Gnosis means knowledge, but not the knowledge of the philosopher ; some god had once directly revealed the secret key of the universe to some chosen soul, and could a man find that knowledge, hidden from other men, he was immune from Fate ; he had short-circuited the stars. They might torment his body, but his soul was beyond their reach ; for Reason was above Fate. Gnosis was to produce some elevated doctrines, but though its roots go back to Hellenism its day was not yet ; all the great systems are essentially later than the Christian era.

No time or country has ever yet been free of magic. But in the second century a fresh flood from Asia poured into the Greek world at astrology's heels ; all the rivers —Assyrian, Babylonian, Anatolian, Persian, Jewish—met in Egypt as in a reservoir, and from Egypt went out to water the earth. Its root idea was, that by employing proper means the hands of the gods could be *forced* ; a formula to compel the Moon says ' You have to do it, whether you like it or not '. To some it was almost like the old Greek will to freedom come to life again in another sphere ; the god or demon could be compelled to alter your fate. But to the mass of people, to whom star-worship meant, not a great oppressive system, but some wandering Chaldean and his horoscopes, magic was merely a short cut to getting some material thing you wanted. Many magic papyri are known, with formulae and cere-monies for every sort of personal advantage ; they will give success in love or money-making, cure disease, exorcise devils, destroy an enemy ; among them are omnibus charms, good for any purpose. All sorts of materials were in vogue, from the humble onion to the formula, probably seldom used, which begins ' Take an emerald of great price and thereon carve a beetle ' ; the sacred ibis, and the baboon, discoverer of Osiris' corpse, naturally played a large part. The demon called might come in many ways ; the magician would see him for you in water or ink or crystal, suggestion playing a considerable part, but he might also be produced in person ; if properly equipped you were for the moment his master, but he might hurt you afterwards, and beside protective charms there are formulae for getting the demon quietly back to his own place again, the side in which mediaeval magic was so lamentably weak. Usually you summoned one of the demons or spirits from the intermediate air ; but a great god could also be called, as in the famous invocation of Typhon. Your best hold over a demon was to utter his true name ; but he probably concealed it with some care, and to make sure you pronounced a vast number, corrupt forms from every language in Asia, with strings of meaningless vocables ; Typhon is called in the power of the ' hundred-lettered name ', Jewish magicians did not scruple to use the name Yahweh, and most potent of all, if a man could learn it, was that Ineffable Name with which Solomon had once sealed up in bronze jars 19,999 demons of the congregation of the Evil One. Some formulae indeed contain nothing but names ; and the Jewish Essenes were sworn never to reveal the names of the angels, which means that they used them for magic. Magic almost became a religious system ; many honestly believed in it, and the papyri contain prayers for deliverance from one's stars. It had relations with the lower forms of Gnosis ; you could compel the god to impart to you his secret knowledge. But Gnosis in its higher forms rejected magic ; Fate, says a Hermetic writing, is not to be compelled.

But far more important than magic were the Hellenistic mystery-religions. Magic might alter your fate, but initiation lifted you above the sphere of Fate altogether ; the god could and would look after his own, and though the stars might work their will on your body, your soul, even in this life, was beyond their reach, and after death would rise above their spheres to the sphere of the divine and dwell with the gods ; you were in fact ' saved '. The universal basis of the mystery-religions was that you sought this *soteria*, ' salvation ', by personal union with a saviour god who had himself died and risen again ; to employ the well-known Orphic phrase, you ceased to be a worshipper, a rod-bearer, and became a Bacchus,—you were as the god himself. Mysteries were an old phenomenon in

Greece ; what was new was the tremendous appeal which, with the breakdown of Greek religion, they now made. Accusations of charlatanry and sensuality were freely levelled against their followers, but a religion is not judged by the bad men among those who profess it. These religions brought to the aspirant a new sense of sin, a new conception of holiness ; and the rite of initiation, culminating in the knowledge that you were saved, was undoubtedly an intense emotional experience. From the second century onwards men's religious sense deepened. There were many mystery-religions, each claiming to possess the original initiation and to be of universal force ; each claimed that the others merely worshipped its own god under other names. The older forms persisted, and Orphism, with its religious ecstasy and its ideas of purity and the antagonism of flesh and spirit, became very widespread ; probably the Orphic hymns took shape at Pergamum. But what must be noticed here are the new forms which entered the Greek world through the occupation of Anatolia and Egypt.

The regular form of the Anatolian mysteries has been recovered by Sir W. Ramsay ; their general likeness to those of Eleusis and Isis needs no comment. At initiation the aspirant stepped into a new life, typified materially at Karakuyu by passing from one part of the Hall of Initiation to another ; he approached the god's throne, received the promise " Happy and blessed, thou shalt be god instead of mortal ", was purified at the sacred pool, and then witnessed a mystic representation of the divine marriage of the god and goddess. In some mysteries he must, before the marriage, have witnessed the death and resurrection of the god, and heard the priest pronounce the message of consolation : " Be of good cheer, mystae, the god is saved ; even so shall we after our troubles find salvation." Doubtless too after initiation was complete the recognition of the initiate as god followed. Ramsay has laid great stress on the phenomenon of the sacred marriage in these mysteries as typifying the growth of morality, civilisation, the higher law, over against the temple prostitutes.  This view has been contested, on the ground that communism of women is not historical ; but a thing need not have existed to exercise enormous influence —the *Contrat Social*, for instance—and the point is simply, did men think there was, or had been, such a thing ?  The evidence seems sufficient that they did.[1]

But of all the mystery-religions that invaded the Aegean world, far the most important was the Egyptian.  The Serapeum at Delos has revealed that the triad who were so to influence Hellenism were not Isis, Serapis, and their son Horus or Harpocrates, but Isis, Serapis, and Anubis, the god who conducted souls to the realm of immortal life ; the religion from the first stressed the fact that its great gift to men was immortality, though Isis also made it clear that she was above Fate, and that over those who came to her Fate had no more dominion.  By the first century it must have seemed that if there were to be a universal religion, it could only be this.  Everywhere men turned to Serapis and Isis as saviours ; their worship had spread far, and its penetrative power was such that Isis alone of foreign deities succeeded in entering Babylonian Uruk.  Serapis, deliberately created by Ptolemy I while still under the influence of Alexander's ideas, is the only god ever successfully made by a modern man ; he was Osiris in his Apis form combined with Greek elements, and was meant to unite Greeks and Egyptians in a common worship.  But Egyptians would not accept him, and though he kept Osirian characteristics and Isis as consort he became the Greek god of Alexandria, he and Isis being represented on earth by the divine Ptolemaic pair.  Zeus, Hades, Asclepius, and others contributed elements to Serapis' nature ; he became the universal ruler, whom his worshippers almost constituted for themselves as they

---

[1] Clearchus of Soli (*F.H.G.* II, p. 319) says Cecrops replaced an original state of promiscuity at Athens by marriage.  Isis claimed to have invented marriage, Dittenberger *Syll.*[3] 1267.  Plutarch, *Moralia* 328 C, says Alexander ' taught the Hyrcanians marriage ' (a tribe practising group-marriage would seem to Greeks promiscuous).

would.  His name (in Greek Sarapis) appears to be unexplained, for some now reject the traditional Osiris-Apis, while the derivation from the cult-name of the Babylonian Ea, *šar apsi*, has not found much acceptance.[1]

Serapis reached Athens and Piraeus before 300, and in the third century there was a lively propaganda in his behalf in the cities of Egypt's sphere ; his worship spread quickly over the Aegean world, and sometimes, as at Eretria, he entered an older shrine of Isis, whose cult had often preceded his own.  At first his worship, like Isis', was confined to private associations ; but later it often became official, as at Athens, Demetrias, Tanagra, and Delos.  At Delos, for instance, an Egyptian priest, Apollonius, introduced him before 300, and after the god had lived in lodgings for two generations Apollonius' grandson built him a house ; by 166 he had three temples, and that year (or earlier) one was taken over by the city ; this official Serapeum was greatly enlarged later.  His two main seats were the temples at Alexandria and Memphis ; and Ptolemy I is said to have brought from Athens the Eumolpid Timotheus to inaugurate his mysteries on the lines of the Eleusinian.  The papyri often allude to some mysterious people called *catochoi* who lived in the precinct of the Memphis Serapeum ; they were probably refugees in the temple asylum who, being unable to leave (through fear of blood feuds or some such reason), did sometimes, to avoid expulsion, dedicate themselves to the god (a thing known elsewhere) and even seek initiation.[2] The destruction of the Alexandrian Serapeum and its statue in A.D. 391 by the bishop Theophilus was taken by the world as the outward sign that Christianity had definitely triumphed.

[1] The name ' Serapis ' applied to some Babylonian deity in Arrian VII, 26, 2, was merely inserted by Ptolemy I in his narrative as propaganda for his god.

[2] Wilcken's view, widely adopted, that they were religious devotees possessed by the god, does not explain why they could not leave if they wished.  The view in the text is from Von Woess and Reitzenstein.

But important as Serapis became, he hardly equalled his consort ; and while he was never invoked without her, she was often invoked alone. Of all the deities of Hellenism, Isis of the Myriad Names was probably the greatest. She was identified with practically every goddess and deified woman of the known world ; she was the one reality which they all imperfectly shadowed forth. She was Lady of All, All-seeing and All-powerful, Queen of the Inhabited World ; she was Star of the Sea, Diadem of Life, Lawgiver and Saviour ; she was Grace and Beauty, Fortune and Abundance, Truth, Wisdom, and Love.[1] All civilisation was her gift and in her charge. Her statues portrayed a young matron in modest dress with gentle benevolent features, crowned with blue lotus or the crescent moon, and sometimes bearing in her arms the babe Horus. Sacrifice was offered to her daily, as to Anaïtis at Ecbatana ; but only at great festivals was her actual image shewn to worshippers, gorgeously robed and blazing with jewels, for her black-stoled priests understood every ceremonial art that might attract men. The November festival, Isia, represented the passion of Osiris,—his death at Typhon's hands, Isis' faithful quest for his body, his divine resurrection ; more magnificent was the spring festival of the Launching of the Ship, when, to celebrate the opening of navigation, the gorgeous procession so vividly described by Apuleius made its way from the temple to the seashore to launch the symbolic ship of the goddess. Her service was typified as warfare ; the initiates were the soldiers in her army. That initiation was no light matter ; the novice might serve for many years before the goddess ' called ' him, and to enter her shrine uncalled was death. It was death too to enter it after call and due instruction by the mystagogue ; but it was death to the novice's old life and birth to a new life, the life of salvation. In the ceremony itself the aspirant was first purified with water, and then wandered in the dark places of the underworld as Osiris had done between his death and resurrection,

[1] See her invocation, *Oxyrynchos Papyri* XI, No. 1380.

submitting to certain trials—possibly he actually ' died '
and was ' buried ', and probably suggestion played a considerable part ; at the end he came out into a blaze of light,
and with the sacred garments on him and a torch in his
hand was exhibited to the congregation as himself a god,
his soul henceforth free from the dominion of fate and of
death.

But there was more in Isis-worship than ceremonial, or
even than the mysteries, important as these things were.
Isis was a phenomenon which had not appeared in the
Mediterranean in historical times, but which, having once
appeared, has never since quitted it : she was the woman's
goddess.  Half the human race had been badly off for a
friend at the court of Heaven.  Athena was uniquely a
man's goddess ; and if women cried to Artemis in child-
birth it was largely because there was no one else.  To
the ordinary decent woman the main facts of life were,
that she was wife and mother ; she had little in common
with a virgin warrior who patronised art, or a virgin huntress,
cold as her own moon ; little with the fertility goddess
of an old matriarchal age, and even less with Aphrodite,
though doubtless people can spiritualise anything.  But
now she had a friend, and the greatest of them all ; one
who had been wife and mother as she was, one who had
suffered as she might suffer ; one who understood.  Isis
herself leaves no doubt on the point ; she is the ' glory
of women ', who gives them ' equal power with men '.
" I am Isis " runs her creed, the Isis-hymn found at Ios ;
" I am she whom women call goddess.  I ordained that
women should be loved by men ; I brought wife and
husband together, and invented the marriage contract.
I ordained that women should bear children, and that
children should love their parents . . ."   In that strength
Isis swept the Mediterranean.  When finally Christianity
triumphed, and Zeus and Apollo, Serapis and the star-
gods, were hurled from their seats, Isis alone in some
sense survived the universal fall ; the cult of the Virgin
had been introduced before the Serapeum was sacked,

and Isis' devotees passed quietly over to the worship of another Mother—how quietly sometimes may be seen from this, that it has been possible to compile a list of her statues which afterwards served as images of the Madonna.

The interest of the Hellenistic religions is that they depict the world in which Christianity arose. That world provided more than the medium of the common civilisation in which Christianity was to spread ; it to some extent paved the way. Men were seeking the unity which must lie behind the different deities and their worships, even as Alexander had once (it was said) called all men sons of one Father ; while the terrible upheaval of the Roman civil wars greatly strengthened the already strong desire for a saviour, for whom many were already looking beyond the sphere of mankind. But though Hellenism supplied the longing, and probably in some a quickened sense of purity (even if only ceremonial) and of faith, there were to be two vital things in the new religion which were not in Hellenism, quite apart from the figure of the Founder, Whose spirit Hellenism did not touch. Plato had declared that all souls were immortal, and a few Jews had grasped the same general idea, while the Stoics gave the souls of the virtuous a limited survival till the end of the world-period ; but to Hellenism generally immortality was only for certain benefactors of their kind or the initiates in some mystery-religion ; it was not for the mass of men, as their epitaphs reveal pathetically enough. And of all the Hellenistic creeds, none was based on love of humanity ; none had any message for the poor and the wretched, the publican and the sinner. Stoicism came nearest ; it did transvaluate some earthly values, and Zeno, at least, gave offence by not repelling the poor and the squalid who came to him ; but it had no place for love, and it scarcely met the misery of the world to tell the slave in the mines that if he would only think aright he would be happy. Those who laboured and were heavy laden were to welcome a different hope from any which Hellenism could offer.

# LIST OF BOOKS

This is not a bibliography, but only some modern references which may help those interested to follow up the various subjects, English works being given where possible. Bibliographies of the period will soon be available in the *Cambridge Ancient History*, which has now (Vol. VI) reached 301 B.C.

CHAPTER I. **Histories, general :** J. G. Droysen, *Geschichte des Hellenismus*, II and III, 2nd ed. Gotha 1877 (to 217); B. Niese, *Geschichte der griechischen und makedonischen Staaten seit der Schlacht bei Chaeronea* II and III, Gotha 1899, 1903; J. Beloch, *Griechische Geschichte*, 2nd ed., IV parts i and ii,[1] Berlin-Leipzig 1925, 1927 (to 217); E. Cavaignac, *Histoire de l'antiquité* III, Paris 1914 ; P. Jouget, *L'Impérialisme macédonien et l'hellénisation de l'Orient*, Paris 1926.—**Special :** E. R. Bevan, *The House of Seleucus*, London 1902, and *A history of Egypt under the Ptolemaic Dynasty*, London 1927 [1]; A. Bouché-Leclercq, *Histoire des Lagides*, Paris 1903–7, and *Histoire des Séleucides*, Paris 1913 ; W. S. Ferguson, *Hellenistic Athens*, London 1911, and *Greek Imperialism*, London–Boston–New York 1913 ; W. W. Tarn, *Antigonos Gonatas*, Oxford 1913 ; G. Cardinali, *Il regno di Pergamo*, Turin 1906 ; M. Holleaux, *Rome, la Grèce, et les monarchies hellénistiques au III^e siècle av. J. C.* (273–205), Paris 1921 ; G. Colin, *Rome et la Grèce de 200 à 146 av. J. C.*, Paris 1908.—**Military matters :** J. Kromayer, *Antike Schlachtfelder* I and II, Berlin 1902, 1907 ; H. Delbrück, *Geschichte der Kriegskunst* I, 3rd ed., Berlin 1920. —**On Hellenism generally,** beside Beloch and Jouguet : P. Wendland, *Die hellenistisch-römische Kultur*, Tübingen 1912 ; U. von Wiliamowitz-Moellendorff, *Staat und Gesellschaft der Griechen*, 2nd ed., Leipzig–Berlin 1923 ; J. Kaerst, *Geschichte des Hellenismus II*, 2nd ed., Leipzig 1926 ; W. Otto, *Kulturgeschichte des Altertums*, Munich 1925 ; M. Rostovtseff, *A history of the ancient world* I, Oxford 1926 ; and on certain points J. B. Bury and others, *The Hellenistic Age*, Cambridge 1923. —Many of these works deal also with the matter of subse-

---

[1] Published too late to use.

quent chapters. The writer is treating the political history
to 217 in Vols. VI and VII (forthcoming) of the *Cambridge
Ancient History*.

CHAPTER II.  **King-worship :**  E. Kornemann in *Klio* I, 1901, p.
51 ;  Kaerst, App. V (see Chap. I) ;  earlier anticipations, O.
Weinreich in *Neue Jahrbücher* II, 1926, p. 633.—**Leagues :**
E. A. Freeman, *History of Federal Government*, 2nd ed. by
J. B. Bury, London 1893 ;  H. Swoboda, *Staatsaltertümer* in
Hermann's Lehrbuch 1⁶ part 3, Tübingen 1913 ;  E. Korne-
mann, κοινόν in Pauly-Wissowa, 1924 ;  G. Busolt, *Griechische
Staatskunde* II, 3rd ed. by Swoboda, Munich 1926.—**The Pan-
hellenic Leagues :**  A. Wilhelm, *Attische Urkunden* I, Vienna
1911 ;  M. Cary, *Class. Quarterly* XVII, 1923, p. 137 ;  P.
Roussel, *Rev. Arch.* XVII, 1923, p. 117 ;  J. A. O. Larsen,
*Class. Philology* XX, 1925, p. 313, and XXI, 1926, p. 52.

CHAPTER III.  Essentially the inscriptions.  On various points :
M. N. Tod, *International Arbitration among the Greeks*, Oxford
1913 ;  E. Ziebarth, *Aus dem griechischen Schulwesen*, 2nd ed.,
Leipzig–Berlin 1914 ;  F. Poland, *Geschichte des griechischen
Vereinswesens*, Leipzig 1909 ;  H. Ormerod, *Piracy in the Ancient
World*, Liverpool 1924 ;  G. Glotz, *Infanticidium* and *Expositio*
in Daremberg-Saglio ;  H. Francotte, *Les finances des cités
grecques*, Liège–Paris 1909 ;  my contribution to *The Hellenistic
Age* (wages) ;  R. von Pöhlmann, *Geschichte der sozialen Frage
und des Sozialismus in der antiken Welt*, 3rd ed. by Fr. Oertel,
Munich 1925, and see on this U. Kahrstedt in *Göttingische Gel.
Anzeigen* 1926, p. 97, and Oertel in *Neue Jahrbücher* III, 1927,
p. 1.  The corn question will be dealt with by A. Jardé in Vol.
II of *Les céréales dans l'antiquité grecque*, Paris.

CHAPTER IV.  **Seleucids :**  Ed. Meyer, *Blüte und Niedergang des
Hellenismus in Asien*, Berlin 1925 ;  U. Kahrstedt, *Syrische
Territorien in hellenistischer Zeit*, Berlin 1926 ;  Fr. Cumont,
*Fouilles de Doura-Europos* (1922–1923), Paris 1926 ;  the works
by Kugler and Kolbe under Chap. VI.—**Land and settlement :**
M. Rostovtseff, *Geschichte des römischen Kolonates*, Leipzig–
Berlin 1910 ;  articles in Pauly-Wissowa, *Katoikoi* (Fr. Oertel),
κώμη (H. Swoboda), *Domänen* and *Bauernstand* (E. Kornemann,
1924).—**Priest-states :**  many studies by Sir W. M. Ramsay
(full list in *Anatolian Studies presented to Sir W. Ramsay*, Man-
chester 1923) ;  Ch. Picard, *Ephèse et Claros*, Paris 1922.—
**Pergamum :**  M. Rostovtseff in *Anatolian Studies*, p. 359
(economics) ;  M. Holleaux in *Bull. Corr. Hell.* XLVIII, 1924,
p. 1 (cities).—Fr. Stahelin, *Geschichte der kleinasiatischen Galater*,
2nd ed., Leipzig 1907.—J. S. Reid, *The municipalities of the
Roman Empire*, Cambridge 1913.

CHAPTER V. **General accounts** : Bouché-Leclercq, *Histoire des Lagides* III and IV ; A. Mitteis and U. Wilcken, *Grundzüge und Chrestomathie der Papyruskunde* I, Leipzig–Berlin 1912 ; W. Schubart, *Einführung in die Papyruskunde*, Berlin 1918. An account of the new material appears periodically in the *Archiv für Papyrusforschung.*—**The economic side** : B. P. Grenfell and J. P. Mahaffy, *The Revenue Laws of Ptolemy Philadelphos*, Oxford 1896 ; M. Rostovtseff, *A large estate in Egypt in the 3rd century B.C.*, Madison 1922, and article in *Journ. Egypt. Archaeology*, 1920, p. 161 ; U. Wilcken in *Schmoller's Jahrbuch* XLV, 1921, p. 349.—**The culture side** : H. I. Bell in *J. Eg. Arch.*, 1922, p. 139, and Fr. Oertel in *Neue Jahrbücher* XLV, 1920, p. 361.—**Alexandria** : E. Breccia, *Alexandrea ad Aegyptum*, English ed., Bergamo 1922 ; W. Schubart, *Ägypten von Alexander d. Gr. bis auf Mohamed*, Berlin 1922.—**On the constitution** : *Dikaiomata*, herausg. von der Graeca Halensis, Berlin 1913.

CHAPTER VI. E. Schürer, *Geschichte des jüdischen Volkes im Zeitalter Jesu Christi* III, 4th ed., Leipzig 1909 ; E. R. Bevan, *Jerusalem under the High Priests*, 5th ed., London 1924 ; E. Meyer, *Ursprung und Anfänge des Christentums* II, Stuttgart–Berlin 1921 ; F. X. Kugler, *Von Moses bis Paulus*, Münster i. W. 1922 ; W. Kolbe, *Beiträge zur syrischen und jüdischen Geschichte*, Berlin–Stuttgart–Leipzig 1926 ; W. Otto, *Herodes*, Stuttgart 1913.—**Citizenship** : H. I. Bell, *Jews and Christians in Egypt*, London 1924 ; M. Engers, *Klio* XVIII, 1923, p. 79 ; G. de Sanctis, *Riv. di filologia* LII, 1924, p. 473 ; H. Stuart Jones, *J. Roman Studies* XVI, 1926, p. 17.—**Literature** : R. H. Charles, *The Apocrypha and Pseudepigrapha of the Old Testament*, London 1913, and the smaller work *Religious development between the Old and New Testaments*, London–New York 1914 ; W. O. E. Oesterley, *The books of the Apocrypha*, London 1915 ; G. A. Barton, *Ecclesiastes*, in the Internat. Crit. Commentary 1908.—**Sabazios** : Fr. Cumont in *Comptes Rendus de l'Ac. des Inscriptions*, 1906, p. 63.

CHAPTER VII. No comprehensive work exists. On certain points : J. Hatzfeld, *Les trafiquants Italiens dans l'Orient hellénique*, Paris 1919 ; M. Rostovtseff, *Arch. f. Papyrusf.* IV, 1908, p. 298 (Red Sea) ; a chapter in G. Glotz, *Ancient Greece at Work*, London 1926.—**Egypt**, see Chap. V.—**Delos** : P. Roussel, *Délos, colonie athénienne*, Paris 1916, and *Délos*, Paris 1925 ; F. Durrbach, *Choix d'Inscriptions de Délos* I, Paris 1921–3 ; Ferguson, *Hellenistic Athens* (see Chap. I). (The whole material is being collected in the French *Fouilles de Délos.*)

CHAPTER VIII. Fr. Susemihl, *Geschichte der griechischen Literatur in der Alexandrinerzeit*, Leipzig 1891 (still indispensable) ; W. von Christ, *Geschichte der griechischen Literatur* II (6th ed. by W. Schmid, in Müller's *Handbuch* VII, ii, 1), Munich 1920 ; U. von Wilamowitz-Moellendorf, *Die griechische Literatur*, 3rd ed., Berlin 1924, and *Hellenistische Dichtung in der Zeit des Kallimachos*, Berlin 1924 ; A. Rostagni, *Poeti Alessandrini*, Turin 1916.—There is no history in English of later Greek literature. On certain sides, see J. B. Bury, *Ancient Greek Historians*, London 1909 ; J. W. Mackail, *Lectures on Greek poetry*, 2nd ed., London 1926 ; J. U. Powell and E. A. Barber, *New Chapters in the history of Greek Literature*, Oxford 1921 ; E. A. Barber on Alexandrian literature in *The Hellenistic Age*.

CHAPTER IX. **Science :** Sir T. L. Heath, *Aristarchus of Samos*, Oxford 1913, and *A history of Greek mathematics*, Oxford 1921 ; J. L. Heiberg, *Mathematics and Physical Science in classical antiquity*, Oxford 1922, expanded as *Geschichte der Mathematik und Naturwissenschaften*, Munich 1925 ; Ch. Singer, *Greek Biology and Greek Medicine*, Oxford 1922.—**Geography :** H. Berger, *Geschichte der wissenschaftlichen Erdkunde der Griechen*, 2nd ed., Leipzig 1903 ; F. Gisinger, *Geographie* in Pauly-Wissowa, 1924 ; W. Capelle, *Neue Jahrbücher* XLV, 1920, p. 305 [Poseidonius) ; O. Viedebant, *Klio* XIV, 1915, p. 207 (earth-measurements).—**Architecture, etc. :** F. Haverfield, *Ancient Town Planning*, Oxford 1913 ; A. von Gerkan, *Griechische Städteanlagen*, Berlin–Leipzig 1924 ; M. Collignon and E. Pontremoli, *Pergame*, Paris 1900 ; Th. Wiegand and H. Schrader, *Priene*, Berlin 1904 ; Th. Wiegand, *Milet*, Berlin (in progress) ; E. Pontremoli and B. Haussoullier, *Didymes*, Paris 1903 ; W. J. Anderson and R. Spiers, *The architecture of Greece and Rome*, 2nd ed., London 1907.—**Restorations of Ptolemaic work :** Fr. Studniczka, *Das Symposion Ptolemaios II*, Leipzig 1914 ; Fr. Caspari, *Das Nilschiff Ptolemaios IV*, Jahrb. deut. arch. Instituts XXXI, 1916, p. 1.—**Sculpture :** Th. Schreiber, *Die hellenistischen Reliefbilder*, Leipzig 1889 ; M. Collignon, *Histoire de la sculpture grecque* II, Paris 1897 ; W. Klein, *Geschichte der griechischen Kunst* III, Leipzig 1907, and *Von antiken Rokoko*, Vienna 1921 ; E. A. Gardner, *A Handbook of Greek sculpture*, 2nd ed., London 1915 (reprinted 1924) ; G. Dickins, *Hellenistic sculpture*, 2nd ed., Oxford 1920. See A. W. Lawrence in *J. Eg. Arch.* XI, 1925, p. 179 (Egypt), and G. Bagnani in *J. Hell. Stud.* XLI, 1921, p. 232 (Cyrene).—**Painting :** E. Pfuhl, *Malerei und Zeichnung der Griechen*, Munich 1923, and the smaller work *Masterpieces of Greek drawing and painting*, tr. J. D. Beazley, London 1926 ; R. Pagenstecher, *Neue Jahrbücher* XLVII–VIII, 1921, p. 271 (landscape) ; Fr. Studniczka,

*Jahrb. deut. arch. Inst.* XXXVIII–IX, 1923–4, p. 57 (the Villa Boscoreale frescoes).—**Mixed art :** K. Humann and O. Puchstein, *Reisen in Kleinasien und Nordsyrien,* Berlin 1890 (the Nimrud-dagh monument) ; *American Arch. Exped. to Syria : Architecture,* by H. C. Butler, New York 1903 ; *Syria II A* (Princeton Expedition) : *Architecture of Southern Syria,* by H. C. Butler, Leyden 1919 ; G. Lefebvre, *Le tombeau de Petosiris,* Cairo 1924.

CHAPTER X. **Philosophy :** E. Zeller, *Stoics, Epicureans, and Sceptics,* Eng. Tr., London 1880 (still indispensable).—**Stoics :** Sir A. Grant's essay in his *Aristotle's Ethics,* London 1885 ; G. H. Rendall, Introduction to his *Marcus Aurelius,* London–New York 1896 ; W. L. Davidson, *The Stoic Creed,* Edinburgh 1907 ; E. V. Arnold, *Roman Stoicism,* Cambridge 1911 (full bibliography) ; E. R. Bevan, *Stoics and Sceptics,* London 1913 ; K. Reinhardt, *Poseidonios,* Munich 1921 (the sequel, *Kosmos und Sympathie,* Munich 1926, I have been unable to see).—**Star-worship :** A. Bouché-Leclercq, *L'astrologie grecque,* Paris 1899 ; Fr. Cumont, *Astrology and religion among the Greeks and Romans,* New York 1912 ; Fr. Boll and C. Bezold, *Sternglaube und Sterndeutung,* 3rd ed. by W. Gundel, Berlin 1926 ; H. Gressmann, *Die hellenistische Gestirnreligion* (Beiheft V zum Alten Orient), Leipzig 1925.—**The mysteries :** R. Reitzenstein, *Die hellenistischen Mysterienreligionen,* 3rd ed., Leipzig–Berlin 1927 ; W. R. Halliday, *The Pagan background of early Christianity,* Liverpool–London 1925.—**Anatolia :** Sir W. M. Ramsay in *Ann. Brit. School Athens* XVIII, 1911–12, p. 37, and *J. Rom. Stud.* VIII, 1918, p. 107.—**Egypt :** P. Roussel, *Les cultes Égyptiens à Délos,* Paris 1916 ; U. Wilcken, *Urkunden der Ptolemaer-Zeit* I, Berlin–Leipzig 1922 ; Meyer and Drexler, *Isis,* in Roscher's Lexicon ; Roeder's articles *Isis* and *Serapis* in Pauly-Wissowa.

# INDEX